PONY EXPRESS

St. JOSEPH, MISSOURI to CALIFORNIA
in 10 days or less.

WANTED

YOUNG, SKINNY, WIRY FELLOWS

not over eighteen. Must be expert riders, willing to risk death daily.

Orphans preferred.
Wages $25 per week.

APPLY, **PONY EXPRESS STABLES**
St. JOSEPH, MISSOURI

Created and Directed by Hans Höfer

**INSIGHT
GUIDES**

CROSSING
AMERICA

Edited by Robert Seidenberg
Photography by Joe Viesti
Updated by Fred Wright

APA PUBLICATIONS

CROSSING AMERICA

Second Edition (3rd Reprint)
© 1992 APA PUBLICATIONS (HK) LTD
All Rights Reserved
Printed in Singapore by Höfer Press Pte. Ltd

ABOUT THIS BOOK

Crossing America is different from the previous titles in Apa Publications' series of internationally acclaimed travel books. It is as much about a journey as about a series of destinations. It captures the spirit and essence of the United States, recaptures the almost mythic quality of trans-American voyages, and maps out travel routes which provide the reader with beautiful sites, fascinating history, worthwhile culture and plain old fun.

The idea for this book was originated by Apa's founder/publisher **Hans Höfer**, and then passed from Apa's American envoy, executive editor **Adam Liptak**, to **Robert Seidenberg**, who took charge of the project in New York City.

Seidenberg has always been fascinated with American culture, history, literature and art, which he studied in the American Studies program at Brown University in the late 1970s. A native of Buffalo, New York, Seidenberg is a writer, editor and aspiring screenwriter who writes frequently about film and pop music. He has served as an editor at such publications as *New York Talk*, *Art Direction* and *TV/Radio Age*. His articles have appeared in numerous publications, including *The New York Times*, *The Village Voice*, *USA Today*, *Rolling Stone*, *Musician*, *Spin*, *The Buffalo News* and *Video Times*.

Rich Taskin ("We're on the Road to Somewhere", "Conquest of Space and Time" and "Poetry in Motion") is currently a visiting lecturer in the History and Political Science Department of North Adams State College. He holds a masters degree in American Studies from Brown University.

Diane Hall ("The North Route"), a freelance writer based in New York City, has traveled extensively in North and South America, Europe, the Pacific and South East Asia. Her work has appeared in *Insight Guide: Canada*, and also in various in-flight magazines and travel publications.

Adam Bresnick and **Nina Tager** tackled the south east route of the grand tour in tandem. Bresnick ("Elvis Presley's Graceland", "Cajun Cuisine" and "Napa Valley"), has published criticism and feature stories on jazz in *Cadence*, *New York Talk* and *Fresh Fruit*. He teaches French at the University of California, Berkeley, where he is a graduate student in Comparative Literature.

Nina Tager took a degree in Religious Studies at Brown and upon graduation, worked with homeless women at the Traveller's Hotel in Manhattan. Tager has written for the *Riverdale Review* and authored several studies for the New York State Department of Mental Health.

Michael Macrone, who tackled the south travel route, is a graduate student at the Univeristy of California English department. He was editor of *Key: This Week in San Francisco* and has published articles and reviews in *High Times*, the (Rhode Island) *Newspaper*, *Weirdo* and *The Comics Journal*.

Ted Greenwald ("Colonial Williamsburg", "Martin Luther King, Jr.", "Las Vegas" and the southwest travel route) is another easterner exiled in sunny California. He lives in Cupertino where he reports for *Keyboard Magazine*. He has worked as recording engineer at Power Station in New York and as arts reporter for *New York Talk*. Greenwald has a degree in music composition from Brown and has done graduate work in film scoring at the University of Southern California."

Joe Viesti was an essential part of this project, having provided photographs for a

Seidenberg

Taskin

Hall

Bresnick

Tager

large portion of the book. He has shot for the National Geographic Society, and his work has also appeared in such publications as *Geo*, *Stern* and *Pacific*, as well as in numerous other *Insight Guide*s. For the past nine years, Viesti has specialized in photographing celebrations around the world. In 1984, his collection was tapped for the UNICEF Engagement Calendar.

The information-packed Travel Tips section of *Crossing America* was composed by **Bob Pfeifer** who has traveled extensively throughout the U.S.A. by automobile – mostly while on tour with his band, Human Switchboard. Since his graduation from Syracuse University and one year of graduate work in Philosophy at Ohio University, he has been writing articles for *The Village Voice* and *BAM*, and more importantly, writing and performing his own music.

Jody Leader ("The Motor City and Henry Ford", "Salt Lake City", "Denver" and "Bryce Canyon") graduated from Oberlin College in Ohio with a degree in English and Dance. She is now first assistant to the entertainment editor at *The Los Angeles Reader* – for whom she also writes reviews of concerts, movies and gallery openings. She is a veteran of Los Angeles Choreographers and Dancers, a professional dance company.

Lauren Bernstein ("Skiing the Rockies"), national regional editor for *SKI Magazine*, was formerly editor of *Art Direction*. She has written for various publications including *Working Woman* and *Cosmopolitan*.

Lorraine Kreahling ("Mighty Mississippi") was educated at Indiana University of Pennsylvania, New York University and Columbia University. Kreahling has worked on and off in publishing since 1980 and frequently travels during her "off" periods.

While many of the photos appearing in *Crossing America* were taken by Joe Viesti, several other contributors deserve special mention. Among them are **Phototheque Vautier-de Nanxe**, an extensive photo library in Paris; **Richard Erdoes**, who has written/illustrated/photographed 10 books on the Southwest and its Native Americans; and **Manfred Gottschalk** in West Germany.

Other valuable contributions came from Lincoln-born **Tom Tidball** who runs the Tidball Photographic Company in Sri Lanka; **Paul van Riel** in Holland; **David Ryan** and his colleagues, **Ray Young** and **Esther Mugar** at the San Francisco Photo Network; Greg Wenger and his colleagues – **Chas D. Benes, Sally Weigand, C & M Shook, Victoria Adams, Jerome Kelly, Robert Bucknam, Joseph Woods, Robert Comfort and Darien Murray** – at Travel Image in California.

Additional contributors were **Michel Hetier** in Paris; **Lee Foster** in Oakland; **Ed Cooper** in Sonoma, California; **Tom Lippert** in Truckee, California; **Pat Canova** in Miami; **Blair Seitz** in Harrisburg, Pennsylvania; **Ed Armstrong** in New Mexico; **Ping Amranand** in Maryland; **Anirut** and **Candy Bunnag** in Maryland; **Photri, Inc.**, an agency in Alexandria, Virginia; **Tony Stone Worldwide** in London; **D. J. Heaton**; and **Paul Von Stroheim**.

Special thanks also to **Bruce Bernstein** for his historical illustrations; the New York Public Library's Picture Collection; and the travel and tourist departments in the following states: Oregon, Washington, California, Utah, New Mexico. Texas, Louisiana, Alabama, Georgia, South Carolina, North Carolina, Virginia and New Jersey.

–APA Publications

Macrone

Greenwald

Viesti

Pfeifer

Leader

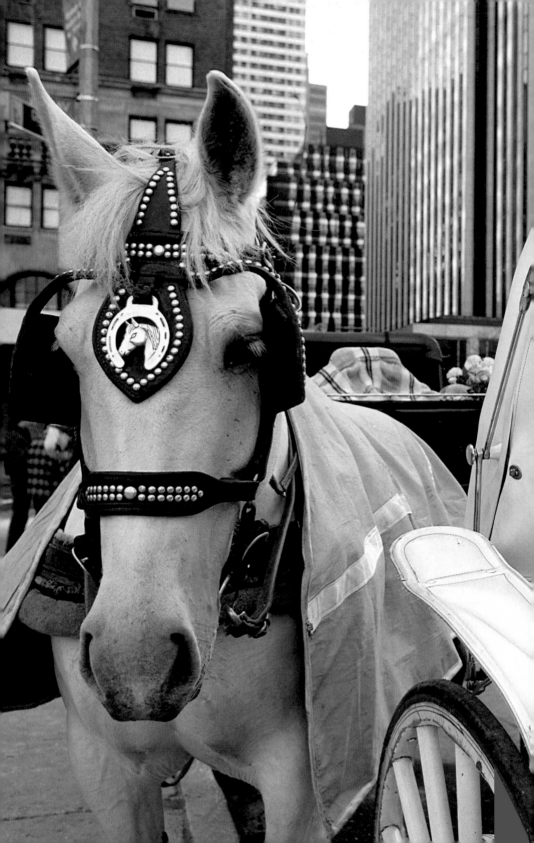

BACKGROUND

THE NORTHERN ROUTE

THE SOUTHERN ROUTE

MAPS

Preceding pages: top-hatted transportation.

TRAVEL TIPS

WELCOME TO AMERICA

The one word that best describes the United States of America is diversity—diversity of peoples, cultures, geographies and climates. Each region of this immense nation exhibits a character and personality all its own. The only way to truly experience and appreciate the contrasts of the country is to drive across it, from the large metropolises of New York and Chicago, to the big sky and open plains of Wyoming and Montana and into the lush forests of the Northwest; or down south through Louisiana's Cajun country, past the Grand Canyon and into California.

Insight Guide: Crossing America is a guidebook for and a story about such journeys. By documenting actual travels across the country, Apa's writers and photographers have created a portrait of the places, sights, people and history of the U.S. *Crossing America* is also a chronicle of life on the road in the U.S., where the sights, sounds and smells continually change as you roll down highways and back roads.

The decision to drive across the country for a book that seeks to discover the true spirit and essence of this vast land is well-grounded. In the book's opening essay, author Rich Taskin discusses how travel and movement are inextricably linked to the history and culture of the nation. The country was settled by groups of people moving westward in search of less crowded and more fertile lands. And travel has informed the arts in America—literature, cinema, popular music—from the very early days.

The travel portion of *Crossing America* is divided into two sections covering two distinct routes: one stretching from New York across the northern states to the northwest corner of the country; the other, a great adventure that begins in New York, cuts down the east coast, across the southern states to the Pacific Ocean and then up the west coast to Seattle. The text recounts the history of each area visited, tells how to get there, relates amusing anecdotes, quotes local citizens, points out worthwhile locales off the beaten track and, on occasion, speaks the ugly truth about popular tourist attractions. The accompanying photographs bring all of this to vivid life.

Interspersed throughout the guide portion of the book are articles about famous Americans (*e.g.* Elvis Presley, Martin Luther King, Jr.), the nation's most breathtaking natural sights, cities not located on one of the routes and such miscellaneous topics as regional American cooking and California wine.

While we at Apa apologize that all areas of the U.S. are not covered in this book (logistically, that would be a nearly impossible task), we are convinced that these two trans-American routes powerfully evoke the character of this nation and all of its infinite variety.

The map overleaf shows the northern route in green. The southern route is divided into three portions: the eastern (shown in blue), southern (in orange) and western (in black). More detailed versions of these maps precede the section of text to which they correspond.

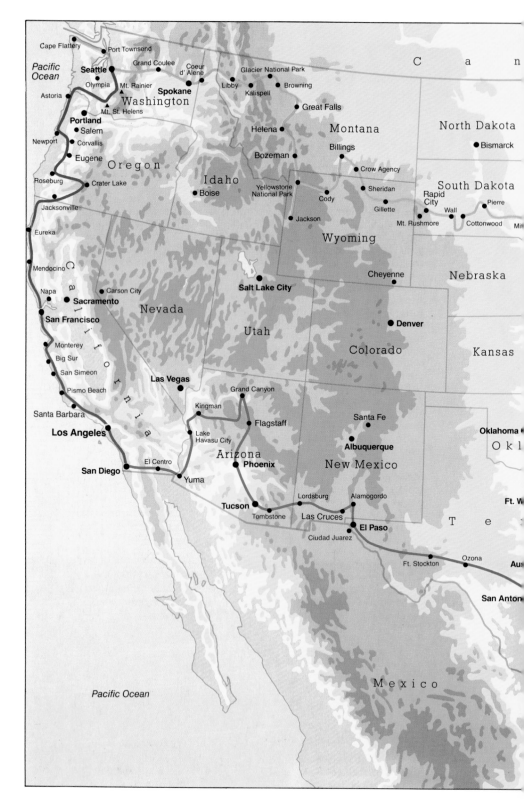

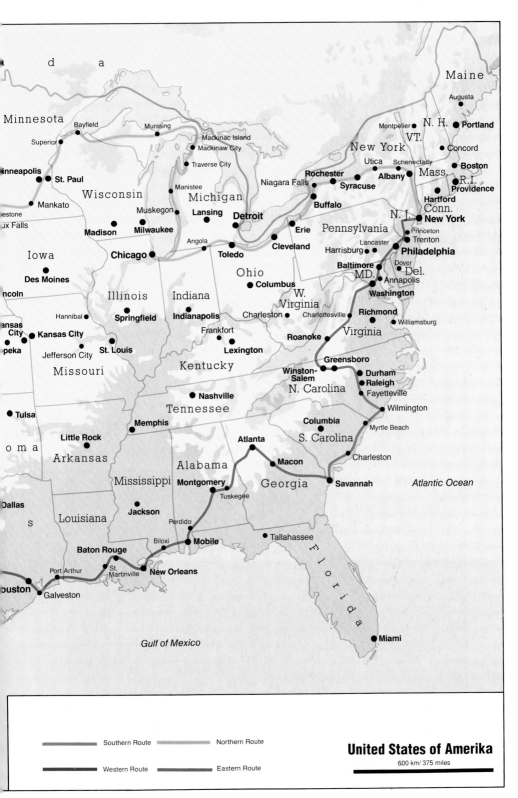

United States of Amerika

600 km/ 375 miles

Southern Route   Northern Route

Western Route   Eastern Route

15

WE'RE ON THE ROAD TO SOMEWHERE

An American will build a house in which to pass his old age and sell it before the roof is on; he will plant a garden and rent it just as the trees are coming into bearing; he will clear a field and leave others to reap the harvest; he will take up a profession and leave it, settle in one place and soon go off elsewhere with his changing desires. If his private business allows him a moment's relaxation, he will plunge at once into the whirlpool of politics. Then, if at the end of a year crammed with work he has a little spare leisure, his restless curiosity goes with him traveling up and down the vast territories of the United States. Thus he will travel five hundred miles in a few days as a distraction from his happiness.

Death steps in at the end and stops him before he has grown tired of this futile pursuit of that complete felicity which always escapes him.

—Alexis de Tocqueville,
Democracy in America

The history of the United States is the story of a people in motion. Movement, mobility and migration are significant forces in American history, and the restless American temperament is a leitmotif of American art. Some of the most basic images of American life—the wagon train rumbling across the prairie, a railroad car speeding through the night, the arrival of immigrants at Ellis Island—are powerful symbols of one nation's timeless obsession with the process of movement. This "restlessness amidst prosperity," identified by the French traveler Alexis de Tocqueville more than 150 years ago as a uniquely American trait, continues to exert an enormous influence upon the American character. Indeed, in a nation where change is the only constant, movement and travel have established the ever quickening tempo of American history.

The meaning of travel is an elusive subject. If the exploration and colonization of America is an example of travel, what about

Preceding pages: Pony Express recruitment poster; Arizona road stretching straight as an arrow; Western horse roundup; American Indian children; "The Scout" keeps watch over Kansas City; Bryce Canyon National Park. The American pioneer spirit is captured in a painting, left, and right, is recalled by a participant in a bicentennial celebration.

the day trip into the country? Can one seriously suggest that the 17th-century Puritan seeking refuge in Boston has anything in common with a 22-year-old computer whiz who moves from Lexington, Massachusetts to Houston, Texas, in search of a higher paying job? Do Lewis and Clark have any common bond with vacationers of the 1950s rolling down Route 66? Such leaps across time and space require a gift for generalization that very few possess. As a general rule, however, it can be stated that travelers everywhere share the belief that movement

may bring prosperity and renewal.

But what's more important than these disparate sojourners is the manner in which we think about travel. For example, travel in pre-modern America was a very serious affair: namely, an essential part of peopling the continent. It is true that some wealthy Americans embarked on European *wanderjahrs*, and some even traveled for pleasure to Newport, Bar Harbor and Saratoga Springs. But it is not these oases of leisure, ease and comfort we associate with the days of old. Rather, we recall Daniel Boone leading pioneers through the Cumberland Gap; young men heeding Horace Greeley's advice and going West to grow up with the country; the Mormons' perilous flight across the

Plains; or the stagecoach company that warned its riders not to "point out where murders have been committed, especially if there are women passengers." We think of travel in early America as a perpetual epic adventure.

Modern Movement

In the late 20th Century, when we go to work, take a trip or run an errand, there is little heroic about it and naturally we flee physical discomfort if at all possible. True, few would deny that Americans are still migrating for economic reasons, particularly to the sunbelt states. But this anonymous and isolated movement of people lacks the drama of the pioneers, or for that matter,

Americans traveled overseas in 1979. By the middle of the decade, when declining fuel prices convinced many Americans that the energy crisis was over, the Automotive Consumer Profile survey revealed that the average American household had more than two vehicles and over one-third had three or more. This growth pattern undoubtedly reflects the expansion of the work force, but it is hard to attribute this proliferation of vehicles simply to economic necessity.

Perhaps an even more impressive index of the migratory habits of the American people is the number of Americans residing in states other than the one in which they were born. Although the unconquered frontier per se may no longer exist, pulling up stakes and heading over the hill for a new start is as

the great Okie migration of the 1930s immortalized in the dustbowl ballads of Woody Guthrie and John Steinbeck's *The Grapes of Wrath*. And yet, it is not unlikely that a 21st Century American historian will judge movement to be as significant a force in the late 20th Century as it was in earlier times.

Certainly that future historian could cite a large body of evidence to sustain the claim that movement and travel remain a key component of the American way. The 1980 census—taken at the height of the energy crisis which sent shock waves through the national psyche—showed Americans on the move at record rates. Not only did the number of registered passenger cars reach a record 121 million, but also some 8 million

common today as it was in the 18th and 19th centuries. In fact, the record suggests it may be more common today than ever before.

In 1850, some 24 percent of the American people were living outside their state of birth, a figure that remained relatively constant for a century. Since 1950, however, the figure has risen steadily and in 1980 reached a record 36.2 percent. So much for the idea that older nations tend to have more stable populations!

Democratized Travel

What do these figures tell us about travel in America today, both permanent and migratory? The sheer numbers involved suggest that the experience of travel is now available to almost everyone. Travel has been democratized, and surely it has played no small role in contributing to the American tendency to view symbols of consumerism (cars, boats and planes) as symbols of equality if not distinction. For better or worse, to be an American is to believe that personal liberty and the freedom to travel, be it on an errand or in search of a slice of utopia, are one and inseparable.

Is there any truth to that belief? Is there a vital link between the uniquely democratic culture of the United States and the transportation revolution of the past two centuries? Michael Chevalier thought so. Chevalier, a French aristocrat sent to the United

building had become a national mania. And Chevalier bore witness to the birth of the age of the railroad, for which he forecast a glorious future.

Riding a steamboat into New Orleans, Chevalier noted that "formerly it was possible only for a patrician to travel, and the great bulk of mankind, were then attached to the globe, chained to the soil by the difficulty of locomotion." But as avenues of economic exchange were opened to more and more people, ideas and populations were transmitted hither and yon along with pelts, peppers and teas. Travel became, in Chevalier's words, a catalyst "to equality and liberty," and he was convinced that modern transportation would "increase the rights and privileges of the greatest number

States in the 1830s to study its public works and who stayed to author a report on its political and social machinery, believed that improved means of travel would hasten the collapse of the old order and play an important role in the emergence of "modern society." During his tour of Jacksonian America, he was amazed by the readiness with which Americans embraced new means of travel: first turnpike roads had been constructed with passionate intensity, then canal

Left, the painting "Manifest Destiny" by Leutze, expresses the eagerness and hopes felt in the early move westward. Right, a modern day camper makes its way across the Badlands of South Dakota.

as truly and as amply as could be done by electoral laws."

Albeit, Chevalier wrote at the beginning of the industrial revolution in America, and he seemed to have drunk rather deeply of the 19th-century faith in progress through science. We now know all too well the mixed blessing of living in a world of rapid transit and rapid deployment systems. We also know that technological achievements have routinized experience while eliminating much physical labor and opening up new paths to the multitudes. But even though the idea that freedom and adventure lie at the end of the road has been partially demystified, the allure of crossing America has lost little of its appeal to restless spirits.

CONQUEST OF SPACE AND TIME: THE TRANSPORTATION REVOLUTION

The transcontinental passenger thinks contracts, profits, vacationtrips, mighty continent between Atlantic and Pacific, power, wires humming dollars, cities jammed, hills empty, and the indiantrail leading into the wagonroad, the macadamed pike, the concrete skyway; trains; planes; history the billiondollar speedup . . .

—John Dos Passos, *USA*

At the beginning of the age of colonization, white settlers generally followed the network of paths that the native Americans had carved out over the centuries. Travel conditions in the early history of the United States were notoriously wretched. It was said that it was cheaper to transport goods across the Atlantic from London to Philadelphia than it was to carry those same goods 100 miles from Philadelphia to Lancaster, Pennsylvania. The big story of 1776. the signing of the Declaration of Independence, took 29 days to reach Charleston. No wonder it was said of the delegates at the Constitutional Convention in 1787 that New England men had more in common with their brethren in England than they did with their fellow countrymen from the Carolina and Georgia.

Fifty years later, when de Tocqueville, Chevalier and a host of European travelers were examining the American experiment in self-government, conditions on dry land were little improved. Whereas the Roman Empire made the construction of great roads an important function of its central government, in 19th-century America laissez-faire attitudes predominated, and the construction of highways was considered a state and local responsibility. Often, what little road work that was done was carried out by farmers and laborers who were unable to meet their tax obligations.

Thus, as a direct consequence of the American belief in "the less government the better," roads suffered from neglect and disrepair. Pioneers such as Abraham Lincoln's father Thomas, who followed the well-worn path from Kentucky to Indiana and Illinois, had to possess courage, physical strength and an incredible tolerance of mud. William Herndon, Lincoln's law partner and biographer, describes the Lincoln family's move from Indiana to Illinois in March of 1830 as one which "suited the roving and migratory spirit of Thomas Lincoln." With the "obscure and penniless" 21-year-old Abe commanding a wagon drawn by two oxen, "the journey was a long and tedious one." Basing his account of the trip upon Lincoln's recollections years later, Herndon memorably evokes the experience of thousands of similar poor whites. "The rude, heavy wagon," he writes, "with its primitive wheels, creaked and groaned as it crawled through the woods and now and then stalled in the mud. Many were the delays."

In antebellum America geography was also a formidable barrier to migration. Even as late as the 1830s, some 80 percent of the American people still resided east of the Allegheny Mountains, and one might have been inclined to agree with Thomas Jefferson's earlier prediction that it would take close to 1,000 years to settle the entire North American continent.

As it turned out, Jefferson was wrong by about 910 years. But his reputation hasn't suffered from this inaccurate prophecy—there is no reason that it should. After all, it was his decision to send those two intrepid travelers, Captain Meriwether Lewis and Lieutenant William Clark, to explore the West and chart the way for settlement of the region.

President Jefferson dispatched Lewis and Clark to the West shortly after the Louisiana Purchase in 1803. His motives for asking for a $2,500 appropriation from Congress to finance the expedition were mixed. Even at this late date it appears that Jefferson had not abandoned all hope that a passage to Asia might be found. He was also confident that the explorers would discover trade routes which would benefit John Jacob Astor and his fellow fur traders. Nor was Jefferson without hope of further expanding what he liked to call the "empire of liberty."

scriptions of what would become the Oregon Trail, but perhaps what one remembers most from sampling their writings are the descriptions of the geology, fauna and wildlife of the West. Their wide range of learning, the courage they displayed in the face of physical deprivation and their eloquence are inspiring. Lewis and Clark were real-life Natty Bumppos, preparing the way for the invasion of the West by white civilization.

By the mid-19th Century, poets and orators—much in demand in a culture that valued the spoken word—matched hyper-

But this is not to say that Jefferson was prevaricating when he explained to the Spanish Minister that the purpose of the mission was the "advancement of science." Jefferson was a child of the Enlightenment, and as such he saw the study of the physical universe as an important chapter in the life of the mind.

And Lewis and Clark did not disappoint Jefferson or posterity on this score. Their voluminous journals provide detailed de-

boles in an effort to describe what one called the "untransacted destiny of the United States." One dimension of this rising glory of the United States would be territorial conquest, and one orator went so far as to forecast that the American lamp of liberty would be visible from Tierra del Fuego to the Aurora Borealis. In the 1840s, the journalist John O'Sullivan popularized the phrase "manifest destiny" to describe this expansionist ideology. Western politicians such as Stephen Douglas based their political fortunes on promoting the future greatness of the West and demanded the construction of a transcontinental railroad to link the nation's rapidly expanding economy. Douglas repeatedly argued during the 1840s and '50s that the

Far left, a remnant of the early railway is kept alive at the Greenfield Village Henry Ford Museum in Dearborn, Michigan. Portraits of American explorers William Clark, left, and Meriwether Lewis, right.

argued during the 1840s and '50s that the West was not only the stage for the nation's future, but also provided the country with an alternative to sectional bickering between the North and South.

Age of the Iron Horse

But before the Union could be linked by rail, the United States was plunged into a bloody civil war. It took four weeks for the news of the opening volley at Ft. Sumter to reach San Francisco, but by the end of the war the nation was forging the bonds of union. The age of the turnpike, steamboat and canal had been overtaken by the iron horse. The war itself may or may not have accelerated the pace of industrialization, but it is widely conceded that the North's superior transportation

ching orders. These robber barons understood that the railroad was the lubricant of both a booming economy and sleazy politics.

The railroad also made long distance travel for pleasure a realistic possibility for middle-class Americans. The creation of the Pullman Palace Car Company in 1868 reflected the growing number of Americans interested in taking vacations. Although an enforced period of rest and relaxation did not sit well with the notorious devotion to work ("the sum of wisdom" according to Emerson, is that "the time is never lost that is devoted to work"), publicists for the new leisure ethic stressed that Americans were growing unhealthy—both physically and spiritually—as a result of their obsession with success. Regeneration through contact with

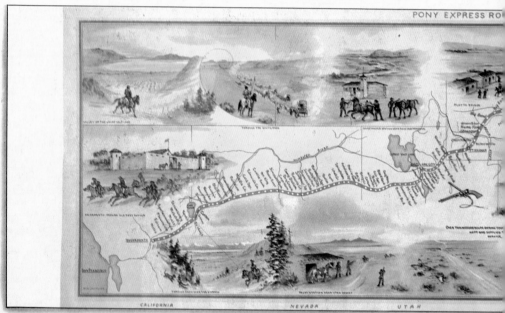

CALIFORNIA   NEVADA   UTAH

system played a crucial role in crushing the rebels. In 1863, the North was able to transport 25,000 troops by rail from Washington, D.C. to Chatanooga to help turn the tide in a major battle.

Mark Twain and Charles Dudley Warner dubbed the final third of the 19th Century "The Gilded Age," an era of conspicuous consumption and corruption. Perhaps the age might better be thought of as the age of the railroad. If one wishes to familiarize oneself with the powers that be in the Gilded Age, one can pretty much ignore the shadow presidencies of Hayes, Arthur and the railroad lawyer Benjamin Harrison and turn to the railroad barons—the Goulds, Huntingtons and Vanderbilts—who gave politicians their mar-

the great outdoors and the vigorous life was a stock promise of popularizers of the West from Teddy Roosevelt to resort owners.

Some intellectuals were particularly disturbed by the implications of the work of Frederick Jackson Turner, a midwestern historian whose landmark 1893 essay, "The Significance of the Frontier in American History," posited that the frontier epoch in the nation's history was at an end. Turner saw the frontier setting as the bedrock of democratic values, and reading his essay through the prism of the chaotic 1890s, it was easy to speculate that the coming century would be one of class conflict and mob rule.

But the same year Turner was delivering his paper at the Chicago World's Fair, two bicycle mechanics, Charles and J. Frank Duryea, were successfully testing the first automobile on the streets of Springfield, Massachusetts.

Car Crazy

Public roads were among the initial benefactors of the age of the automobile. The movement to upgrade the quality of American highways had begun during the 1880s when bicycling organizations like the League of American Wheelmen led the call for improved roads. When automobiles began to appear in the streets and villages in greater numbers after 1900, the drive for surfaced roads attracted increasing support. The instinctive American distrust of federal intrusion into the lives of its citizens was

greatest share of credit for democratizing the automobile and travel is Henry Ford, who introduced to the industry the assembly line which revolutionized the production and sale of cars. In 1922 he sold an astonishing 1.3 million Model Ts. And while their uniformity would soon make them obsolete, the Tin Lizzie had made the automobile a badge of social distinction as well as a necessity.

The impact of the widespread ownership of cars upon travel cannot be overstated. It was probably the single most important factor in the opening of American life not only to travelers seeking remote scenes, but also to 20th-century movers and migrants.

What would the 1930s have been like, after all, if Tom Joad and his fellow wandering poor could not have climbed into a car and headed

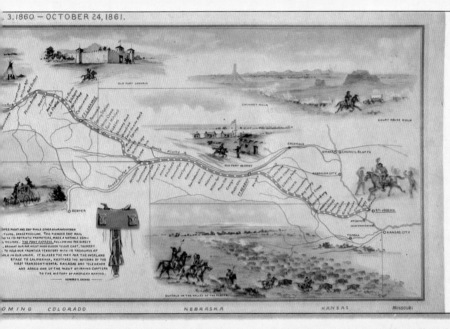

overcome by the politically popular demand that the U.S. Mail ought to be delivered directly to rural Americans over improved roads. In 1916, President Wilson signed a Federal Aid Road Act which was the first of a series of occasions when federal intrusion into the nation's transportation system met with widespread public approval.

The constituency for such governmental action grew larger with each passing decade. And the person who probably deserves the

A map of the mid 19th-Century Pony Express route that stretched from St. Joseph, Kansas to Sacramento, California, connecting Midwest and West.

for California where, as one Jimmie Rodgers song promised, the "water tastes like cherry wine?" The increased mobility the automobile offered underscores the judgement of George F. Pierson, who in his book *The Moving American* describes this lateral freedom as "the great American permit to be both more free and more equal than our contemporaries could manage to become in the more static societies of Europe."

In the 1980s, people began traveling faster and farther than ever in greater numbers, and de Tocqueville's American who traveled "five hundred miles in a few days as a distraction from his happiness" now has been replaced by a globe-trotter pursuing equally elusive dreams.

POETRY IN MOTION:
AMERICAN ARTISTS AND THE ROAD

*I'm going down that long,
    lonesome road
And I ain't gonna be
    treated this a-way.*

—"Lonesome Road Blues," better
known as "Going Down the Road
                    Feelin' Bad"

*Within me, latitudes widen,
    longitude lengthens.*

—Walt Whitman, "Salutau Monde!"

American artists seem to be perpetually on the run. Their work epitomizes to an extreme the wanderlust of the American people, the belief in movement for movement's sake. "The sound of a jet," John Steinbeck wrote in 1961, "an engine warming up, even the clopping of shod hooves on pavement brings an ancient shudder, the dry mouth and vacant eye, the hot palms and the churn of stomach high up under the rib cage."

Over a century before, Herman Melville depicted travel as a balm to a depressed soul. "Whenever I find myself growing grim about the mouth," he muses in the famous first paragraph of *Moby Dick*, "whenever it is a damp, drizzly, November in my soul; . . . whenever my hypos get such an upper hand of me, that it requires a strong moral principle to prevent me from deliberately stepping into the street, and methodically knocking people's hats off—then, I account it high time to get to sea as soon as I can." In the classic American fiction of Melville, Edgar Allan Poe, James Fenimore Cooper and Twain we repeatedly encounter characters fleeing the inertia of polite society for a jaunt into the wild. Nineteenth-century romanticism celebrated the arcadian, rural world over that of the hypocritical, acquisitive city, and of course American writers could also draw from Greek and Roman models in devising fiction of the open road and sea.

"I wish for a change of place," J. Hector St. John de Crevecoeur wrote in the final chapter of *Letters From an American Far-*

Left, a rebellious Marlon Brando "hits the road" in the 1954 film *The Wild One*. Right, Walt Whitman, one of the greatest American poets, was a preeminent celebrator of individual freedom and democracy.

mer. "The hour is come at last, that I must fly from my home and abandon my farm!" To be sure, Crevecoeur's threat to flee into the Indian territory "and revert into a state approaching nearer to that of nature, unencumbered either with voluminous laws, or contradictory codes" was pure fiction, no more likely to occur than Mark Twain hooking up with Huck Finn a century later when Huck threatened to "light out for the territory." But Crevecoeur was one of the first of a lengthy procession of American writers to celebrate the movement away from the com-

plexity of modern life.

The desire to travel afar in search of spiritual and physical revitalization did not simply express itself as a desire to move across land. Particularly in the mid-19th Century it seemed to observers like de Tocqueville that the American people "were destined to be a great maritime people . . . born to rule the seas as the Romans were to conquer the world." The desire to see what Herman Melville liked to call "the watery part of the world" was an animating force behind Melville's sea novels as well as those of Poe, Cooper and Richard Henry Dana.

But whether on land or sea, the great writers of 19th-century America viewed travel as a "stay against confusion" in a

Left, a rebellious Marlon Brando "hits the road" in the 1954 film *The Wild One*. Right, Walt Whitman, one of the greatest American poets, was a preeminent celebrator of individual freedom and democracy.

society committed to material gain. When they were too old to sail before the mast, Melville, Nathaniel Hawthorne and Cooper sought refuge in foreign travel. Like the Parisian expatriates of the 1920s, they felt alienated from the climate of the times.

Poet of the Open Road

Their despair with the democratic masses stand in marked contrast to one of the greatest American poets of the open road, Walt Whitman. The journey along the open highway perfectly suited his desire to know and comprehend the whole of life. The casual meeting, the encounter between the eye of the seer and the landscape and the timelessness of nature are recurrent themes in Whit-

also,
I think I could stop here myself and do
*   miracles,*
I think whatever I shall meet on the road I
*   shall like, and whoever beholds me*
*   shall like me.*
I think whoever I see must be happy.

The use of the voyage as metaphor for change is part of the achievement of Mark Twain. It was Twain who in his greatest novel, *The Adventures of Huckleberry Finn*, made it clear that the voyage was a learning experience and a rebellion against conventional morality. Some of the most moving passages in the book are Huck's descriptions of life on the river. Every adventure, however, requires a return, and each time Huck and the escaped slave Jim touch base with

man's work, and together are part of his quest for cosmic harmony.

Although Whitman's mentor, Ralph Waldo Emerson, would insist in "Self-Reliance" that the "soul is no traveler; the wise man stays at home," Whitman saw the open road as the passage to wisdom and fraternity. The act of traveling itself is a democratic gesture to Whitman, a source of poetic inspiration and a symbol of his personal liberty. Not only were the "American people the greatest poem," but the American environment itself was an incubator of freedom and unity. As he wrote in "Song of the Open Road":

I think all heroic deeds were all conceiv'd
*   in the open air, and all free poems*

people on shore, trouble, trickery and cruelty predominate. The book ends with Huck's famous vow to flee civilization and its hypocrisy. But, of course, the old-fashioned frontier was disappearing when Twain was writing in the 1880s, and Huck's dream of flight belonged to a vanishing world.

The elegiac note that closes *Huckleberry Finn* brings to mind another characteristic of American literature from Cooper through Twain right down to Jack Kerouac and William Kennedy: loneliness, and the traveler as a solitary figure.

It is not just our literary artists who have sung of the loneliness and vagaries of the open road. Country music in particular often focuses on that "lonesome guy" Hank Williams sang about on "the lost highway." Old Irish and English ballads about murder and betrayal were often reworked by cowboys who sang at night to fight off despair and to keep the cattle from stampeding. It should come as no surprise to learn that much of the music produced under such circumstances was often grim and filled with resignation. In the 20th Century, singers such as Gene Autry and Roy Rogers evoked the nostalgia of the open range: truck drivers. These mod-confined by harsh economic circumstances to lives of poverty and loneliness.

Not all country music is downbeat, however. A whole genre of country has arisen devoted to the lives of those modern riders of the open range: truckdrivers. These mod-ern folk figures form a loyal audience for

some Highway Blues" the man fleeing the hellhounds and slave-catchers is "feelin' bad," perhaps because he understands something about the paradoxical nature of freedom.

In the 20th Century, artists such as Robert Johnson evoked the road as a haunting meeting place. In his highly influential song "Crossroads," it is hard to say exactly why "he got down on his knees and prayed"—perhaps because the crossroad is where the bodies of suicides are often buried?—but what is clear is Johnson's anguish and fear.

This Land is Your Land

But if Walt Whitman is the most buoyant celebrator of the open road and Robert

country music, and songs like the much recorded "Six Days on the Road" are Whit-manesque whoops of triumph over the gov-ernment, the cops and anything else in the way of seeing "my baby tonight."

The road is often the scene of terror and flight in blues music. The escaped slave literally saw the open road as the path to freedom, but in such songs as the "Lone-

Left, Peter Fonda and Dennis Hopper on the move in the 1969 film *Easy Rider.* Center, American writer John Steinbeck, best known for his 1939 novel *The Grapes of Wrath.* Right, folk singer and composer Woody Guthrie.

Johnson the most serious habituate of the dark side of the street, surely Woodrow Wilson "Woody" Guthrie is the bard of the open road. Even a simple listing of some of his best known songs—"Dust Bowl Re-fugees," "I Ain't Got No Home," "Walkin' Down the Railroad Line," "Will Rogers Highway," "So Long," "It's Been Good to Know You," etc.—suggests the prominence he assigned to "walkin' down the line." Like Whitman, he attempted to capture the whole of America in his verses. At times, as in "This Land is Your Land," he succeeded as few have or will. Occasionally, in songs like "The Great Historical Bum," he was able to laugh at his persona as the roustabout poet of the open road:

I'm just a lonesome traveler, the great
    historical bum,
Highly educated from history I have come,
I built the Rock of Ages, it was in the
    year of one
And that's about the biggest thing that
    man has ever done.

Guthrie lived the life he wrote about after his middle-class family was destroyed by tragedy and disease. The best of his songs are timeless—not surprisingly many of his tunes borrow heavily from hymns and old ballads—and will live as long as there are roads to walk and people to sing.

The great road films of Hollywood probably are the sagas of the open plains. People all over the world think of the United States as a land of wide open spaces thanks to the image of America they receive from the films of John Ford and countless other Western movies. Here again we encounter solitary figures who have an uncomfortable relationship with polite society. Ready to right wrong wherever they find it, the cowboy must move along in the last reel.

Clint Eastwood's *Pale Rider* attempted to revive this formula in the 1980s, but since the 1960s the cowboy has been replaced by motor-driven outlaws as the star of mythic road films. From Marlon Brando in *The Wild One* to Mel Gibson in *The Road Warrior*, films set on the road have focused upon wandering anti-social, anti-heroes who take the alienation of the cowboy to an emotional extreme.

Perhaps *Bonnie and Clyde* takes this aspect of the road picture genre to its tragi-comic limit. The story of Clyde Barrow and Bonnie Parker seems like a folk tale of the Depression '30s viewed through the counter-cultural lens of the 1960s. Bonnie and Clyde rob banks that rob the poor of their dreams and make their getaway to the sound of rebellious country music. They seem like two kids who went to the movies to learn how to get in the money, but rather than dying with their boots on they're gunned down alongside their last stolen car.

Bonnie and Clyde brought the road film skidding into the tumultuous '60s. But probably no film of the recent past inspired more real-life voyages than *Easy Rider*. Those who see the film as a period piece and high camp have no idea how its original viewers saw it. It was probably the most powerful advertisement for the counter-culture to appear in movie houses throughout the heartland of the nation. Even to this day,

there are middle-aged blue-collar workers who dream of throwing away their beepers and multifunctional wrist watches, climbing aboard a Harley motorcycle and retracing the voyage of Captain America and Billy to New Orleans.

Since World War II, the accelerated pace of travel has produced a literature equally frenetic. The most famous road book of the age has, of course, been Jack Kerouac's *On the Road*, the definitive statement of beat culture and the McGuffrey's Reader of cultural radicals of the 1960s and '70s. Kerouac's prose and the quality of his mind may impress us less as we grow older, but his celebration of the possibilities of finding spiritual truths while racing across the continent makes his work compelling in ways that transcend literary canons.

James Dean, the rebel without a cause, reclines outside a Texas mansion in the 1955 film *Giant*.

Kerouac's work continues the tradition of artist as pathfinder and spiritual voyager into the late 20th Century. William Least Heat Moon's *Blue Highways* extends that tradition into the 1980s. Moon traversed the nation in his van "Ghost Dancing" after being laid off from his job at a small college in the Midwest. His report is both a rumination on travel literature in general and one of the most revealing studies of the state of the nation since de Tocqueville. Whereas Kerouac filters all experience through his ahistorical frame of mind, Moon, by letting people speak for themselves, captures the diversity of the landscape that overwhelms the trans-American traveler.

Sometimes, in fact, the complexity of the American experience is more than one mind can absorb. John Steinbeck's best-selling *Travels With Charley* is an honest effort by a great American writer to take stock of his country in 1960, but the book seems overly restrained. As Steinbeck drove the nation's highways in his van "Rocinante" with his faithful poodle Charley, perhaps he realized that the America he knew and described with such searing realism in the 1930s and '40s was as distant to him as the Hannibal of antebellum America was to Mark Twain in the 1880s.

The swoop of history follows us down every highway, and the traveler has many teachers to choose from before embarking on an adventure. For William Moon, Walt Whitman served as the model. For the incurably romantic Steinbeck, Cervantes was his inspiration. As you head out on the human highway, reader and friend, listen to those voices speaking to you, but know that there is no experience like an original one.

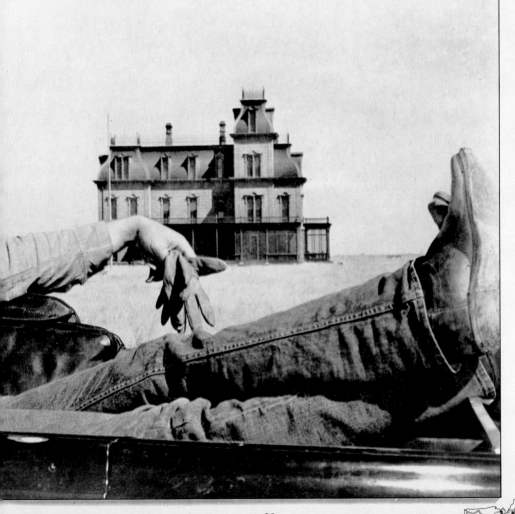

THE NORTHERN ROUTE

The northern route across the U.S. is framed on either side by the nation's largest metropolis and some of its most unspoiled lands. It is the shorter, more direct of the two trans-American tours in *Crossing America*, but it is by no means a straight line between two points. On the road between New York and the Olympic Peninsula you will encounter a fascinating collage of farmlands, ranches, wilderness, port towns, declining industrial cities, reborn urban centers and constant reminders of the nation's history.

The first half of the journey is marked and guided by water. From New York City the route swings north along the shores of the Hudson River into the industrial triangle of New York State and alongside the once-bustling, now-dormant Erie Canal. Then you will come upon the Finger Lakes and the cities of Syracuse and Rochester before reaching Lake Erie and Niagara Falls.

The Great Lakes dominate the next portion of the trip. The shores of Erie are dotted with industrial cities—Buffalo, Erie, Toledo—that have seen better days but are attempting revitalization. Next you will reach Chicago, the midwestern crossroads, a city of marvelous architecture at the southern tip of Lake Michigan. From here to the thriving twin cities of Minneapolis and St. Paul the tour cuts through cities and towns that owe their existence—as vacation spots, fishing villages and ports—to the Lakes.

Once you reach western Minnesota, however, the character of the land begins to change. As you cut into South Dakota, the geo-

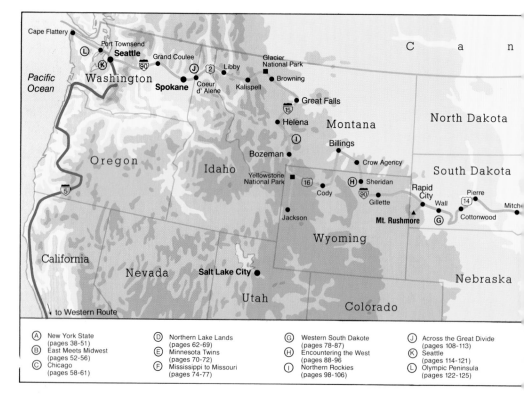

graphy overwhelms. Rising out of the prairie are the otherworldly Badlands, the Black Hills and Wounded Knee, a reminder of the nation's brutal treatment of Native Americans.

Next, along a legendary stagecoach route, come towns of the notorious Wild West that were once inhabited by the likes of "Wild Bill" Hickok, Calamity Jane and "Buffalo Bill" Cody. The sky here is huge and the land seems vast, populated mainly by small buttes, sagebrush, cattle and deer. The route through this area of Wyoming and Montana passes the site of General Custer's last stand against the Indians and stops at an actual cow camp.

From here the tour passes into the northern portion of the Rocky Mountains, and the main attractions are the gorgeous national parks of Yellowstone, Grand Teton and Glacier. Crossing the Continental Divide on paths previously traveled by mountain tribes, trappers, traders, gold and silver prospectors and homesteaders, the northern route cuts through the forests of Montana, the Idaho panhandle and into the state of Washington, where the land modulates between deserts, canyons and irrigated farm land.

The final portion of the route shoots westward toward the Pacific into the very livable, cosmopolitan port of Seattle and then onto the Olympic Peninsula, the northwesternmost outcropping of the coterminous U.S. This is among the nation's most remote, exotic and wildly beautiful spots, an ideal place to reflect upon your just-completed trans-American journey.

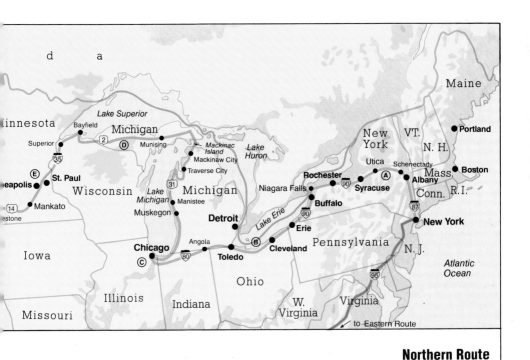

Northern Route

600 km/ 375 miles

NEW YORK: THE STATE

Oh the Er-i-ee is arisin'
And the gin is agettin' low
And I scarcely think we'll get a drink
'Til we get to Buffalo
—Old Erie Canal Song, 19th century

Buffalo, New York is not the destination it once was. As the 19th-century terminus of the Erie Canal, it served as a funnel through which raw materials, pioneers and immigrant laborers flowed into the midwestern states.

The idea of a canal connecting Albany, on the Hudson River, and Buffalo, on Lake Erie was greeted with skepticism and derision at first. Detractors called it "Clinton's Ditch" after De Witt Clinton, champion of the project. Completed in 1825, and eventually bypassed in the early 20th century, the Erie Canal was responsible for the settling of the Midwest and the rise of the state of New York. The old canal towns, once the sites of boisterous activity, are quiet now, many down on their luck.

Tracing this great inland water route along the Hudson from New York to Albany then west toward Buffalo is not the shortest distance between two points, but is well-worn and rich with history. The river, so majestic it inspired a school of painting, is lined with stately mansions and manor houses, towns, palisades and wooded groves. Place names recall earlier inhabitants of the region, from the eastern Woodland Indians to the early Dutch settlers.

If you're traveling north, **Broadway** is a good road to follow out of New York City. This city's manic and overstimulating version of Main Street, is a year-round midway along which every manner of life unfolds. Basically, it parallels the **Hudson River**. Broadway continues north past the stately George Washington Bridge and the Cloisters. It crosses the Harlem River into the Bronx, passes Van Cortland Park and enters Yonkers, the start of suburban Westchester County. Broadway changes names a few times as it makes its way upstate. At times it's known as Albany Post Road or US 9, but it retains its status as a main thoroughfare throughout Westchester County.

Yonkers suffers from identity problems, with one foot in the Bronx and one in Westchester. On the suburban side, it is home of St. Andrew's Course, where golf was introduced in the United States. West of Broadway, in a pastoral setting overlooking the Hudson and New Jersey's Palisades, is the Hudson River Museum housed in the historic Glenview mansion.

As Broadway continues north it passes through towns, villages and hamlets which are greener, less populated and generally well-heeled. Many have hyphenated names ending with the words "on-Hudson." Between Hastings-on-Hudson and Ardsley-on-Hudson, the road passes by the **Ardsley Club**. Organized by a group of millionaires in 1895, it was America's third golf course. According to local history, its founders were also early owners of automobiles which they tested for pos-

sible commercial value—perhaps racing up and down Broadway.

Sleepy Hollow

Tarrytown lies at the opposite side of the Tappan Zee Bridge, and as its name implies it's a good place to stop. Washington Irving made his home here in the 1800s and set several of his stories here including "Rip Van Winkle" and the "Legend of Sleepy Hollow." Tourists can visit the writer's home, **Sunnyside**, and find it much as it was over a century ago. Whimsical in design, Irving called it "... as full of angles and corners as an old cocked hat!"

Broadway continues north through **Ossining**, home of the infamous Sing Sing penitentiary, now closed. The folks at the local Chamber of Commerce would rather send you up the river to the **Old Croton Aqueduct**.

Nearby **Croton-on-Hudson** was settled by Irish and Italian laborers who came here to build Croton Dam, which in turn created a reservoir of the same name. This water supply for New York City gave rise to the term "Croton bug" for a type of cockroach which thereafter began proliferating in the city. In the 1910s, an exodus of intelligentsia from Greenwich Village trickled upriver to this peaceful community, creating quite a stir in the process. Among them were Max Eastman, Edna St. Vincent Millay and radical journalist John Reed, who was reintroduced and romanticized by **Warren Beatty** in his film *Reds*. The town later became suburbanized and considerably more complacent.

Farther north, State 9D splits from US 9 and follows the river's course more closely. **Garrison** takes you to **Boscobel**, a gracious Federal-style mansion built in the 19th Century, complete with herb and rose gardens and an orangery. Nearby, the riverfront village of **Cold Spring** is a haven for browsers, with antique and other specialty shops housed in 19th-century buildings. Across the river is the **U.S. Military Academy at West Point**, known to military insiders simply as "The Point."

Left, a young couple smiles over New York champagne. Right, a Halloween grimace at a roadside farm.

State 9D rejoins US 9 south of Poughkeepsie and brings you to the **Hyde Park** mansion of Franklin Delano Roosevelt (FDR), the 32nd U.S. president. The views of the Hudson from this national historic site are magnificent, and the grounds are open year-round until dusk. The home, which remains as it was at the time of FDR's death in 1945, can be toured in combination with the **FDR Library and Museum** and the neighboring **Vanderbilt Mansion**, built in the late 19th Century. All three are located along US 9, as is the **Culinary Institute of America**. The Institute runs three fine restaurants (reservations essential) on its 75-acre (30-hectare) campus overlooking the Hudson.

Rhinebeck, farther along US 9, boasts the oldest hotel in the nation (1700). But most people come here to visit the **Dutchess County Fairgrounds**, site of the annual county fair and regional craft. Visitors will also find the **Old Rhinebeck Aerodrome**, with its collection of vintage flying machines spanning the era from 1908-1938. Be prepared to see white silk scarves trailing in the wind (perhaps your own); air shows are staged on weekends, and open-cockpit biplane rides are available for spectators.

At Rhinebeck, State 9G splits off from US 9, with less traffic and greater proximity to the river. You'll pass by orchards on both sides of the road. This is McIntosh apple country, and you can obtain the local delights at numerous roadside stands, or better yet, you can pick your own at many local farms. Just south of Germantown is **Clermont**, once the estate of Robert R. Livingston, who helped draft the Declaration of Independence, and now maintained as a historic and recreational facility.

About 10 miles (16 km) north is **Hudson**. Beyond the Rip Van Winkle Bridge, just south of town, is **Olana**, the Persian-style former home, studio and estate of artist Frederic E. Church of the Hudson River School. Set on a hilltop over the river, the house provided the artist with an ideal vantage point from which to paint his favorite subject. The

Left, a country-fair Uncle Sam signs autographs. Right, a vintage plane at the Rhineback Aerodome.

grounds are as wonderful as the mansion—perfect for picnics in spring and summer. In winter, the pond is for ice skaters and the carriage trails are an open invitation to cross-country skiers.

Downtown Hudson has undergone a facelift intended to preserve its heritage as an old waterfront town and whaling center. Henry Hudson himself landed the "Half Moon" here in 1609. At one time a bustling saloon town filled with sailors, it is now a peaceful community with a keen sense of its own history.

North of Hudson, State 9J steals the distinction of being closest to the river away from 9G. The stretch of road from here to the industrial Capital District traces the Hudson and is particularly beautiful. Along this route, just south of **Kinderhook**, is **Lindenwald**, the home of eighth U.S. president Martin Van Buren. The Van Alen House in Kinderhook is representative of early Dutch architecture in the region.

Albany, Troy and Schenectady are points of a triangle formed by the convergence of the Hudson and Mohawk River. Although no longer the booming metropolises they once were, the three cities have managed to maintain their vitality through difficult times.

US 9 and its tributaries converge and cross the Hudson at Rensselaer, heading straight into the granite and marble heart of **Albany**, the state capital. Albany shouts its importance with its buildings. The 96-acre (39-hectare) **Governor Nelson A. Rockefeller Empire State Plaza** is a governmental and cultural conglomerate that has replaced the State University campus designed by Edward Durrell Stone as the most imposing and futuristic show in town. Over 40 stories high, the Plaza's **Tower Building** offers a stunning view of the city.

But Albany is more than a collection of impressive buildings. It also has a historic and human side that is often overlooked. Few people know that Albany is the second oldest permanent settlement in the 13 original colonies. Henry Hudson explored the area, and Dutch traders established an active trad-

New York State's picturesque Hudson River.

ing post here before the arrival of the "Mayflower." Although few structures remain from this era, travelers can visit **First Church**, one of the oldest houses of worship in the country. Visitors interested in architecture of a later period will find the 19th Century especially well-represented. Two buildings are of special interest, the Romanesque Revival **City Hall**, where the carillon rings out daily, and the **State Capitol**, whose steps become a farmers' market during the growing season.

For travelers who want to get a feel for more current history, there is perhaps no better source than William Kennedy's *Ironweed*, winner of the 1984 Pulitzer Prize. Kennedy deals with Albany's 20th-century human landscape, probing corners of the city's social history that are often neglected by visitors and residents alike. North of Albany on the other side of the Hudson is **Troy**, a key site during America's Industrial Revolution. This old canal town and inland port was also once the home of author Herman Melville.

On the north side of town is **Oakwood Cemetery**, the site of "Uncle Sam's grave. Sam Wilson was a Troy meat packer who provisioned the U.S. Army during the War of 1812. The "U.S. Beef" stamp was interpreted as "Uncle Sam's Beef," and Sam's caricature, commanding in red, white and blue, later became a symbol of the United States.

Crossing Rivers

US 4 leaves Troy and crosses the Hudson to **Waterford**, America's oldest incorporated village. A guided tour of the village's historic district can be arranged by contacting the village historian (common in many upstate villages). From Waterford, another road takes you across the Mohawk to **Cohoes**, situated at the point where the rivers converge and create lovely waterfall. Known locally as "Spindle City," it rose to prominence in the mid-19th Century as a center for cotton knittings.

Leaving the Hudson behind now,

The face of government in Albany. Left, the State Office Building. Right, the Capitol.

Crescent Road follows the Mohawk River out of Cohoes and crosses at the first of many river bends to **Crescent**. A starlight cruise along the Mohawk River, spiced with information about the old **Erie Canal**, departs from the end of the bridge here. From Crescent to Vischer Ferry and Rexford, River View Road follows the course of the river as it curves westward. Vestiges of the Erie Canal can be viewed along this route.

Vischer Ferry is an old canal town on the banks of the Mohawk, much of it unchanged since its 19th-century heyday. Once known as Amity, the hamlet was anything but friendly, for the canal spawned continual trouble. You can spot the remains of aqueducts and low-slung farmers' bridges along River View Road. But the canaller's call of "Low bridge! Everybody down!" no longer rings through the valley.

At Rexford, State 146 crosses the Mohawk to the town of **Niskayuna** on the south shore. This was once the site of a thriving Mohawk Indian agricultural community, later settled by the Dutch in 1640. Today it is the home of General Electric's (GE) Research and Development Center, one of the world's largest such facilities. Due east of Niskayuna is **Schenectady**. A plaque in this town sums up its early history: "Settled by Van Curler 1661. Burned by French and Indians Feb 8, 1690."

Because it was the farthest west of all Dutch settlements in the New World, the town's settlers built a stockade around the land which was bounded by the Mohawk River and the Binne Kill. The stockade is now gone, dismantled during the American Revolution; but the area it protected is still known as the **Stockade** and is now a historic district containing an eclectic array of buildings spanning three centuries.

Schenectady's strategic riverfront location has historically made it an important center for commerce and transportation. The city supplied Revolutionary troops battling in the Mohawk Valley, and in the 19th Century it was a major port. In 1931 it became the terminus of the nation's first passenger steam

Waterside living on the Finger Lakes.

train, the "DeWitt Clinton," an innovation stimulated by the protracted process of traversing the 23 locks between Albany and Schenectady.

Schenectady has not been exempt from the exodus of industry out of the Northeast. In the 19th Century it progressed from being a center for the manufacture of brooms, broom corn thrives along the Mohawk to "the city that lights and hauls the world." The Schenectady Locomotive Works (later the American Locomotive Company) opened in 1851, followed by Edison and his Machine Works, (which later became GE). The Locomotive Company pulled out of town in 1970, but the lights are still on at GE.

Leatherstocking Trails

New York's heartland is generally considered to begin west of the industrial triangle of Albany, Troy and Schenectady. This essentially rural area north of the Catskill Mountains and south of the Adirondacks is also known as the **Leatherstocking District**, after the protective garb once worn by trailblazers. Native son James Fenimore Cooper immortalized the region in his *Leatherstocking Tales* and his other works. And the numerous Revolutionary War battles that took place throughout the Mohawk River Valley are the subject of Walter D. Edmonds' historical novel, *Drums Along the Mohawk*.

Schenectady's Broadway leaves town in a southwesterly direction (State 7). It passes through Rotterdam and Duanesburg, where State 7, US 20 and I-88 converge. From there US 20 travels to **Esperance** on Schoharie Creek. This pleasant town features old houses, antique shops and the obligatory country store. About eight miles (13 km) south of here along State 30, which follows the creek, is the town of **Schohairie**, the third oldest village upstate. Its **Old Stone Fort Museum Complex** started as a church in 1722, became a fort during the Revolution and has served as museum and library specializing in early American since 1889.

The Erie Canal at Rome, a manmade passage through the countryside.

An interesting chapter out of Schohairie's past includes the Middleburg and Schohairie Railroad built in the late 1860s. This short, 5.7-mile (9.1-km) run down the Schohairie Creek Valley transported hops and other local products. The railroad's president was fond of pointing out that although it wasn't as long as other railroads, it was just as wide. In its last days the line's single locomotive faltered physically and financially, and operation were finally stopped in 1936.

US 20 west of Sharon and Sharon Springs is one of the loveliest stretches of road in central New York, providing a panoramic view of **Cherry Valley**, the site of an infamous massacre in 1778, now crimson only in autumn. At **Richfield Springs**, known for its sulfur springs and fossil-hunting grounds, State 167 travels north toward **Little Falls**. Not far up the road, is the **Russian Orthodox Holy Trinity Monastery**. It is startling to the eye in this land of colonial history, 19th-century buildings and rustic farm houses.

Little Falls' **Herkimer Home** the former residence of Revolutionary War hero Brigadier General Nicholas Herkimer, provides a glimpse of colonial life—from maple sugar gatherings to sheep shearing. This canal town once had the world's highest lock, at 41 feet (12.5 meters). West of here along State 5 is Herkimer, named after the general whose statue still commands attention. The **Herkimer County Courthouse** was the site of the Gillette murder trial which inspired Theodore Dreiser to write *An American Tragedy*, depicting the dark side of the American dream. George Stevens' film version, *A Place in the Sun*, featured Montgomery Clift (never more tortured), Shelley Winters (never more pathetic), and Elizabeth Taylor (never more luminous).

Between Herkimer and **Mohawk** along State 5S is the **Fort Herkimer Church** built in 1730. But Mohawk's most unusual attraction is **Dorothea's Christmas**, an estate overlooking the Mohawk Valley that harks back to 1790. The front parlor and ballroom of

Expert brewmaster tappin' the keg at Utica's F.X. Matt Brewery.

46

the 23-room house contain 20 Christmas trees decorated with European glass ornaments and antique miniatures. This fanciful indoor forest is open from May Day to Christmas Eve.

Ilion, a small industrial pocket, is located just beyond Mohawk. The **Remington Firearms Museum** here is devoted to the great guns made by Remington Arms Company, past and present. Continuing west, the road terminates in **Utica**, the only city of any size since Schenectady.

Utica, once named Fort Schuyler, is rich in colonial and revolutionary history. But perhaps the biggest attraction here is the **Munson-Williams-Proctor Institute**, reputed to have one of the finest collections of 18th- through 20th-century American and European art in the northeast, housed in a building designed by Philip Johnson. On a less cultural note, Utica's **F.X. Matt Brewery**, maker of Utica Club, gives the beer away at their Victorian era tavern. it's all part of a brewery tour that culminates in a trolley ride to the tavern.

State 69 leaves Utica for **Rome**, best known for its crucial role in the building of the Erie Canal. Beyond this point there were no continuous natural water routes westward. This is where excavation began. Commemorating this important chapter in its history is the **Erie Canal Village** a reconstructed 1840s village near a refurbished section of the old canal. The biggest draw here is the "Independence," a packet boat towed down the canal by horses. In winter the village features sleigh rides.

The canal brought industry to Rome, some of which remains. There is also a military presence here—the Strategic Air Command's 416th Bombardment Wing at Griffiss Air Force Base. Tours of the base are available in the summer.

Rome has always been serious about America. You will find a reconstruction of 18th-century Fort Stanwix and the Tomb of the Unknown Soldiers of the American Revolution. And this is where native son Francis Bellamy wrote the "Pledge of Allegiance." Actually, there is no respite from patriotism;

Waterways manufactured and natural: left, the Erie Barge Canal at Little Falls; right, cascading water at Chittenango Falls.

even Fort Putt Miniature Golf provides a crash course in American history along its 18 holes.

State 46 takes you from Rome to **Oneida**, still home to the Oneida Indians. The Oneida Community, associated with this town but actually just southeast in Sherrill, was established in the mid-19th Century by John Humphrey Noyes and his followers. Calling themselves perfectionists, they adhered to a strict sexual code as part of a community-determined system of selective breeding. In their spare time they produced high quality silver-plated flatware. The community was dissolved in 1881, but the silver-plate business continues to thrive.

Chittenango is a short drive from Oneida along State 5. (If you can't wait for Niagara Falls, head straight for **Chittenago Falls**). In town, don't be surprised to see a yellow brick sidewalk, for this is "Oztown, USA." The sidewalk is a tribute to L. Frank Baum, author of the beloved *Wizard of Ox*. State 5, leads to Syracuse.

Finger Lakes: The Northern Tips

Following hot on the heels of the Leatherstocking region are the **Finger Lakes**, a series of 11 watery depressions created by glaciers. This region is characterized by vineyards, gracious inns, myriad freshwater pursuits and ballooning hot-air.

Syracuse is the urban gateway to the Finger Lakes. In Syracuse, State 5 becomes Erie Boulevard and cuts through the heart of the city along a path carved by the Erie Canal. The Greek Revival **Weughlock Building**, built in 1849, once weighed canal boats for the purpose of toll collection. At the turn of the century it was converted into an office building, and in its latest reincarnation it serves as the **Erie Canal Museum**.

Syracuse was once a center for the salt trade and some still refer to it as "Salt City." The town boomed during the 19th and early 20th centuries, as its well preserved architecture demonstrates. The **Landmark Theatre**, an ornate "fantasy palace" built in the

Autumn in the woods of the Finger Lakes region.

48

1920s, has been renovated and functions now as a multi-dimensional entertainment center.

Syracuse University, elevated on a hill above the city, draws crowds of sports fans and other audiences to its huge **Carrier Dome**. For the more sedate, it offers the **Joe and Emily Lowe Art Gallery**. Art-lovers should not miss a visit to the **Everson Museum of Art**, designed by I.M. Pei.

State 5 leaves Syracuse on its way to **Camillus**, where you can canoe to your heart's content along seven miles (11 km) of navigable canal in the **Camillus-Erie Canal Town Park** which includes Nine-Mile Creek Aqueduct. Farther along, the road merges with US 20, a route that strings together the northern tips of the largest Finger Lakes.

Past Cayuga Lake US 20 follows the Seneca River to **Seneca Falls**, where the First Women's Rights Convention was convened. The site has been developed into a National Historic Site and includes the **Women's Hall of Fame Waterloo**, also in between fingers,

prides itself on being the birthplace of Memorial Day. The road through here passes the Scythe Tree upon which local farm boys planted their scythes on their way to war. Seneca Lake follows, the town of **Geneva** its jewel, replete with elegant inns and mansions.

Approximately 20 miles (32 km) west of Geneva is **Canandaigua**, on the northern tip of Canadaigua Lake. Of particular interest here is the Federal-style **Granger Homestead** built in 1816, with its collection of 40 horse-drawn vehicles. North of town on State 21 are the **Sonnenberg Gardens**, 50 acres (20 hectares) of Victoriana with a mansion incorporating the Canandaigua Wine Tasting Room.

State 21 passes through Shortsville on the way to **Palmyra**, a pilgrimage site for Mormons. This was the home of Joseph Smith, who, according to Mormon belief, received and translated ancient records in the Book of Mormon, buried them here and subsequently founded the Church in the 1820s. Religious sites and Smith's restored farm

Syracuse architecture rich with history: left, the Syracuse Savings Bank and right, the Gridley Building.

homestead are open to the public, as is the **Martin Harris Landmark Cobblestone House**. Built in 1850, the house is typical of the farmers' homes that sprang up along the Erie Canal.

It's about 20 miles (30 km) from Palmyra to Rochester along State 31. The names of the towns along the way are perhaps more exotic than the towns. After Palmyra comes Macedon and Egypt, where the New York State Barge Canal steps in for the Nile.

Like other upstate cities, **Rochester** thrived during the canal era and suffered economically with the advent of alternate modes of transportation. But it has adjusted to change better than its siblings and is on the upswing as a center for high-tech industries, while preserving much of its 19th-century architectural ambience. Eastman Kodak is the big name in Rochester, so big that they call it "Picture City." Kodak offers tours to its facilities.

The former mansion of George Eastman, who founded Kodak, now houses the **International Museum of Photog-** raphy, devoted to the history of this art and science. The **Eastman School of Music** sponsors musical events from jazz to symphonic works, and the **Eastman Theatre** is the home of the Rochester Philharmonic. For those who still enjoy childish things, the **Margaret Woodbury Strong Museum** has the most extensive collection of dolls in the western world.

Winters are severe in Rochester, thanks to its northern location on Lake Ontario, the easternmost Great Lake. But in late May, **Highland Park** is abloom during the annual Lilac Festival—featuring the world's largest display of these blossoms—when Rochester is truly "pretty as a picture."

On to the Falls

State 31 continues along the path of the Erie Canal from Rochester to Niagara Falls. The names of the towns along this route, including Spencerport, Brockport, Middleport and Gasport, continue to remind us of the importance

Old and new styles mingle in the cityscape of Rochester.

of the canal. But there are other reminders as well. **Medina** has its cobblestone buildings and Culvert Road, which passes under the canal. **Lockport** also has its share of cobblestone houses but is best known for its magnificent flight of five locks.

From Lockport, State 31 (Saunders Setara Settlement Road) travels directly to **Niagara Falls**. Once known as America's "Honeymoon Capital," the town is now fond of referring to itself as an international tourist destination. It is one of the top three in the United States despite hard times and endless tackiness. Quite simply, the 700,000 gallons (3 million liters) of water that plummet here each second are a wondrous assault on the senses. For reasons that are dubious at best, some people have been inspired to cross over the falls in a barrel or on a tightrope.

The natural beauty of this site might have been irreparably violated were it not for the efforts of landscape architect Frederick Law Olmsted, artist Frederic Church and others. Their "Free Niagara" (from commercialism) campaign resulted in the establishment of the Niagara Reservation in 1875.

One of the best ways to experience the falls is by donning foul weather gear (provided) and taking a boat ride on the **"Maid of the Mist,"** or drive across the river to Canada for what many consider a superior view.

River Road hugs the eastern branch of the Niagara River, past the falls and through the industrial Tonawandas to **Buffalo**, on the eastern tip of Lake Erie. Like other industrial giants past their prime, New York's second largest city, has acquired a bad reputation. Still there are plenty of reasons to stop for a visit.

For one thing, you can eat well and cheaply here. A specialty is spicy chicken wings, elsewhere called "Buffalo wings," but here simply "wings." They are available all over town, or you can go to the source—the **Anchor Bar**, where Theresa Bellissimo is said to have invented the dish.

As terminus of the Erie Canal and major inland port, Buffalo was a center for raucous entertainment during the heyday of canalling. An early minstrel troupe known as the Christy Minstrels was organized here, and in the 1920s an opulent movie palace called **Shea's Buffalo Theatre** was built. It's been refurbished and is back in business along with its Wurlitzer, one of the largest pipe organs ever built.

One survey has determined that Buffalo has the highest number of library volumes in the nation and its **Albright-Knox Art Gallery** is considered to have one of the finest collections.

Rochester may have Kodak, but Buffalo has **QRS Music Rolls** on Niagara Street. QRS manufactures music rolls for players pianos. It's done this since 1900, longer than anyone else in the business. While keeping up with modern times (the operation is now computer enhanced, and the latest chartbusters are made into music rolls), the shop appears much as it might have in the beginning. A small family of employees operates the ingenious machines. The company cat stands idly by, preferring the role of mascot to mouser.

Shea's Buffalo Theatre, one of the great movie palaces, looks now as it did in the 1920s.

EAST MEETS MIDWEST

Buffalo was an important point of departure for 19th-century settlers heading for the Midwest. From Buffalo they traveled to major ports of the Great Lakes in order to start their new life.

Today, the road from Buffalo to the midwestern states follows the shore of Lake Erie through New York, Pennsylvania and Ohio. Although known primarily as an industrial area, there are still some unspoiled stretches of coastline that are remarkable for their beauty. At Toledo the highway diverges from the shoreline on its way to Chicago.

South of Buffalo along US 62 is the town of **Hamburg**, where the hamburger, perhaps America's greatest contribution to world cuisine, was purportedly invented in 1885. In celebration of the centennial of this event, J. Wellington Wimpy came to town and was honored as the undefeated hamburger-eating champion of the world. Essentially a rural town, Hamburg has been host to America's largest county fair since 1868. It's only about five miles (eight km) from here to Lake Erie, where you can pick up State 5, a lakeside road that takes you to Ohio.

Lake Erie has suffered more than its sister Great Lakes at the hands of industry, yet miles of its beautiful sandy, ocean-like shoreline are still unspoiled. The stretch from Silver Creek, New York to the Pennsylvania border has been called the "antique trail" for the abundance of antique shops located just off the road. But more importantly, it cuts directly across a region devoted to the gentle art of viniculture.

State 5 takes you past terrain blanketed with grape vines and other fruit trees. In **Silver Creek**, go straight to Jackson Street, site of the **Skew Arch Railroad Bridge**. Built on an angle in 1869, it is one of only two such bridges in the world—the other is in the U.S.S.R.

Dunkirk and Fredonia follow, in the heart of the Concord Grape Belt (the world's largest) which extends into

Pennsylvania. **Dunkirk**, with its natural harbor, is also a center for boating and the "Chautauqua (County) wine trail." **Fredonia**, to the south, is home of Grange Number One, America's first such farmers' organization. This town is also known for having the nation's first gas well dating from 1821.

Continuing along the lake, the road passes **Lake Erie State Park** in **Brocton**, where campers will find a pleasant place to pitch their tents.

Westfield follows, calling itself "The Grape Juice Capital of the World." The town is dominated by the various processing and production facilities of Welsh Foods, Inc., makers of a popular grape jelly. Combined with peanut butter and two pieces of bread, this vies with Hamburg's hamburger as the quintessential American food.

There is no obvious transition between New York and its western neighbor other than a town named State Line, Pennsylvania. The landscape remains the same—the lake on one side and vineyards on the other. In season, road-

Left, Niagara Falls, a truly spectacular sight. Right, a friendly smile from a native Midwesterner.

side stands sells grapes, in every imaginable form.

Only 63 miles (100 km) of Lake Erie shoreline prevents Pennsylvania from being a landlocked state, and she knows just what to do with it. Past State Line is the town of **North East**, the center of the state's tiny wine industry. Several wineries do business here and all offer tours and tastings.

About 15 miles (24 km) west of wine country is the city **Erie**, off whose shores Commander Oliver Hazard Perry's fleet defeated the British in the Battle of Lake Erie during the war of 1812. Despite his motto, "Don't give up the ship!" the flagship *Niagara* was left to sink in what later became known as **Misery Bay**. That bay is now a quiet fishing cove off Presque Isle, and the ship was rescued a century later. A reconstructed *Niagara* now sits high and dry along the Erie waterfront.

On the other side is Erie's finest physical feature, **Presque Isle**, a claw of land (almost an island) reaching out into the lake. You can drive its length, pass Presque Isle Lighthouse, and then loop around along the southern end past Misery Bay. You'll find lovely sand beaches, wooded trails, fishing holes, lagoons and a statue of the Commodore.

The Top Of Ohio

Before you can say "knee high by the Fourth of July," you're in Ohio, the far eastern portion of the Midwest. I-90 cuts through the gently rolling farmland of this part of the state past Ashtabula, Geneva and Euclid, before reaching Cleveland. Aged A-frame homes, the fumes and smokestacks of heavy industry and a lot of American flags (the largest in front of a Honda car dealership) all crowd into the view of the city.

Despite popular notions to the contrary, Cleveland has its share of high culture including the world-renowned Cleveland Orchestra and the **Cleveland Museum of Art**, which is especially well-known for its extensive Chinese collection. And like other cities characterized by ethnic diversity.

Fishing in Misery Bay, Lake Erie.

54

State 2 leaves Cleveland on its way west. At Ceylon it turns to Lake Erie and bridges Sandusky Bay to the Marblehead Peninsular. State 165 takes you to land's end and reveals the peninsula to be slightly run-down and refreshingly unpretentious, full of lively harbors, the Prehistoric Forest, orchards and fruit stands ("Take a peach to the beach"). At its rocky tip is **Marblehead Lighthouse**, in continuous use since 1821, longer than any other beacon on the Great Lakes. And with good reason, for this is considered the most treacherous outcropping along Lake Erie. Off the peninsula State 2 proceeds toward Toledo. This region was once part of the **Black Swamp**, a refuge for wildlife which extended from Sandusky to Detroit. Small remnants of the swamp have managed to survive along this route.

The road emerges from the swamp and continues straight as an arrow to **Toledo**, past bait shops, drive-through package stores and drive-in movies. The "Toledo Strip" was once the subject of a border dispute between Ohio and Michigan. When Ohio got the Strip, Michigan got its Upper Peninsula from Wisconsin Territory as compensation.

At first, Toledo seems like an industrial wasteland. But early signs of rejuvenation, just beyond the International School of Meat Cutting give way to full-fledged restoration and redevelopment in the downtown riverfront area. The river is the Maumee and the massive project is called **Portside**. It's worked wonders for the city. One resident proclaims, "I've lived in Toledo all my life and it's just starting to get fun."

Leaving Toledo and Lake Erie behind, US 20 heads due west, cutting straight through Ohio farm country to the Indiana border, a distance of about 60 miles (100 km). The highway parallels the Michigan border, which is just a few miles north.

They call Indiana the Hoosier state and native Indianans Hoosiers. Some people say the name comes from a common inquiry from the pioneer days, "who's yer?" Others say the nickname comes from a canal-builder named

Sunset over Cleveland.

Samuel Hoosier, who liked to hire Indiana men over other workers. The workers became known as Hoosiers, and the the name stuck.

Ten miles (16 km) inside the state at Angola, leave US 20 for I-69 south. Fifteen miles (25 km) later, cut over to US 6, which will carry you westward through northern Indiana to Illinois. Around Kendallville, there is some agricultural diversification, but just past **Brimfield** it's corn and more corn, as far as the eye can see.

South of Brimfield is **Chain O'Lakes State Park**, a refreshing string of oases in the middle of Noble County. This county was once home of the "meanest man in the world," according to Indiana's contribution to the WPA American Guide Series. Legend has it that this man divorced his wife, after which she landed in the poorhouse. For funds, the institution would farm people out to the highest bidders, and when his ex-wife was put on the auction block, the "meanest man" purchased her to do the housework that his second wife refused to do.

Back on US 6, tiny towns punctuate this land of corn. One of them, near **Buzzard Hill**, includes among its few enterprises a business devoted to "odd size shoes." This is the southern corner of Elkhart County, known for the productivity of its land and for its considerable Amish population. The Amish, or Mennonites, have been in this area for over a century. These inventive, industrious people go about their business while shunning worldly things such as buttons, zippers, electricity and motor vehicles. **Amish Acres** in **Nappanee** is a historic farm homestead which interprets the Amish lifestyle for visitors. For a more intimate experience, its organizers have also developed an Amish Bed & Breakfast network.

Drifting along US 6 like the "Windiana winds" through the last of rural Indiana before Chicago's industrial fringe, takes you over the Kankakee River (a good fishing stream) and on to **Westville**, home of **Pat's Favorite Flea Market**.

Calm canoeing at Chain O' Lakes State Park.

THE MOTOR CITY & HENRY FORD

Were it not for the city of **Detroit**, Michigan and Henry Ford, this book might never have been written.

Every American adult drives an average of 7,767 miles (12,500 km) per year. And there are so many cars in the United States that the entire population could go driving at the same time and not one person would have to sit in the back seat. A good portion of those millions of back seats (and front seats, carburetors, fan belts and tire treads) are made in the Motor City.

The first automobile was a tricycle topped with a one cylinder engine created by Carl Benz in 1885. But Ford came out with the first *practical* motorcar eight years later. It had two cylinders and looked like an old-fashioned buggy. He formed the Ford Motor Company in 1903, and six years later he had 10,000 orders for his newest car, the Model T. In 1919 Ford sold 1 million cars.

Ford introduced the hand crank starter, the factory assembly line and, in 1914, established the five-dollar-a-day/six-day workweek. His innovations bolstered Detroit's economy, gave more people more jobs and made cars more desirable. But there was a dark side to this technological proliferation.

Ford never cared much for his workers until he was forced to. The assembly line might have cut a car's total production time by 12 hours, but it sapped the life out of the lowly worker who struggled to keep up with car after car after car. Safety devices were rare at Ford, and for years the founder kept the union out of his company.

The **Renaissance Center** built in the 1970s, signaled the rebirth of downtown Detroit. This $350 million complex of shops, restaurants, cultural facilities and offices encloses a half-acre lake complete with a waterfall and a plethora of exotic vegetation.

Nearby **Hart Plaza** is the site of a dozen ethnic festivals from late April to mid-September. And **Belle Isle**, in the Detroit River, also attracts summer crowds to its parks, Safari Trail Zoo, Blue Heron Sanctuary, the Dossin Great Lakes Museum and the Whitecomb Conservatory's dazzling orchid collection.

Finally, there are two museums in Detroit well-worth a visit. The **Detroit Institute of Arts** crams more than 35,000 works into 101 galleries and is home of the Detroit Film Theatre, Youtheatre and several musical series. The 260-acre (105-hectare) **Henry Ford Museum and Greenfield Village** complex in nearby Dearborn is the world's largest indoor/outdoor museum. The Ford Museum holds Henry's collection of wheeled technology and decorative arts, including locomotive steam engines, farm implements, ox carts and early automobiles. The Village houses recreations of famous businesses and residences, including Thomas Edison's Menlo Park laboratory. Blacksmiths, glass blowers and weavers work in restored 19th-century shops and sell their wares to visitors.

CHICAGO: MIDWEST-ERN CROSSROADS

No other city has as long a list of aliases on its record. Hog Butcher for the World (bestowed upon it by Carl Sandburg), the Windy City, the Crossroads of the Midwest, the Second City—the list goes on.

Chicago's status as hog butcher is now merely symbolic, its famed stockyard having been shut down in 1971. These days you can drive into town and see it before you smell it. And 21 U.S. cities are windier, though the windy city appellation was reputedly an epithet tossed at the city before the turn of the century by a New York journalist. He was not referring to the weather.

Chicago's reputation as midwestern crossroads, however, is indisputable. Its railroad yards are the largest in the world, and O'Hare is the world's busiest airport. Even the Art Institute of Chicago straddles train tracks.

Los Angeles has now superseded Chicago as the second largest U.S. city. This is probably just as well; the city has never worn its secondary status very comfortably, and its' grown tired of constant comparison with the "Big Apple." Chicago is a tough, political, literary, ethnic, cosmopolitan midwestern city. It isn't New York, and as a unique entity it's second to none.

The site, at the confluence of the midwestern prairie, the Chicago River and Lake Michigan, was an obvious place for a town to spring up. With the building of a canal in the 1840s—essentially linking the Great Lakes with the Mississippi River drainage system—followed by the advent of railroading, Chicago grew like wildfire as commerce and masses of immigrants descended upon it. Then in 1871, as the story goes, Mrs. O'Leary's cow knocked over a lantern, starting a disastrous fire known as the "Great Chicago Fire." The cow shed long gone, is now home of the **Chicago Fire Academy**, graced with an outdoor sculpture depicting a giant flame. (Chicago is crazy about outdoor sculpture and all the big

names are represented: Oldenburg, Calder, Picasso, Miro and Dubuffet, to mention a few. Some of their pieces have been known to sport Chicago Cubs baseball caps.)

The Great Fire signified the beginning of a new era in Chicago. The city became the workshop of architects like William LeBaron Jenny (the father of the skyscraper), Louis H. Sullivan, Frank Lloyd Wright and later Ludwig Mies van der Rohe. From the **Chicago Water Tower and Pumping Station**, the only public building to survive the Great Fire, to the **Sears Tower**, one of the tallest buildings in America.

Progress has swung the wrecker's ball at many low-rise 19th-century masterpiece. The **Prairie Avenue Historic District** has managed to survive. Once known as the "Avenue of Avenues," home to the rich and famous, it experienced a mass exodus during the early part of this century and many of its limestone and brick mansions were demolished or defaced. But those that remain are now being restored and protected.

All rails lead to Chicago. Left, the city has the world's largest railyards. Right, a genial resident offers an alternative way to go.

On the Waterfront

It's old hat now. Even Toledo has fixed up its waterfront. But Chicago has made the most of its magnificent lakeshore since the turn of the century.

A huge front yard encompasses 29 miles (46 km) of beaches, wonderful parks with distinct personalities and some of the nation's finest cultural institutions: the **Museum of Science and Industry** on the South Side, **Field Museum of Natural History, Shedd Aquarium** and **Art Institute of Chicago**, all in **Grant Park**. The Art Institute is particularly known for its collection of French Impressionists and is also home of that stoic couple, Grant Wood's "American Gothic." Behind the Institute is the bandshell, summertime the site of concerts and picnics.

Oak Street Beach, on the North Side, is Chicago's version of muscle beach, a multi-ethnic mass of humanity going about the very serious business of playing. You have to squint across Lake Shore Drive periodically to remind yourself that this is truly a city.

Chicago is the ultimate film noir city. Never has a place been so closely associated with gangster and political corruption, the latter almost an institution. Eternally proud of those things that set it apart, the city has made little attempt to dispel these images. Those who have never been here, but who have watched their share of movies, probably come here expecting to see the likes of George Raft, Edward G. Robinson and all those other "mugs"—maybe even a reincarnated Al Capone.

Politics are a way of life in Chicago. Jesse Jackson came up here and Richard J. Daley—gone but not forgotten—pulled the strings of this town for so long that time is now sometimes measured in years A.D. ("After Daley").

Chicago is also a writer's town, as articulate as it is brash. A steady stream of writers have interpreted their hometown for the rest of the world, from James T. Farrell and Nelson Algren to Richard Wright, Saul Bellow, Studs Terkel and David Mamet.

A jazz trio plays against a modern Chicago backdrop.

If you happen to find yourself in a residential neighborhood on Chicago's North Side and you notice signs that read "NO LIGHTS," be assured that this has nothing to do with poor electrical service. It is one side of a continuing and impassioned debate over **Wrigley Field**, smack in the middle of the neighborhood, the only major league baseball park without lights. Games that run into extra innings on this hallowed diamond are sometimes called darkness. Bands of diehard Cubs fans want to keep it that way. Television networks and baseball executives, on the other hand, feel the situation demands illumination.

Dark and smoky blues clubs have long been part of the Chicago scene. Players and singers of the blues came to this city from the deep rural South. Hear all about it at **B.L.U.E.S.** on North Halsted, or the **Checkerboard Lounge** and **Theresa's Lounge** on the South Side, where generations of University of Chicago undergraduates learned about life from Muddy Waters.

The communities flanking Chicago are among the oldest and most affluent American suburbs. **Glencoe**, to the north, is familiar to many as the home of Joel, a fictional teenager played by Tom Cruise in the movie *Risky Business* who submerges his father's Porche in Lake Michigan and gets into lots of trouble.

Land locked **Oak Park** is located west from Chicago's Loop via I-290, on the other side of the city limits. Hemingway grew up here and Frank Lloyd Wright lived and worked here during the early part of his career. Wright moved to Wisconsin, leaving his wife, children and 25 buildings in Oak Park, making the town the repository of the world's largest collection of his work. Many of these buildings were "bootleg" houses, designed independently and clandestinely for extra income.

Wright's home and studio, built in 1889 but continually reworked, is perhaps most revealing of his personality and genius, from the distinctive and now world-renowned Prairie Style to the Scottish proverb carved over a fireplace and the electrical wiring.

A sunlit game at Wrigley Field.

NORTHERN LAKE LANDS

The Great Lakes, those magnificent inland seas, have brought centuries of explorers and settlers to what is now the Midwest. Every state washed by these waters has been deeply influenced by their presence. Even Indiana, with only 45 miles (72 km) of Lake Michigan shoreline, has been affected.

A full spectrum of life thrives along the shores and through the fields and forests of the northern lake lands, from industry and international port cities to bustling fishing villages, farms, sand dunes and long stretches of beautiful wilderness.

While hardly in a league with neighboring Michigan, which abuts four out of five Great Lakes, Indiana makes the most of its 45 miles of Lake Michigan shoreline. From the South Side of Chicago, US 12 follows the lakeshore through Indiana to the Michigan border.

First part of this route, through east Chicago and Gary, is characterized by heavy industry, punctuated here and there by a beach or park. But beyond County Line road, the natural landscape begins to shine with sandy beaches, dunes, ponds, forests, wetlands and prairie that comprise **Indiana Dunes State Park and National Lakeshore**.

A story is still told in these parts of a hermit who became known as "Diana of the Dunes," discovered at Ogden Dunes in 1916. The solitary activities of this beautiful woman made her the subject of publicity and subsequently a target for marriage proposals. She married a man from Texas but succumbed to a mysterious illness and died before she could join him there.

Michigan is known as the Wolverine State, but as one resident complains, "Just try and find one." It's also called the Great Lake State, an appellation that fits like a glove. Obtained as consolation after losing Toledo to Ohio, the huge mit-shaped Lower Peninsula and the wild Upper Peninsula (U.P.) have a combined shoreline greater than the coastal distance from Maine to Florida.

US 12 out of Indiana, bound for Detroit, abandons Lake Michigan just past the border. To follow the lakeshore north, I-94 travels a short distance to meet US 31, which strays far from the lake on its way to the northern tip of the Lower Peninsula. As US 31 puts distance between itself and Chicago the pace becomes less frenetic. Pleasant towns and a string of state parks along the shore are a haven for city dwellers.

Benton Harbor, about 30 miles (48 km) north of the Indiana border, is known for its huge fruit market where local growers sell directly to the public. At the turn of the century it was home of the House of David, a religious cult founded by a man who called himself "King Ben." The group was later dissolved under a cloud of controversy.

You'll come to the towns of **Douglas** and **Saugatuck**, facing each other on opposite banks of the Kalamazoo River. A hand-cranked ferry covers this distance, as it has for more than 100 years. Also anchored in Saugatuck is the "Queen of the Saugatuck," a true sternwheel paddleboat that plies the Kalamazoo and sometimes ventures out into the lake. Saugatuck itself is a pretty town, with country inns, antiques, crafts and other such enticements.

The road turns inland a bit at **Holland**, site of a mid-19th century Dutch settlement that has clearly not forgotten its roots. They still make wooden shoes here, the old windmill is authentically Dutch and fully operational, and each May brings the Tulip Time Festival.

Back toward the lake is the town of **Grand Haven**, where you'll find the world's largest musical fountain, and farther north, **Muskegon**. Once a logging port, this is the biggest city on this stretch of the coast and gateway to the **Manistee National Forest**. On the other side of this sizable woodlands is the town of **Manistee**. Its name derived from the Ojibwa meaning "spirit of the woods." The town is a gem of Victoriana, having been rebuilt in this style following a devastating fire in 1871.

The northwestern region of the peninsula north of Manistee is morel country. These wild mushrooms, prized by

A misty sunrise over Michigan's Upper Peninsula.

gourmets and gourmands, bring out the morel squad each spring.

Leelanau, Leelanau, Land of Delight

Past Manistee, US 31 heads for a Michigan treasure: the **Leelanau Peninsula**, named "delight of life" by the Ojibwas. Fortunately, State 22 winds around its erratic coastline, traveling through the beautiful country side of Benize and Leelanau Counties, rich in lakes and orchards, and past the highest sand dunes in America. Little known outside the Midwest, the Peninsula is delightful year round.

From the start, State 22 showcases cherries, a local crop produced in greater quantities in this part of Michigan (about a third of total world production) than anywhere else in America. In season—which peaks in July—you'll see them weighing down trees and overflowing boxes at roadside stands in every shade of red. And they're not the only fruit around. **Elberta** welcomes

motorists with a sign calling itself "a peach of a place," and vineyards cover many peninsula hillside.

Beyond Elberta and Frankfort, a road skirts **Crystal Lake**, while Lake Michigan peeks out from behind the forest to remind you of its great size. An excursion to the eastern end of Crystal Lake takes you to the towns of **Benzonia, Beulah** and **Honor**. Craftspeople have long been attracted to the solitude of these tranquil communities.

Back on State 22 along Lake Michigan just past Crystal Lake is **Point Betsie**, whose signature is a lighthouse built in 1858. Father Jacques Marquette, credited with having discovered the Mississippi River, is believed to have died nearby in 1675. A couple of miles down the road is the beginning of **Sleeping Bear Dunes National Lakeshore**, with 34 incredible square miles (8,800 hectares) of dunes (some of them atop bluffs rising 350 feet [100 meters] above the lake), forests, lakes and two offshore islands.

The town of **Empire**, which punctuates the National Lakeshore, was once a major lumber center and was named for a schooner that became ice-locked off its shores in 1865. North of town, State 109 branches from State 22 and takes you to the **Dune Climb**, a 150-foot (45 meter) trek up a steep, seemingly endless pile of sand. People are transformed into tiny silhouettes at the summit, later disappearing to catch their breath while wandering across more dunes high above the lake.

State 109 puts you back on State 22, a road that could tell many stories. You may notice a roadside stand different from the others; nobody is there to make sure you don't squeeze the tomatoes or to take your money. Instead there's a little sign, "God knows everything. Please be honest," a logbook to record transactions, a box for the money and a bowl of change. The proprietor farms his land alone now, something he had once done with his father and later with his sons. His sales strategy seems motivated more by world-weariness than optimism, as he laments, "I don't know what's wrong with people today.

A sampling of Michigan's cherry crop shines bright as candy.

They're fallin' to pieces."

Still traveling along State 22 up the western aspect of the peninsula brings you to **Leland**, built around an inlet that joins the "Big Lake" and Lake Leelanau. It's an attractive town with an abundance of shops and restaurants aimed at the summer tourist trade, but there's also **Fishtown**. Unconcerned with appearances, this little waterfront parcel dutifully goes about the business of fishing.

Around the other side of Leelanau, now skirting Grand Traverse Bay, is **Peshawabestown**, an Ojibwa Indian village. At the base of the peninsula is **Traverse City**, the Cherry Capital of the World and as American as cherry pie. With each July comes the National Cherry Festival, perhaps best known for the cherry pit spitting and pie eating contests. The latter, a children's event, brings out the worst in parents in much the same way as Little League baseball. "Shove it in, Katie!" "Ma I don't like cherry pie." Veterans of the event have clearly refined their techniques over the years. Joey of Traverse City, a perennial winner, finds that thumping his chest with considerable force after the final gulp works for him.

US 31 zips up the western shore of Grand Traverse Bay, passing Elk and Torch Lakes, to **Charlevoix**. Situated between Lakes Michigan and Charlevoix and surrounding Round Lake, the town enjoys an influx of population during the summer.

Residents like to refer to their town as "Charlevoix the Beautiful," and they work hard to keep it that way, each year planting petunias along four miles (6.5 km) of US 31. In the early 1920s, realtor Earl Young began doing his part by building rather unique homes and a couple of motels—30 of them over a period of 40 years—called the "stone cottages." With no architectural training, Young built his free-form structures using large boulders for the exterior walls because he "liked rocks." A drive along Park Avenue will demonstrate what Earl meant by this.

Around the other side of Lake Char-

A painted barn on the Leelanau Peninsula.

levoix is **Horton Bay**, a place where Ernest Hemingway spent a good part of his youth. This and other pockets of northern Michigan show up prominently in his Nick Adams stories. He once wrote of a fictional character. "Of the place where he had been a boy he had written well enough. As well as he could then." He was most likely writing about himself.

From Charlevoix, US 31 curves around Little Traverse Bay through commercialized Petoskey and the much quieter Bay View with its cool, wide-porched bungalows and gingerbread cottages. **Mackinaw City**, on the Straits of Mackinac, is only about 30 miles (48 km) north. In Mackinaw City you can watch the sun rise over Lake Huron and set over Lake Michigan. Although it was founded by the French in the early 1700s as a fort (Fort Michilimackinac) and trading post, military operations were later relocated to **Mackinac Island**. The island later became a key fur-trading post, but after the regional beaver population was de-

pleted, that era came to a close. It has been a resort ever since.

Mackinac Island is accessible by ferry from either Mackinaw City or St. Ignace (at the southern tip of the U.P.). It's a small island with intact Revolutionary-era and 19th-century buildings that can be explored in the course of a day. Despite a law prohibiting motor vehicle, the main drag is overcrowded with tourists, bikes and horsedrawn carriages. The aroma of fudge mingles with that of horse manure. In fact, fudge is so common in northern Michigan resort towns that tourists are called "fudgies." The manure, on the other hand, is kept under control by diligent horsesweepers.

Away from the center of commerce, the island comes into its own. The unspoiled beauty of the other side of the island is complimented by a magnificent old fort and a number of historic churches, one of which was dragged across the ice from the mainland. This is also the site of the magnificent **Grand Hotel.** This stately structure, built in the

Lovely Mackinac Island, once a key fur trading post, is now a popular resort.

late 19th century from native white pine, is said to have the world's longest porch, as panoramic as its view.

The U.P.

Suspended across the five miles (eight km) that separate Michigan's two peninsulas is the **Mackinac Bridge**, or "Mighty Mac." The fact that this magnificent structure was not built until 1957 accounts in large part for the U.P.'s isolation.

This northernmost piece of the state, once considered worthless, has seen voyagers, missionaries, fur traders, lumberjacks and miners come and go. Sparsely populated with much of its wilderness intact, it now seeks to attract its share of visitors. Many consider it a sportsperson's paradise. You will not encounter crowds here, except for possibly at the start of the hunting season.

The bridge leaves you in **St. Ignace**, founded by French Jesuit explorers more than 300 years ago. The **Hiawatha National Forest**, extending up to Lake Superior, begins at the edge of town. Driving north about 10 miles (16 km) on I-75 takes you to State 123. which cuts through the deep forest and along Whitefish Bay to **Paradise**. This rustic little town, where you can hunt for agates along the lakeshore, greets visitors with a sign, "Glad you made it."

West of Paradise along the same road, hidden among hills of pine, are the beautiful Upper and Lower **Tahquamenon Falls**, said to have inspired Henry Wadsworth Longfellow to pen *The Song of Hiawatha*. The Tahquamenon River (meaning "black waters"), cascading along its circuitous route to Lake Superior, is thought to be the river where Hiawatha built his birch canoe; the "Shining Big-Sea-Water."

State 123 loops past the falls and south through Newberry (exactly half way between Lakes Michigan and Superior) to State 28 on its way to **Seney**, the "Sin City of the North." The town gained its reputation as the toughest place in northern Michigan during its late 19th century logging heyday.

The "Shining Big-Sea-Water" of Tahquamenon Falls.

The most noise to be heard today is from the Canadian geese, bald eagles and other migratory birds who nest at the **Seney National Wildlife Refuge.**

From Seney, the road leads to **Shingleton**, gateway to another section of Hiawatha National Forest. It continues northwest to **Munising**, home of **Gitchee Gumee Lounge/Lanes**, one of many *Song of Hiawatha* spin-offs. On the way out you get a good look at Lake Superior and a glimpse of the **Picture Rocks National Lakeshore** to the north. These naturally sculpted, multihued cliffs are best seen from a boat.

West of Munising is **Christmas**, a town that celebrates its name in every way conceivable, such as, "Last gas 'til Christmas." Along this far northern, coastal section of State 28, you'll notice larger stockpiles of firewood than elsewhere, attesting to the length and severity of U.P. winters.

State 28 is characterized not only by firewood and forests, but by deer crossings and tiny pockets of local color. Passing through the **Ottawa National Forest**, which extends nearly to the Wisconsin border, will take you to **Kenton and Happy's bar**, which calls itself "The Kenton Hilton." One of the road's more intriguing signs proclaims, "Welcome to **Ewen**—Home of the 1893 **World's Fair Load of Logs**." A spin around the block will satisfy your curiosity. Here, guarded by a steel fence, are 50 perfect white pine logs chained to a sleigh. The chain alone weighs 2,000 pounds (900 kg). It was pulled over ice and snow all the way to Chicago and back and still manages to withstand the test of time. If you're ready for a bite to eat try **Big Mama's Cafe** and the **South Branch Saloon**.

Every town around here has its claim to fame, and **Bessemer** boasts having "The most scenic little league field in America," as well as being "Home of the Speedboys." From Bessemer it's less than 10 miles (16 km) to **Ironwood** and the Wisconsin border. Once a mining boom town, you can now drive through Ironwood without seeing a soul. One citizen speaks his mind with a

The 1983 World's Fair Load of Logs in Ewen.

sign on his antler-cluttered porch: "Restore the Constitution."

Wisconsin: Big Cheese on the Big Lake

Hurley, just inside Wisconsin, was a tough turn of the century boom town, with a reputation for trouble worn well into the 20th century. The majority of its business establishments were bars, many of which masqueraded during Prohibition and continued to thrive. Clean-cut skiers now descend upon the town in winter, bearing little resemblance to the booze runners, gamblers and criminals of an earlier time.

US 2 travels from Hurley through the **Bad River Indian Reservation** to **Ashland** at the head of Chequamegon Bay. The town is characterized by lumber-yards and cheese stores. In January you can catch the annual dogsled races.

State 13 leaves Ashland and winds around the **Bayfield Peninsula**, where every town features sandstone buildings. The sandstone was quarried locally and shipped to New York and Boston, where it was used in constructing "brownstones" around the turn of the century.

Prior to the Great Depression, **Bayfield** was a bustling port town devoted to lumber, fishing and wealthy vacationers. Today it's a small fishing village of considerable charm and head quarters for excursions to the **Apostle Islands**, an archipelago in the deep waters of Lake Superior. Twenty-two islands comprise the group; all but two are part of National Park System. The stand-out is **Madeline Island**, the largest of the bunch and the only one with year-round inhabitants.

Visiting the Apostles gets you out into Lake Superior, the world's largest body of fresh water. Oceanic in scale and temperament, it is the deepest, most beautiful and most treacherous of the Great Lakes. Seamen respect these waters. In the words of Herman Melville's Ismael in *Moby Dick*, "they are swept by Borean and dismasting waves as direful as any that lash the salted wave. They know what shipwrecks

are." The last ship to go down off the Apostle Islands was a Canadian "Prohibition wreck" carrying, among other things, 10 cases of fine Scotch Whisky.

North of Bayfield along State 13 is the **Red Cliff (Objibwa) Indian Reservation**, followed by **Cornucopia**, Wisconsin's northernmost village. The road follows the Brule River, a fine trout stream, returning to the lake at **Superior**. Lakers and freighters from around the world clog the harbor, in the shadow of the world's largest grain elevators. The city has declined along with the mining and steel industries, and its streets reflect a mood of desolation.

From Superior, State 35 plunges into the emerald land of dairy farming, leaving the North Woods behind and heading straight toward Minnesota's Twin Cities. The transition is as sudden as it is refreshing. Past Cozy Corners and Dairyland, and on to Luck and Centuria, you'll find towns with Lutheran churches and populations of 700 to 800 people. Past Centuria the road heads west toward the St. Croix River.

Big Bill, a rough looker passing through Superior.

MINNESOTA TWINS

Because of their proximity, **Minneapolis** and **St. Paul**, on opposite sides of the Mississippi, will eternally be known as Minnesota's "Twin Cities." Fraternal rather than identical, they are like sides of the same coin: different, yet inseparable.

St. Paul, the more conservative, ethnic and parochial of the two, presents an earthier and more weatherbeaten appearance. Minneapolis, more competitive and cosmopolitan, dresses for success while living and breathing the concept of quality time. Local radio humorist Garrison Keillor puts it this way, "The difference between St. Paul and Minneapolis is the difference between pumpernickel and Wonder Bread."

It's the traits they share—springing from their pioneer heritage and strong northern European roots—that are responsible for this urban success story, the envy of every overcrowded and crime-ridden metropolis. Minnesota pioneers were forced by circumstances to cooperate with one another, and a spirit of cooperation and friendliness toward strangers prevails to this day. Characterized by common sense, morality, tolerance and unflagging civic-mindedness, people here put a lot of stock in politics and have developed a distinct political style. While Chicago spawned the likes of Richard J. Daley and Jesse Jackson, Minnesota nourished the careers of Hubert Humphrey and Walter Mondale.

Minnesotans also love to play. Combining their innate talent for invention (transparent adhesive tape was born here) with a philosophy of making the most of what they have gave rise to both snowmobiles and waterskiing.

Without its waters, Minnesota wouldn't be Minnesota; the name itself comes from the Sioux, meaning "skyblue water." The shore of Lake Superior marks the border of its northeast corner and the Mississippi River courses down its eastern flank.

Modern Minneapolis reflected in the mighty Mississippi.

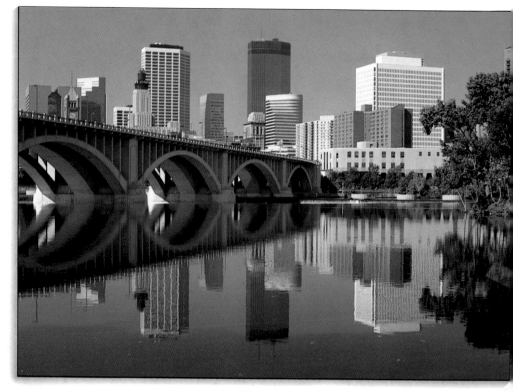

70

State license plates affirm, "Land of 10,000 Lakes," but there are more.

In the 18th century French explorers stumbled onto this region and named it *L' Etoile du Nord*, the Star of the North. Over the next 150 years, the Sioux and Ojibwa Indians who originally occupied the territory were set upon by hundreds of settlers, and as competition for land became more critical, violent clashes between the groups grew.

In order to protect the early settlers and establish a secure trading station, Fort Snelling was built in 1819, high on the bluffs overlooking the convergence of the Minnesota and Mississippi Rivers at the site of what is now Minneapolis. By 1865, the situation had become unbearable for the Sioux and the fort was nearly overrun by a group of rampaging Indians who cut a 300 mile (500 km) swath of violence and destruction across the plains, driving white farmers to the fort for refuge. The Minnesota Massacre, as it came to be known, was only the first bitter sparks of a conflict that would ultimately devastate the Indians' way of life.

Today, Fort Snelling has been reconstructed and staffed with actors who give visitors a first-hand glimpse of frontier life, circa 1827. "Soldiers" here go about the business of soldiering and participate in special events, such as the annual Fur Traders' Rendezvous.

Pig's Eye

An increase in commerce along the river gave birth to the towns of St. Paul and Minneapolis. The former sprang up as a local center of navigation and was originally known as Pig's Eye, after "Pig's Eye" Parrent, proprietor of a riverfront saloon. Seeking a better image, its residents renamed it St. Paul.

Ever-industrious Minneapolis, "city of water," evolved upstream around **St. Anthony Falls**, source of power for sawmills and gristmills. Both towns were flooded with a wave of immigrants, mostly northern Europeans, on their way to harvest the bounty of the Great North Woods: lumber and iron

The cannons still boom at Fort Snelling.

ore. In the wake of the Homestead Act, settlers came to cultivate a sea of wheat.

In the years following the turn of the century, Minneapolis and St. Paul grew rapidly. The two cities were gateway to the northern Great Plains and one of the nation's foremost centers of agricultural products, such as grain and flour.

The Twin Cities' status in the world of agriculture is never far from the minds of Minnesotans. Reports from the Minneapolis Grain Exchange, the nation's largest cash market, monopolize the local airwaves. General Mills and Pillsbury are headquartered here, and generations of Twin Cities homemakers have turned their ovens into "test kitchens" and their families into guinea pigs. The magnificent grain elevators, standing tall above the Mississippi, vie for attention with **St. Paul's Cathedral** and the **Capitol Building**. Minneapolis' **Investors Diversified Services** (IDS) building, the tallest building between Chicago and San Francisco.

Industry has been kind to the Twin Cities, Minnesota Mining and Manufacturing Co. (3M), who gave the world Scotch-brand adhesive tape and post-it notes, is as diversified as it is successful. It also provides employees with country-club-like facilities for golf, skiing, tennis, etc, while allowing plenty of room for its corps of engineers and scientists to brainstorm.

The Good Life

Characterized by clean industry, stable neighborhoods, fine cultural institutions, superbly planned public places and open spaces, the Twin Cities combine to make a metropolis that works. Many are struck by the cleanliness of this place, something that makes the muddy Mississippi appear off course. Minneapolis has cleaned up its act even further with **Riverplace**, a waterfront marketplace and condominium, complex along Historic Main Street at **Lourdes Square**.

They've given a lot of thought to the weather here, and over the years Twin City dwellers have refined their meth-

ods of dealing with a typically cruel and unrelenting winter season. Ever expanding glass-enclosed skywalks radiate from the Crystal Court of the IDS building, as they do in downtown St. Paul. Yet the people here are proud of their ability to withstand recordbreaking temperatures, and they celebrate the ice and snow at St. Paul's Winter Carnival. Some residents, however, would rather be at Minneapolis' summer Aquatennial Festival.

The **Walker Art Center** is a forum for contemporary visual and performing arts. *The New York Times* calls it, "one of the best contemporary art exhibition facilities in the world." The Center incorporates the **Guthrie Theatre**, indisputably one of the premier repertory theatres. The **Northrup Dance Season** puts together one of the most impressive dance series. And there's more—film, classical music and jazz. At **Mendota**, a tiny riverfront community just west of the Mississippi, you'll find the **Hall Bros. Emporium of Jazz**, said to be the oldest jazz club.

Wheatfield of St. Paul

MIGHTY MISSISSIPPI: THE BIG RIVER

Most modern travelers will never know the communion the legendary Huckleberry Finn and his companion, the escaped slave Jim, felt with the majestic **Mississippi River.** Today's Mississippi is crossed over 30 times by modern bridges, and these extensions of westward-bound highways zoom travelers over the river before songs can change on the car radio. Cruising on dry surface above the mighty Mississippi's frequently brown waters makes the infamous strong, dangerous currents seem an exaggeration. But bargemen, lockmen and freshwater fishermen voice a humble respect for the river's many-faced character. Echoed in one lockman's advice to the captain of a small craft, "respect her or she'll do you in."

The Spanish explorer DeSoto's claim to "discovering" the river in 1541 would have surprised the Algonquian Indians who had already lived near it for more than 1,000 years, and from whom the name "missi" [big] "siippii" [river] seems to have come. In 1682, while the Indians worshipped a temperamental river god who offered both food and flood, the French explorer La Salle traveled down the river, claiming the entire territory for the French. In another 40 years, New Orleans, Prairie du Chien and St. Louis would be founded along with a number of other river basin settlements. And in 1803, the French sold the river as part of the Louisiana Purchase.

The mighty Mississippi, the third largest river system in the world, begins as a small stream at **Lake Itsaca** in northwestern Minnesota. For 512 miles (842 km) it gathers force, slowly becoming the cool blue giant that roars over the falls of St. Anthony in Minneapolis.

In the course of its 1,840-mile (2,962-km) journey, the river forms the partial borders of 10 states and receives the Wisconsin, Ohio, Missouri, Arkansas and Red Rivers before reaching the crow's foot delta in Louisiana and the Gulf of Mexico. Here the once cold blue river is called Old Muddy for obvious reasons.

Today's traveler to rivertowns frequently finds a less-than-romantic scene. Modern communities turn their back on the "old town" that grew up on the river. Landmark-quality buildings, remnants of another era of river glory and wealth, lie in a state of disrepair. Often levees separate the town from the river; abandoned button factories blink broken panes over shoreline yards of riddled clam shells, and indigent community members still catch their living outside their riverside tarpaper shacks. Meanwhile, most townsfolk have migrated down the highway to be close to the new town square: the shopping mall.

The auto traveler determined to see more of the Mississippi can take the **Big River Road** which runs faithfully along the river's west shore, occasionally offering spectacular scenic overlooks, as at **Lake Pepin**. Those who want a change and feel like abandoning their cars can find a variety of scenic boat rides departing from the major cities, including a round trip from Dubuque to Davenport, Iowa on a paddle-wheel steamer.

THE MISSISSIPPI AND THE MISSOURI

The region extending from the Mississippi River in Minnesota to the Missouri River in South Dakota marks the transition from the midwestern to the western states—geographically, culturally and spiritually.

The transition can be subtle. If you listen to the car radio, up-to-the minute reports from the floor of the Minneapolis Grain Exchange will be heard with progressively less frequency. Western idioms begin to turn up in small farm towns. The changes in geography are more abrupt, the Missouri River serving as a boundary between the Grain Belt and the West.

Minnesota: Southern Exposure

The region of Minnesota southwest of "The Cities" is unmistakably farm country. This land was settled by European and Scandinavian immigrants during the latter half of the 19th century. Some called them "sodbusters;" they deforested the land and penetrated the virgin sod, exposing the rich soil of the midwestern prairie. Many of their grandchildren and great-grandchildren still farm the land here, an occupation known these days as agribusiness.

The founders of **New Prague**, a town dominated by **St. Wenceslaus Church**, clearly had no desire to hide their Eastern European heritage. West of the town, along State 19, are peculiarly medieval-looking outbuildings with domed roofs, in the midst of all American corn country.

Those who believe the Valley of the Jolly ("ho-ho-ho") Green Giant to be a mythical place created by advertising executives are mistaken. At **Le Sueur**, (renowned for its peas), US 169 intersects the Minnesota River and passes through the lush, green valley itself. You will know this, because the **Green Giant** sprouts from the top of a billboard and welcomes all motorists.

Branching farther west towards **Mankato**, the road enters Blue Earth country across the **Blue Earth River**. This is some of the most productive farmland in the state, a green expanse interrupted only by lakes. Modern farming is still a family business, and it is not unusual to see an entire family out in the fields manning various pieces of machinery.

Continuing west through **Windom**, where a statue atop a municipal building waves you on, the lay of the land becomes somewhat hillier, but no less cultivated. Satellite dishes dot the landscape and even the shortest of Main Streets has its video shop—the changing face of rural America. Past **Fulda**, the fields create an optical illusion, as bold green strips kaleidoscopically merge into a solid blanket.

In **Pipestone** (near the South Dakota border), the strong suit is Sioux quartzite, not agriculture. Buildings constructed from this local, pinkish stone appear up and down historic Main and Hiawatha Streets; significant not only because they are lovely to look at, but because they are among the last of their

Left, signs of Minnesota's original "sodbusters" remain amid the lush green of new crops. Right, much modern farming is still a family affair.

kind. (The use of Sioux quartzite is no longer considered cost-effective.) But for a period of less than 20 years before the turn of the century, Pipestone went to town with it—the **County Courthouse**, the **Public Library**, the **Bank Building**, the **Calumet Hotel** and most impressively, **Moore Block** (c. 1896). L.H. Moore embellished the block bearing his name with fanciful images of the sun, angels, gargoyles, jester, and devil.

Underlying and veining Sioux quartzite is a material called pipestone, also known as catlinite (after George Catlin, artist and student of Native American cultures, who documented the quarrying of pipestone here in 1836). The tepees at the northern edge of town are not there to impress tourists; they are authentic.

Longfellow's *The Song of Hiawatha* tells of "...the great Red Pipestone Quarry." The quarries in Pipestone and the land which surrounds them are sacred ground of the Sioux and other Native Americans; a land of legend and tradition, now a national monument.

The **Circle Trail** travels a mile loop through the prairie surrounding the quarries, past **Hiawatha Lake**, **Winnewisa Falls**, quartzite cliffs and wind-carved formations known as **Old Stone Face** and the **Oracle**. A stone inscription along the trail documents the past presence of the Nicolet expedition, members of which traveled through here in 1836 while exploring the Upper Mississippi region.

The road between Pipestone and **Jasper** (which also has its share of quartzite buildings) accentuates an element common to all rural landscapes: the unity of structures, equipment and the land. They do not tear down old barns here, nor do they haul old reapers off to a junk pile. Everything is left to decay, eventually becoming one with the soil.

South Dakota: East River

The South Dakota Department of Highways chose to make use of the locally plentiful quartzite, and so a pink road unfolds at the border. It takes you

Fanciful images carved from quartzite in Pipestone.

to **Garretson**, known for its **Devil's Gulch**. The Gulch is a sliver in the quartzite cliffs that loom above **Split Rock Creek**. According to one legend, the rocks were split by the Great Spirit's tomahawk. According to another, outlaw Jesse James jumped across the gap while being pursued by a posse. Fortunately, modern travelers can now cross the gap over a short bridge.

Devil's Gulch lends Garretson an Old West image, but it is primarily a small farming community, visually dominated by grain elevators. **Tom's Bar** offers both Grain Belt beer and Tombstone pizza, perhaps the perfect fare to accompany a "Spaghetti Western."

The prairies of eastern South Dakota and the pioneers who settled this land have been immortalized both on canvas and in popular literature. The paintings of Harvey Dunn, son of homesteaders and sodbusters, depict the reality and the dignity of these people; themes mirrored in the work of Laura Ingalls Wilder, author of the beloved *Little House on the Prairie* and other books concerning life in De Smet.

I-90 cuts through eastern South Dakota in a nearly straight line, through terrain that is a bit hillier and less green, as the cultivation of hay and wheat is mingled with corn. These crops will eventually move through **Sioux Falls**, the commercial center. Farther west, in **Mitchell**, they have created a monument to and with all the amber grains. It's called the **Corn Palace**. This is one of a few reasons to stop at Mitchell—not the least of which is a much needed break from the Interstate. The Corn Palace is most certainly the world's only Byzantine structure decorated with murals of corn and other grains.

As I-90 approaches the Missouri River, which divides South Dakota into "East River" and "West River," a different type of terrain lies ahead. Rolling, multicolored hills littered randomly with cylinders of hay take over the landscape. As you pass through the gently sloping prairie of **Fort Pierre National Grasslands** on your way to the city of **Pierre**, the West begins to reveal itself.

Mitchell's extraordinary Corn Palace.

WESTERN SOUTH DAKOTA

Western South Dakota is unquestionably where the West begins. Visually, the Badlands and the Black Hills rise out of the prairie and hit you with a one-two punch. They are equally unexpected and stunning. But there is more to these regions than their beauty. They have been witnesses to a tumultuous modern history that has molded them.

West of Pierre and the Missouri River, US 14 appears as a silver ribbon, unraveling over velvet mounds of prairie grasses. It coincides with a section of the **Old Deadwood Trail**, a legendary wagon-train and stagecoach route.

The stagecoaches were destined for "uncivilized" parts; nevertheless they had certain rules. "If you must drink, share the bottle." Chewing tobacco was permitted, but it was requested that you spit "...with the wind, not against it." And specified topics of conversation were forbidden: stagecoach robberies and Indian uprisings.

The road cuts due south and then west again toward **Cottonwood**, foretold by grove after grove of cottonwood trees. Continuing west, motorists are besieged by signs imploring them to stop at Wall Drug, located in **Wall** on the northern edge of the Badlands. Depending on your degree of thirst, hunger, illness or defiance, you can continue west and arrive at Wall in no time at all, or turn south at Cottonwood directly into the Badlands.

A gravel road from Cottonwood goes due south hugging the hills that comprise **Buffalo Gap National Grassland** where the U.S. Forestry Service is attempting to restore the natural prairie grass destroyed by uncontrolled grazing and other abuse. Looming up on the horizon, west of the road, is an extraterrestrial landscape: the **Badlands.**

The Dakota, or Sioux, Indians called it (roughly translated), "land bad." French trappers in the early part of the 19th century described it as "a bad land to cross." Many contemporary travelers must concur, for they bypass the Badlands (rarely visible from the Interstate) while rushing to the Black Hills to see the stone faces of Mount Rushmore.

This constantly eroding landscape has served as a symbol of youthful malaise and rootlessness. Bruce Springsteen sang about it ("Badlands," 1978), and Terence Malick used it as a title for his acclaimed film (*Badlands*, 1973). But despite all the discouraging words, there is striking beauty to be found in the desolation of the White River Badlands.

The region has been described as, "Hell with the fires burned out," but fire has played no part in it; it has been shaped by wind and water. Spires, turrets and ridges comprise a silent skyline, which changes with each gust of wind and each torrential (though infrequent) downpour. The colors of this uninhabited city are the delicate earth tints of a watercolorist's palette.

Badlands National Park is not one large rectangular piece of land but several chunks of land loosely strung to-

Hold-overs from a wilder past: the sheriff of Deadwood flashes a toothless grin, left. Right, a Buffalo bull grazes in the Black Hills, where his ancestors once roamed in abundance.

gether and carved out of Buffalo Gap National Grassland and the Pine Ridge Indian Reservation. It is possible to drive through rolling grasslands and suddenly be confronted with Badlands terrain, as car and driver find themselves dwarfed by sand-castles or on the edge of a canyon wall. A 40-mile (64-km) loop road travels through the park and provides access to spots of geological and paleontological interest.

Life in the Badlands

It was once the stomping ground of ancient camels, three-toed horses and saber toothed tigers, whose fossilized remains continue to be uncovered by the elements. Many of these fossils, dating back to the Oligocene Epoch, 25 to 35 million years ago, have been preserved by the **South Dakota School of Mines and Technology** and are exhibited at their **Museum of Geology** in Rapid City. The largest of the Oligocene mammals was the titanothere, the subject of Sioux mythology as Thun-

derhorse. It was believed that this creature descended from the heavens during thunderstorms and killed buffalo.

Fossil hounds were on the way toward cleaning out the Badlands prior to federal protection but the abundance of wildlife that once roamed here was largely gone by the 1890s—depleted by the throng of humanity en route to the Black Hills in search of gold. Thanks to reintroduction and protection, the park is today a sanctuary for pronghorn antelope and buffalo. Prairie dogs also thrive here in their own metropolis. These peculiar rodents employ an elaborate system of tunnels, entry holes and sentries; a shrill "barking" rings across the prairie if you venture too closely.

These dogs are one of the many banes of area ranches' lives (cattle can be severely injured by stepping into their holes). Another is the weather, as severe as it is unpredictable. Old-timers still talk about the blizzard of May, 1905 when the weather progressed from balmy to icy. Thousands of head of cattle and horses drifted south with the

Biking through the Badlands.

80

wind and fell to their death over the north wall of the Badlands.

For Some a Home

Comparatively few people visit the badlands, and those who do, keep their visits short. Even fewer call this inhospitable landscape home. One of the most hospitable people who does, is Lavanne Green, the proprietress of the **Woodenknife Drive-Inn** in **Interior** (population 70). You can't miss the Woodenknife. Its neon signs beam across the barren landscape, addressing the most primal of needs: "EAT" and its companion, "FOOD."

Lavanne grew up in Interior and says that she "...couldn't wait to get out." Get out she did, only to return in 1975, after many years. Her Indian tacos, which come with a rarely applied, money-back guarantee allow her to survive happily in Interior. They are also her passport to meeting people from across the U.S. and around the world, something she obviously thrives upon.

When asked about neighboring town **Scenic**, she merely laughs and advises that you not miss it. "What's between here and Scenic? There isn't a *dog* between here and Scenic."

Scenic, South Dakota is a ramshackle place named by someone with a sense of humor. In the same spirit, a sign along the main road ("Business District") signals your arrival. There is a tiny church, a few abandoned shacks, several vintage mobile homes, a hole-in-the-wall U.S. Post Office, a heap of junked cars and on the edge of town, the place people come here to see: the **Longhorn Saloon**.

The Longhorn was established in 1906, and the ankle-deep sawdust on the floor has been collecting ever since, as have the bullet holes and cattle brands on the ceiling. Always the site of a recent shootout, discomfort pervades the atmosphere. Tractor seats mounted on metal barrels serve as bar stools. Its facade features longhorn skulls and a weather-beaten sign "no Indians allowed." But the bartender and a woman

A lone church overlooks the site of the Wounded Knee Massacre.

customer are both Oglala Sioux from the nearby Pine Ridge Reservation.

The **Pine Ridge Reservation** surrounds the southern tier of Badlands National Park and coincides with Shannon County, which has the lowest per capita income in the United States, a fact that should surprise no one. On this land, **Wounded Knee Creek** bleeds off from the White River to the site of the infamous massacre of Dec 29, 1890—the last tragic episode of the Indian Wars and an enduring symbol of unfathomable loss.

Wall Drug, in the town of the same name, did for drugstores what Phil Spector's "Walls of Sound" did for rock-and-roll. Never has there been a more elaborate drugstore. Located on the northern wall of the Badlands alongside the interstate, it is difficult to pass through this part of South Dakota without dropping in. For one thing, there are those ubiquitous signs. Apothecary Ted Hustead began posting them along the highway in the early 1930s, inspired by the old Burma Shave signs. By the Missouri River, even the most stoic of travelers perceives a need for a glass (or a jug) of Wall Drug's free ice water.

What began as the only drugstore in a small, dusty town became famous as the "Ice Water Store." It now takes up most of Main Street in Wall. You can still buy aspirin here and you can wash them down with free ice water.

Wall Drug has, among other things, a chapel for those in need of solace a clothing and boot shop for those in need of Western duds a fine bookstore a harness shop for serious riders, an art gallery and a staggering assortment of Western "attractions" from a replica of Mt. Rushmore (for those tired of driving) to a six-foot (two-meter), "jackalope," a mounted buffalo and life-sized carvings of Butch Cassidy and the Sundance Kid. Donuts and coffee are free for hunters, skiers, honeymooners, missile crewmen and 18-wheelers.

Approximately 20,000 folks stop by Wall Drug on a good day. It is an American success story, and Ted Hustead defines the lesson of his success in this

Longhorn skulls adorn the roof of the saloon in Scenic.

82

way: "....that there's absolutely no place on God's earth that's godforsaken."

The ride from Wall to **Rapid City** is approximately 50 miles (80 km) of rolling, treeless prairie and wheat fields. Rapid City, settled by prospectors in 1876, is the gateway to the Black Hills.

Paha Sapa

"...as long as rivers run and grass grows and trees bear leaves, Paha Sapa—the Black Hills of South Dakota—will forever be the sacred land of the Sioux Indians." (excerpt, 1868 Treaty between U.S. Government and Sioux Nation)

"There's gold in them thar hills." (attributed to U.S. Army scouts, 1874)

These words, taken together, summarize the course of late 19th century history in the **Black Hills**, and indeed throughout the West; an era characterized by greed, deception and bloodshed. The Sioux were "granted" eternal rights to this land that held little interest for the white man until the discovery of gold.

George Armstrong Custer led an army reconnaissance expedition through here in 1874. The presence of gold was barely confirmed before the deluge of humanity swept through the Hills, leaving the treaty of 1868 drowned in its wake. Years of bloodshed followed, and the Sioux would never regain exclusive rights to their sacred *Paha Sapa*.

A steady stream of humanity continues to flow through the Black Hills—mostly past Mount Rushmore, the "shrine of democracy" that was, ironically, never completed.

Past Rapid City and all the commercialism of US 16, you'll encounter a road of another color, a 17-mile (27-km) corkscrew known as the **Iron Mountain Road**. It is one of the spectacular, specially engineered Black Hills highways. They were built in the 1930s and intended for pleasure driving, with the Black Hills as their showcase. The inspiration of Highway Commissioner Peter Norbeck, the roads are characterized by hairpin turns,

Old-fashioned filling station near the South Dakota-Iowa border.

switchbacks, granite tunnels (which are placed to provide remarkable vistas) and pigtail bridges which utilize native pine columns in place of steel.

Rather than sashaying around the mountain, Iron Mountain Road heads straight for the top. It passes by **Mt. Rushmore**, which first appears framed at the end of a tunnel. This sight is akin to watching Hitchcock's *North by Northwest* (1959) on television from across the room. You may find yourself squinting to see if those specks up there are actually Cary Grant and Eva Marie Saint escaping across the six-story, granite faces. But you will not see them—or anyone else for that matter. Climbing the memorial is strictly prohibited. For a view of the presidents it is necessary to hire a helicopter.

Rushmore, the mountain, was purportedly named for Charles E. Rushmore, a New York attorney who visited here in 1885. Upon inquiring about the name of the (then-nameless) peak, a local obligingly replied, "Mount Rushmore."

In the 1920s, Doane Robinson, the official historian of South Dakota, was considering various projects aimed at attracting visitors to the Black Hills. He decided on the concept of a colossal mountain carving, envisioning statues of legendary mountain men such as Jim Bridger, John Colter and Kit Carson. But the more universally admired presidential subjects (George Washington, Thomas Jefferson, Abraham Lincoln and later, Theodore Roosevelt) were finally chosen, and in 1927 sculptor Gutzon Borglum (then 60 years old) was commissioned to do the work. The enormous endeavor took him the remainder of his life. Work on the mountain came to a halt following Borglum's death and the attack on Pearl Harbor. Borglum had intended the figures to be carved to the waist. Had he worked from the opposite direction, the U.S. would have been left with a rather peculiar shrine of democracy.

The project was plagued by controversy throughout and a subsequent lack of funds, largely as a result of

Mt. Rushmore National Memorial.

84

SALT LAKE CITY AND THE MORMONS

Tourism is the largest single industry in **Salt Lake City**, Utah, but not because it's the home of Donny and Marie Osmond. The city is also the home of **The Church of Jesus Christ of Latter Day Saints**.

Marking the day Brigham Young founded the Mormon Kingdom of Deseret and Salt Lake City, **This Is The Place Monument** stands at the mouth of Emigration Canyon at the western base of the Wasatch Mountains. Eighteenth-century Spanish explorers and 19th-century fur trappers had preceded them, but Mormon pioneers were the first to establish a white settlement here. They had been fleeing religious, political, social and economic persecution since Joseph Smith established the Church in Fayette, New York in 1830. When Smith was murdered by angry non-believers, Brigham Young took over as prophet (Mormons believe that Jesus Christ is alive and guides his Church through living prophets) and led the Mormons to the valley of the Great Salt Lake. On July 24, 1847, in a moment of enormous historical significance, Young touched his cane to the earth and said, "This is the place."

Today, the headquarters of the Church lies at the center of Salt Lake City. **Temple Square** is ten lushly landscaped acres scattered with monuments, statues and more than a half dozen church buildings (including the mighty **Mormon Temple**), all enclosed by a 15-foot (five-meter) wall. Atop the tallest of the six spires that crown the Temple is a 12½-foot gilt, copper statue of the trumpet-bearing angel **Moroni**. It is this spirit that appeared to young Joseph Smith in 1830 and led him to discover several inscribed gold plates which he translated into the Book of Mormon.

Violence is rare in this peaceful, clean city of 167,000 people, 56 percent of whom are Mormons. Liquor is hard to come by (the Church's "Word of Wisdom" requires abstinence from alcohol, caffeine and tobacco), and the divorce rate is the lowest in the country. For Mormons the family is extremely important. They are encouraged to marry young and have sex only as often as they want children, which is a lot. Polygamy was practiced by several early Church leaders (Brigham Young was rumored to have 27 wives) until it was outlawed in 1890.

There *are* parts of the city that have little or nothing to do with the Church. Sporting a copper dome and nestled among brilliant flower gardens, the **Capitol** is one of the prettiest in the country. There's the **Salt Palace** (seating 28,000 for rock concerts and other events), the **Bicentennial Center for the Performing Arts** and **Pioneer Trail State Park** (10 renovated buildings from the pioneer era).

The Great Salt Lake lies 20 miles (32 km) northwest of the city. Biologically dead, this sticky, salty, warm mass stretches for 73 miles (117 km). If one can bear the omnipresent brine flies, a short dip is recommended.

[Salt Lake City is located in north-central Utah, at the junction of I-84 from Boise, Idaho, and I-15 from Butte, Montana.]

Borglum's artistic temperament and egotism. Some say that he pushed for the inclusion of Roosevelt because he considered the presidents's spectacles to be a particular challenge to his skills. He also planned a 500-work chiseled inscription to be written by President Calvin Coolidge—an idea aborted following a ruthless and undiplomatic edit by Borglum. But the sculptor's ambition and talent were of the highest order and the memorial is a testament to his own peculiar genius.

Visitors flock to **Mt. Rushmore National Memorial**, necessitating a band of parking attendants to oversee what looks like a recreational vehicle (RV) dealership. At times the parade of tourists from all over the world are as much of an attraction as the sight they have come to visit.

Crazy Horse

Mt. Rushmore is not the only mountain carving in the Black Hills. There is also the **Crazy Horse Memorial**, a work-in-progress by the late Korczak Ziolkowski. Whereas Mt. Rushmore remains incomplete, Crazy Horse, even more ambitious in scale, is still in its infancy. Ziolkowski left detailed plans and instructions behind, and the grounds—the town of Crazy Horse now—are literally abuzz with workers.

Ziolkowski was engaged to carve this depiction of the great Sioux warrior by Chief Henry Standing Bear so that the white man might know that "...the red man had great heroes, too." Although nearly 8 million tons of rock have been blasted off the mountain since 1949, it is still impossible to visualize a figure on horseback without the aid of a 1/34th scale plaster model. But come anyway, not necessarily to look at the mountain, but to visit the ever expanding **Indian Museum of North America**, as well as Ziolkowski's studio.

Learning about the sculptor, his life and his ambitions for this place is time well spent. Ziolkowski was a fascinating giant of man, as a father, artist and humanitarian. He liked to think of him-

The Crazy Horse Memorial, an unfinished tribute to a Native American hero.

self as a "storyteller in stone," and these are words he personally inscribed on the door of his tomb.

South of Mt. Rushmore and Crazy Horse is **Wind Cave**, the first cave to be named a National park. Wind Cave and **Jewel Cave** (its sister to the west) are the eighth and fourth largest caves in the world respectively. They are characterized by calcite crystals and honeycomb formations known as "boxwork," found extensively here than anywhere else.

North of Wind Cave in the direction of Lead is **Needles Highway**, another Black Hills driving experience. The road was built to show off the Needles, granite spires which reach for the sky. Frank Lloyd Wright called it "...an endless supernatural world more spiritual than Earth, but created out of it." The highway meanders and climbs several miles up into the firmament, at times through tiny granite tunnels. You must sound your horn before proceeding.

Past Needles Highway, continuing north toward **Lead**, the aroma of pine pervades the atmosphere as the road passes through thick, dark stands of ponderosa pine. The appearance of these trees from afar gave the Black Hills its name. Lead, (pronounced *leed*), named for a lode or vein of ore, is the site of **Homestake Mine**, which today produces more gold than any other gold mine in the Western Hemisphere. It is definitely a company town. Although all mining now takes place underground, the town's main aboveground attraction, the town's main aboveground attraction is the old **"Open Cut"**—a gash in the side of the mountain where gold was originally found in 1876. The people of Lead like to call their home a "four-dimensional city": over a mile high, over a mile long and over a mile deep.

Deadwood, just northeast of Lead, is the other Black Hills town that gold built. It was the center of gold mining activity until being upstaged by Lead. In the 1870s Deadwood gained its reputation as the quintessential Wild West town through the likes of "Wild Bill" Hickok, Calamity Jane and others. Wild Bill and Calamity are buried beside each other in **Mt. Moriah Cemetery** high above town in accordance with Jane's last wishes. Today it is a lovely town with an historic Main Street, nestled high in the hills and devoted to perpetuating its "Wild West" image.

Deadwood has a sheriff who looks as if he has seen his share of shoot outs and barroom brawls. He claims, "There was a shoot out just last week."

You can visit **Saloon #10**, where Wild Bill was fatally shot by Jack McCall. It's billed as "Home of the Deadman's Hands" and "The Only Museum in the World With a Bar." There are numerous places in town to buy Black Hills gold jewelry in the traditional tri-color grape leaf design. You will also find the **Green Door Brothel** and the **Bela Union Theatre**, which fomerly served as church, courthouse and town hall. Still, the people of Deadwood only take their myths half-seriously. One establishment places a chair out front with a sign reading: "The only chair in Deadwood that Wild Bill was shot in."

Portrait of a 19th-century Sioux warrior by Mark R. Stewart.

WYOMING AND MONTANA

Quite simply, the West is not like the rest of the country. For one thing, the number one professional sport here is neither football nor baseball, but rodeo. This is a land of last stands, last chances and lost dreams. it is also a region of sparsely populated open spaces characterized by a wild natural beauty.

"Big Wyoming" and the "Big Sky Country" Montana are quintessential western states. They lead all others in the field of statistical extremity—the most bars, drive-ins, gas stations, cars and mobile homes per capita. But more importantly, the myths of the West live on here in the hearts and lives of the people who call this vast country home.

Descending from the Black Hills of South Dakota by way of the spectacular Spearfish Canyon brings you right to I-90, less than 10 miles (16 km) from the Wyoming border. The "Cowboy State" greets you with a sign, "Howdy, you're in Big Wyoming." And while South Dakota has chosen somber presidential faces for its license plates, this state has opted for a silhouette of a cowboy riding a bucking bronco.

Wyoming has a small piece of the **Black Hill National Forest**, one of few small things about this state, located not far from the border outside of **Sundance**. Hardy Longabaugh, known as the "Sundance Kid," presumably shot a deputy sheriff near here and subsequently entered the infamous **"Hole-in-the-Wall"** hideout about 150 miles (240 km) southwest of here. Once little known outside the West, his memory now lives on, his name a household word, thanks to George Roy Hill and Robert Redford, director and actor of the movie *Butch Cassidy and the Sundance Kid*. Past Sundance, US 14 loops up toward the Black Hills and **Devil's Tower**, that object of obsession depicted in another very popular movie, *Close Encounters of the Third Kind*

It can be seen from almost 100 miles (150 km) away. This 860-foot (260-meter) fluted, butte-like rock formation (the tallest of its kind in America) stands on the other side of the Belle Fourche River, where the Black Hills meet the gullies and grasslands of the plains.

The first white men to explore this region, supposedly misinterpreting a benign name ascribed to it by Native Americans, called it Devil's Tower. It held a prominent place in the folklore and legends of the Sioux, and it later served as a landmark for those traveling west, just as it does today.

You can hike around the base of the Tower (beware of rattlesnakes), most people simply stare at it. It is an extraordinary sight, almost supernatural in shape and dimension and particularly luminous at sunrise or by the light of the moon. The sight of it impressed Teddy Roosevelt enough to make it the nation's first national monument in 1906.

South of the monument the road loops back to I-90 at **Moorcorft**, an old cow town. The old Texas Trail made its way through here in the 19th Century, trampled by cowboys driving cattle all the way to Montana. Farther west,

Left, a neon cowboy points the way west, and right, the real thing at the TX Ranch, Montana.

through **Gillette**, the plains are vast and beautiful. Before crossing the Powder River and its tributary the Crazy Woman Creek, you will see the distant snow-streaked peaks of the **Bighorn Mountains.**

Traveling westward, the Bighorn Mountains are the first range you encounter. They were named for bighorn sheep, once prevalent here but now rarely seen. As abrupt as they are majestic, the Bighorns foretell the Rocky Mountain ranges beyond. The eastern foothills are traversed by I-90, as they once were by the Bozeman Trail, a bloody shortcut in the 19th century push westward through Sioux, Crow and Cheyenne hunting grounds.

Buffalo, where the road bends north, was strangely named after its sister city in New York, not for those most quintessential of American beasts who once thundered across the plains. It was one of the earliest settlements in this part of Wyoming, it's main street was formerly an old trail that negotiated Clear Creek.

The road from Buffalo to Sheridan passes near the remains of **Fort Phil Kearny**, now a national landmark. This was the most hated army outpost along the Bozeman Trail, and when it was finally abandoned in 1868, it was immediately burned to the ground by local Indians.

About 20 miles (32 km) south of the Montana border is the small city of **Sheridan**, the county seat in a region once inhabited by the Crow Indians and now a major cattle-producing area. The railroad came to town in 1890, following the discovery of coal and continued to play a major role in the development of this city. Although cattle is of primary importance here, the city is perhaps best known for its annual July celebration, American Indian Days and for its hotel, the **Sheridan Inn**.

Right across the street from the railroad station in Sheridan is the Sheridan Inn, opened in 1893 by the Burlington Railroad and Sheridan Land Company. This gracious structure, with its long, cool, inviting front porch, fell into disuse and was scheduled for demolition in

The historic Sheridan Inn, Buffalo Bill's home away from home.

90

the mid-1960s. Fortunately, it was saved by Neltje Kings an area rancher who considered it more than just an old building. He felt its loss was akin to tearing out the most important chapters of history. It is again open for business, and it functions as a living museum.

The Sheridan was modeled after a Scottish inn, and most of the materials used in its construction were shipped from the East by rail. In its day, it was considered to be the finest hotel between Chicago and San Francisco. Presidents stayed here; so did such celebrities as Ernest Hemingway, General Pershing and Will Rogers. Aside from celebrities, ranchers would travel for days to spend a weekend of festivities here and many of their wives would keep a trunk of fancy clothes at the inn.

The inn was the first place in the area to feature bathtubs and electric lights. The lights were powered by an abandoned threshing machine and were illuminated from dusk until midnight when a whistle was blown to warn of the impending darkness. Later there was a

telephone, the only one in the county, which was a direct line to the drugstore. But the inn's pride and joy was its bar, constructed in England from oak and mahogany and still in use today. It arrived from the East before the railroad was completed as far as Sheridan, so they lugged it from Gillette by ox team. It's known as the **"Buffalo Bill Bar."**

William F. "Buffalo Bill" Cody made the inn his second home and even owned a share of it. It was customary for him to sit back on the long porch and audition acts for his Wild West Show.

Indian Wars

Along I-90 north of Sheridan in the direction of Billings, Montana, are two of the most infamous sites of the 1860s "Indian Wars" in an area of lush ranchlands where herds of buffalo once roamed. **Ranchester** is the site of **Connor Battlefield**, where General Patrick E. Connor led a division of more than 300 soldiers in an ambush of an Arapaho encampment. The Arapaho lost 64

Left, Buffalo Bill posing with Chief Sitting Bull, and right, a painter's portrait of Cody.

of their people and their camp was virtually destroyed. Women and children were massacred here, and as a result Connor lost his command.

Just north of Ranchester is the Montana border and the **Crow Indian Reservation**. The road here traces the Little Bighorn River into a land of lush, rolling grasslands.

The town of **Garryowen**, named after an Irish drinking song leads you into the legendary **Custer Battlefield**. The Battle of Little Bighorn, better known as "Custer's Last Stand, took about as long as it takes for a white man to eat his dinner, according to one observer. But the Sioux and Cheyenne who fought that day were to lose the greater struggle. Two-hundred-sixty white marble stones now sanctify this place along with the words of Oglala Chief Black Elk, in Lakota and English: "Know the Power that is Peace."

Beyond the battle site is **Crow Agency**, headquarters of this 2.5 million-acre (1 million-hectare) reservation. Originally, a treaty designated 38 million acres (15 million hectares) as Crow land. The area, bisected by the Bighorn River and characterized by rolling hills was described by Crow Chief Rotten Belly in the 1830s as being "exactly in the right place. Everything good is to be found there. There is no country like the Crow Country." From Crow Agency to Billings, I-90 skirts the northern boundary of the Crow reservation. Before crossing the Yellowstone River into Billings, civilization again assaults the senses in the form of several malodorous meatpacking plants.

Anything is possible in America. You can find yourself one day pushing papers, meeting deadlines, squeezing into subways or conforming to whatever routine you call your own, and the next day you can be riding the open range, punching cows and maybe even wielding a branding iron.

The adventure begins at **Billings Logan International Airport**, where a group of individuals from various walks of life meet and wait for Abby Tillett to take them to cow camp.

An artist's depiction of "Custer's Last Stand."

92

The Tilletts, an extended ranching family in the western tradition operate the **TX Ranch**. Based in **Lovell**, Wyoming, just south of the Montana border, their summer cattle range takes them north into Montana where Abbey and her cowboy son Hip have cow camps set up especially for the tenderfoots.

The camps are deep within the sage and grass-covered foothills of the Crow Indian Reservation, between the Bighorn and the Pryor Mountains. On the way, road surfaces deteriorate in direct proportion to the degree of isolation—pavement, dirt roads, followed by trails that is best negotiated on horseback.

Don't expect to find the comforts of home. The TX is not a dude ranch, but a working ranch where you'll live and work like one of the hands. No beds (you'll sleep in a tent), no electricity, no telephones, no running water. There is an outhouse, where the coffee can on the wall intended to hold a spare roll of toilet paper has been usurped by a family of wrens. If you want a shower after a hard day in the saddle, you can fill a plastic bag with water from the creek in the morning, let the sun warm it during the day and hang it from the roof of a shack. But people find exactly what they are looking for here, and they are more rejuvenated after a week of hard riding than they would be after a vacation at Club Med. Many return yearly for a dose of the Old West.

The TX Ranch isn't the only working ranch open to visitors. New York City-based Adventure Guides can set you up at a number of other ranches throughout the West.

Ancient Medicine Wheel

Approaching the Bighorn Mountains via I-90 from Montana to Wyoming, you begin to see a road switch backing its way up the snow-streaked slopes. Traveling west from Ranchester to Lovell allows you to experience this firsthand.

US 14 out of Ranchester ascends Bighorn National Forest past bullet-ridden signposts to **Burgess Junction**.

The ancient Indian Medicine Wheel; its creators and purpose are unknown.

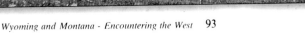

The road is treacherous beyond this point. Several runaway truck ramps and brake-cooling turnouts are also available to help negotiate the steep grades and sharp turns.

About 20 miles (30 km) beyond Burgess Junction is a three mile (5 km) gravel road leading to the **Indian Medicine Wheel**. Although well paved, the road is extremely narrow and winding, at one point crossing a narrow ridge. But the views from these highest reaches of the Bighorns are stupendous, and the immediate country-side is sprinkled with lovely wildflowers. Near its end, the road forks and presents you with a clear choice: the 20th century radar facility to the left or the ancient medicine wheel to the right.

This medicine wheel is the most elaborate of a series of stone circles found east of the Rocky Mountains, its 28 spokes forming an almost perfect circle 74 feet (22 meters) in diameter. It is thought to be about 600 years old, but its creators and its purpose remain a mystery. According to Crow legend, the wheel was here when they arrived in the 1770s. Today it serves a ceremonial function for Native Americans. One visitor, looking over at the radar station, wonders how *that* structure might be interpreted centuries from now.

Past the Medicine Wheel, US 14A plunges directly down the mountain into the **Big Horn Basin**. Protected by the mountains, this region enjoys a milder climate than the rest of Wyoming. It is a prime cattle producing area which saw one of the last great range wars between cattlemen and sheepherders in the early part of the 20th Century.

US 14A travels from Lovell to Cody through Shoshone River Valley. **Lovell**, a well-groomed town, was founded by ranchers in the 1870s and remains identified with cattle though it is also known as the "Rose Town of Wyoming". Past Garland, the Rocky Mountains loom into view for the first time with square-topped **Heart Mountain** in the foreground. A short drive from here is **Cody**, a town named after William F. "Buffalo Bill" Cody.

Old trail town, Cody.

Buffalo Bill's Town

"He has been more than picturesque; he has been worthwhile."
—Chicago Evening Post, 1911.

You can't pass through Cody without confronting the memory of Buffalo Bill, that one-time Pony Express rider, soldier, buffalo hunter, Army Chief of Scouts, ranchers, frontiersman, actor and showman. He has accurately been called a "kaleidoscope of white man's western experience." Through his Wild West Show, his own screen roles and other films that dealt with his character (he's been played by everyone from Roy Rogers to Charlton Heston and Paul Newman), he has, more than any single person, influenced the world view of the American West—for better and for worse. And he certainly left his mark on Cody.

Cody is unquestionably tourist crazy. When Yellowstone attained national park status this town jumped right in, billing itself as gateway to the park. Today there are so many tour buses, tourist attractions and so much hoopla that the inclination is to step on the gas toward Yellowstone. But if you can withstand the phony facade, you'll discover a treasure trove of the Old West.

Most prominent is the **Buffalo Bill Historical Center**, which is actually four truly outstanding museums in one. The **Buffalo Bill Museum** is devoted to the man's vast collection of memorabilia. He was known for his flamboyance and excess, and the collection is all the better for it.

The **Whitney Gallery of Western Art** spans the period from the 1800s to the present. All the greats are represented—Catlin, Bierstadt, Moran, Remington, Russell and others. Remington's studio has been recreated here, and it is a stunning achievement. The **Plains Indian Museum**, displays one of the world's finest collection of Sioux, Cheyenne, Shoshone, Crow, Arapaho and Blackfeet artifacts. Perhaps most fascinating is a series of precise pictographs executed by Sitting Bull while imprisoned at Fort Randall

An original poster advertising Cody's show, from the Buffalo Bill Historical Center.

in 1882. Drawn on fort Randall stationery, they depict what he considered to be the important events in his life. Finally, the **Winchester Arms Museum** displays a collection of more than 5,000 projectile weapons. Although the center is closed from December to February, it is open the rest of the year from 7 a.m to 10 p.m. You can easily spend a day here.

Cody is also known for its **Night Rodeo**, a long standing tradition which along with the annual Fourth of July Cody Stampede, legitimizes the town's claim to "Rodeo Capital of the World."

Old Trail Town, including the **Museum of the Old West**, is located west at the original town site. The beloved obsession of Bob and Terry Edgar, this is an impressive collection of authentic frontier buildings, horsedrawn vehicles and other artifacts from Wyoming's past. The **"Hole in the Wall Cabin,"** used by Butch Cassidy and the Sundance Kid, is here, marked by a rock with the oldest inscribed date in northern Wyoming (1811).

A number of legendary frontiersmen have been reburied here, among them John "Jeremiah Liver-eating" Johnston, portrayed by Robert Redford in the film *Jeremiah Johnson*. Johnston died in an old soldiers' home far from the mountains where he lived, and his reburial was marked by a moving ceremony featuring Robert Redford and the Utah Mountain Men as pallbearers. The plaque on his grave reads, "No More Trails."

Us 14 west out of Cody follows the north fork of the Shoshone River winding through the colorful formations of **Shoshone Canyon** and past the **Buffalo Bill Dam**, the world's first concrete arch dam. It then tunnels through **Rattlesnake Mountain**, which supports the northern end of the dam, and continues on through the **Wapiti Valley** with its irrigated pastures and sage brush hills. This is the land of the **Shoshone National Forest** (the nation's first), and as you take leave of it you'll find yourself at the entrance to Yellowstone National Park.

Shoshone
National
Forest
Wyoming.

DENVER: MILE-HIGH CITY

Denver, Colorado is the home of the first ice cream soda and the first bowl of shredded wheat. Walter L. Hakason invented softball in the Mile High City, and the infamous "Denver boot" was created there to tackle illegal parking offenders tardy on their fine payments. The idea of the shopping mall originated in Denver, and in 1967 the nation's first abortion law was passed within the walls of the Colorado State Capitol.

Two-hundred-and-fifty ounces of 28 carat gold leaf cover the dome of Denver's **Capitol Building** and serve as a lasting reminder of the Gold Rush that built the city. In the mid-1800s the first settlement was established by gold prospectors and several officials appointed by Kansas Territorial Governor James W. Denver. Gold dust was the common currency back then, and for a pinch between the thumb and forefinger a letter could be delivered back East. Weary, unlucky

prospectors flocked to the city from all over for guns, booze and women; the gambling halls never closed. Rumor has it that a county probate judge gambled away 30 town lots in less than 10 minutes.

Thus the city thrived despite population decline, the catastrophic fire of 1863 and the flooding of Cherry Creek the following year. Between 1880 and 1890 money from the silver camps bolstered the city's economy, and the population increased nearly threefold. This marked the beginning of Denver's urbanization. Since then the city has become a major center of trade, food distribution, banking and transportation.

The Denver metropolitan area is flavored with such popular attractions as the **Coors Brewery** (free samples), the **U.S. Mint** (producing more than 5 billion coins annually, no free samples) and **Casa Bonita**, the second largest volume restaurant in America, where cliff divers perform every three minutes from a real 25-foot (eight-meter) indoor waterfall.

Denver's newest addition is the **16th Street Mall**. Spanning 13 blocks, this pedestrian walkway of shops and restaurants is one mile long and serviced by free shuttle buses.

The city boasts the world's largest collection of Indian art. The 10-story, 28-sided **Denver Art Museum** houses much of this collection, specializing primarily in Asian, pre-Columbian and native American art. This unusual building is covered with a million gray glass tiles and perforated with oblong windows strategically placed to prevent any natural light from damaging the art work inside.

By far Denver's most outstanding feature is its natural setting. Not only are the **Rocky Mountains** less than one hour away, but the Denver city park system is the largest in the country. More than 450 acres of urban respite are scattered throughout Denver proper. Even the city's most popular concert hall is a natural outdoor wonder— **Red Rocks Amphitheater** was hollowed out of the pre-existing red sandstone on a site high above the city.

[Denver is located in north-central Colorado, about 100 miles (161 km) south of Cheyenne, Wyoming, on I-25.]

THE NORTHERN ROCKIES

The national parks of the northern Rockies—Yellowstone, Grand Teton and Glacier—are regions of breathtaking natural beauty, vignettes of primitive North America.

These mountain parks share an abundance of wildlife. But they are not identical. Yellowstone has its geysers; Grand Teton encompasses the incomparable Teton Range rising above cattle country, and Glacier has its spectacular mountain passes.

The route between Yellowstone and Glacier passes through the westernmost **Great Plains**, the traditional hunting grounds of the Plains Indians. First described by Lewis and Clark in the early part of the 19th Century, and later depicted by Charles Russell, the landscape is now dominated by cattle ranches and wide open fields of wheat.

Yellowstone is both symbol and sanctuary. Located in the northwest corner of Wyoming, it was the world's first national park and for many people it is still the most magnificent. This primitive landscape, forged by fire and water, has been called the "greatest concentration of wonders on the face of the earth," its shapes and colors "beyond the reach of human art." It is a hotbed of geothermic activity, with more than 10,000 thermal features, as well as one of the last remaining of the grizzly bear in continental U. S. All this, and enough canyons, cliffs and cataracts to please the most jaded eye.

Though Native Americans hunted here for centuries, credit for the region's discovery goes to John Colter, the first white man to set foot in what is now Wyoming. Later in the 19th century, trappers and prospectors passed through, among them Jim Bridger, celebrated mountain man and teller of tall tales. Impressed by the petrified trees of **Specimen Ridge**, he embellished his description a bit, raving of "petrified trees full of petrified birds singing petrified songs." In 1870, Henry Washburn the Surveyor General of Montana Territory, headed up a more illustrious expedition endeavoring to set the record straight, they returned awe struck and committed to the creation of a "nation's park"—a dream realized in 1872.

Yellowstone encompasses an area of more than 2 million acres (800,000 hectares). Those who prefer being at one with nature can rest assured that 95 percent of this area is backcountry. For the less intrepid, there are nearly 300 miles (500 km) of roads. The **Grand Loop Road** provides access to most major attraction, from **Yellowstone Lake** and the **Grand Canyon of Yellowstone** to **Mammoth Hot Springs** and **Old Faithful**. All are magnificent.

Many visitors view Old Faithful's performance with a sense of obligation. Although not as faithful as it once was, the geyser pleases the crowd regularly—21 to 23 times daily. This is also a prime location for people-watching a chance to glimpse a real slice of American life frozen in anticipation.

Some come here primarily to view wildlife, and few depart disappointed. Stopped cars along the road generally indicate that some large mammal is grazing nearby. Unfortunately for both man and beast, visitors tend to forget their natural fear of and respect for these truly wild creatures. A park ranger relates that people who would ordinarily be reluctant to pet a neighbor's dog have no qualms about posing for a snapshot with a wild animal twice their size. Bison gorings are quite common and can be serious. These wounds usually occur in the same part of the human anatomy, inflicted from behind during a chase. The ranger stresses that a lone bison is alone for a good reason. "...because he wants to be." Greatest concern to park officials are the bears both black bears and grizzlies, the latter more dangerous and more endangered.

One way to avoid bears is to visit the park in winter, a time of hibernation. This season comes early to Yellowstone. Many feel that the park is never more beautiful than when it is clothed in white. Snowmobiles and snowcoaches provide limited access, but probably the best way to explore this quintessential

Artist's Point, Yellowstone National Park, Wyoming.

winter wonderland is on skis. Kick and glide your way to the thermal areas, good places to spot wildlife warming their hooves and paws.

Nature and Nightlife

With the coming of winter, the Yellowstone elk population leaves the high country and heads for the National Elk Refuge outside of Jackson, Wyoming. Though not exactly following in their hoofprints, US 89 south nevertheless takes you from the southern boundary of Yellowstone, through Grand Teton National Park and Jackson Hole, alongside the Refuge, to Jackson, the perennial boomtown.

If the Rockies are the crown, then the **Teton Range** is its jewel. Exquisitely beautiful, amethyst-tinged, jagged, snowcapped and hypnotic, they loom above the horizon west of the highway. The **Snake River**, running true to its name, intervenes. The Tetons and **Gros Ventre** ranges encircle the **Jackson Hole** valley. Trappers worked this terri-

tory in the early 19th Century and it was named for David E. Jackson, a prominent member of the trade. Settlers came in the 1880s as outlaws, homesteaders and ranchers. This is gorgeous country, never more visually stunning than in the 1953 movie *Shane*, filmed on location here. It is still cattle country, though tourism has become the mainstay economically. People flock from all over the country to play here and skiing is the name of the game.

One Jackson local defines spring as "two weeks of poor skiing." Nearby **Rendezvous Mountain's** claim to fame is its vertical drop—the greatest of any U.S. ski resort. This can be appreciated even in summer by taking a ride on the aerial tram with a sheer ascent of nearly a mile (1.6 km). The view from the summit is stupendous—Grand Teton and far beyond.

The Old West and the New West have converged in **Jackson**, land of condos and cowboys. (Some of the cowboys here wear Vuarnet sunglasses.) This is a big-name resort with its share of local

Misty steps of stone, Yellowstone.

color; you just have to look for it. Look beyond the boutiques, the ski chalets, the nightly "shoot-outs" and the stagecoach rides. Bars are generally the best place for this sort of quest, so pull up a saddle (mounted on a bar stool) at the **Million Dollar Cowboy Bar** and hoist a few with the locals.

North of Jackson is the **National Elk Refuge**, established in 1912 and now the winter habitat of a herd some 8,000 strong. Once the victims of starvation and disease the elks are now protected and nourished. Regularly scheduled sleigh rides transport visitors briefly into the company of these graceful creatures. In spring the elk shed their antlers, which are expeditiously retrieved by area Boy Scouts and later auctioned off at considerable profit. Bidders include those from the Far East, who grind the antlers into a powder valued as an aphrodisiac. Perhaps in response to all of this, the elk soon abandon their winter home and head for the hills.

Gardiner, Montana, sits along US 89 just north of Yellowstone on the south-ern fringe of **Gallatin National Forest**. Out of Yellowstone, the road passes through barren plains and irrigated farms before reaching the forest, rich in minerals. It plays hide and seek with Yellowstone River before intersecting with US 10 at **Livingston**. Livingston was put on the map by both the Northern Pacific Railroad and Yellowstone, just 56 miles (89 km) to the south.

Further west along US 10 is **Bozeman**, nestled in the Gallatin Valley. This was known as the "Valley of Flowers" by the Blackfeet, Piegan Crow, Cheyenne and Snakes who hunted here. William Clark passed through here with their blessing in 1806 on the return trip of his path finding expedition. John Bozeman and Jim Bridger later guided wagon trains through in direct violation of treaty, and therefore at considerable risk. The trail became Bonanza Trail, the Bridger Cut-Off and the Bloody Bozeman—a treacherous shortcut for impatient pioneers.

Like so many other western cities, Bozeman has a historic main street. It is

An elk flaunts his impressive headdress.

also a college town and site of the **Museum of the Rockies**, an institution devoted to the physical and cultural heritage of the northern Rockies. Bozeman's "boot hill" is **Sunset Hills Cemetery**, the final resting place of native sons, journalist Chet Huntley, John Bozeman and Henry T.P. Comstock of Nevada mining fame, who committed suicide while passing through in 1870.

Northwest of Bozeman is Manhattan where there is not much of a skyline followed by the town of **Three Forks**, just the other side of the Madison River. This town was named for the Missouri Headwaters—the Gallatin, Madison and Jefferson Rivers—all three named by Lewis and Clark. Meriweather Lewis and William Clark led their historic expedition here in July 1805. They had accepted the challenge of exploring the recently acquired Louisiana Purchase by tracing the Missouri River and its tributaries, with a view to discovering the elusive Northwest Passage. By the time they reached the Tree Forks area, they realized that the Missouri drainage system did not in fact lead to the Pacific. Nevertheless, the success of their expedition remains undisputed. They opened up the West for a generation and for all-time. A deluge of exploration and exploitation soon flowed.

Gone today is the abundance of wildlife that Lewis and Clark found at the headwaters, although a state park has been developed, commemorating and interpreting its historical significance. Here, you can have a picnic at the very spot where the expedition stopped for breakfast on July 27, 1805 at nine a.m. or you can climb up to **"Lewis Rock,"** where Lewis sketched a map of the surrounding countryside. At the entrance to the park are the remains of a ghost town, **Second Gallatin City**. The town moved here from across the headwaters to be astride the main stagecoach route, after having been abandoned by the steamboat. But its existence was short-lived, bypassed by the next wave of transportation: the railroad.

A few miles west of Three Forks on I-

Touring on horseback through Teton National Forest.

90, the color suddenly changes to the gold of wheat, and US 287 enters, going north toward Helena. Past **Townsend**, **Canyon Ferry Lake** appears to the east of the road like an oasis on the prairie. Behind it stand the **Big Belt Mountains**. US 287 continues north and merges with I-15, skirting **Helena**, the seat of government.

In Helena they continue to make Lewis and Clark Bourbon and there is still talk about **Last Chance Gulch**, although now it is a pedestrian mall. Charles M. "The Cowboy Artist" Russell fans will want to stop at the **Montana Historical Society**, which houses a collection of his work. Esteem for Russell runs high in Montana, and one of his masterpieces graces the chambers of the House of Representatives—an enormous mural with a name to match, "Lewis and Clark Meeting the Flathead Indians at Ross' Hole."

Outside of Helena, the road passes through Montana's version of suburbia. The consummate beauty and endless expanse of the treeless plain is clearly violated by tract housing, but only briefly. Near **Wolf Creek**, the road starts climbing circuitously past multicolored ledges and then descends, meeting the Missouri river.

Exiting at **Ulm**, just before Great Falls, a gravel road travels for several miles, past the **Lazy J Ranch**, to Ulm *Pishkun*, meaning buffalo jump. Prior to the acquisition of horses, Native Americans hunted buffalo by stampeding them over cliffs to their deaths. Stone tools were used to slaughter and dress the animals at the base of the cliff. Several hundred of these sites have been identified in North America, most of them in Montana. Ulm *Pishkun* is now silent, the chaos, blood and deafening roar of the buffalo kill obscured by the passage of time.

Out of Ulm, the route follows the **Lewis and Clark Trail** to **Great Falls**, the center of Charles Russell country. A museum devoted to his work and that of his contemporaries is located here, incorporating his home and log cabin studio. The **Mint Bar** was once also a

Bisons grazing peacefully on the Montana plains.

major repository of his paintings—some traded for drinks—until they were purchased by a collector.

Russell came to Montana at the age of 15, and during the course of his life he witnessed the transformation of this land. A rare combination of authenticity and romance, his work reflects the passion, beauty, action and soul of the Old West. The country around Great Falls, first described by Lewis and Clark, served as a backdrop for most of his paintings. Preserved on canvas are the herds of buffalo, the vast grasslands upon which they grazed, the open range, the bluffs and the buttes.

Out of Great Falls, US 89 travels northwest toward Glacier National Park, roughly paralleling the **Continental Divide**. Known meteorologically as the "Northwest Chinook Zone," this is a region of abrupt and record-breaking changes in temperature caused by the geographical transition from the Great Plains to the Rockies. Geometrically, the road approximates the base of the "Golden Triangle," a rich, grain-producing area where towering elevators announce the next town.

Past **Fairfield**, "The Malting Barley Capital of the World," with its obligatory **Silver Dollar Bar**, the setting sun scorches the white line of the highway as black-eyed Susans look on. Close the car windows and step on the gas while passing the Custom Feed Lot north of Choteau. Beyond **Bynum** (a grocery store, a bar, a couple of nondescript buildings), the road winds through countryside which is a showcase for the art of strip cropping.

North of **Dupuyer**, a tiny town devastated by flood in 1964, the road enters the **Blackfeet Indian Reservation**. The Blackfeet journeyed from the East stopping here at the foothills of the Rockies. According to legend, they walked across charred prairies.

Browning is the headquarters of the Blackfeet Reservation and location of the **Museum of Plains Indians**, which houses the most comprehensive collection of Blackfeet artifacts. Also of interest is the **Museum of Montana Wild-**

Natural Montana: Gallatin National Forest and a grizzly bear wanders through the field.

life and **Hall of Bronze**, featuring the work of local sculptor and taxidermist Bob Scriver. The biggest event of the year occurs each July, when Browning hosts **North American Indian Days**, one of the largest gatherings of its kind.

About 12 miles (19 km) northeast of Browning is "Camp Disappointment." Hoping that the headwaters of the Marias River would rise north of the 49th parallel, effectively extending the boundary of the Louisiana Purchase, they were disappointed upon discovering that it rose to the west. This, along with dismal weather and a shortage of game, gave the camp its name.

The drive from Browning to **St. Mary**, at the eastern entrance to Glacier, is dramatically beautiful. From Browning to Kiowa, the road heads due west and appears as a straight black arrow pointing to the mountains, silhouetted against the setting sun. North of Kiowa, US 89 bends Northwest and ascends rapidly, winding as it goes. Thirty m.p.h. road signs are riddled with bullet holes and appear to advise driving 38 m.p.h. Farther north, the highway descends precariously toward St. Mary, with a prayer and several runaway truck ramps.

Glacier National Park

The small town of St. Mary separates Lower St. Mary Lake from St. Mary Lake proper, and is best known for being at the eastern end of **Going-to-the-Sun Road**. It is a friendly town, attentive to the needs of visitors to **Glacier National Park**. The park cafe, outside the park entrance, obliges with 13 varieties of homemade pies and Mexican-inspired breakfasts that will knock your socks off.

Opened in 1933 Going-to-the-Sun Road is the only road that crosses Glacier, bisecting it into two nearly equivalent sections. It has been called "... the most beautiful 50-mile stretch of road in the world." These 50 miles (80 Km) pass through the heart of Glacier, one of the North America's wildest and most unspoiled mountain preserves. The

Columbian ground squirrels in Glacier National Park.

two-lane highway climbs the mountains beyond St. Mary to **Logan Pass**, **Garden Wall** and the shore of **Lake McDonald** before reaching the town of **West Glacier**.

Glacier is more remote and less crowded than Rocky Mountain park, Yellowstone, yet traffic can be heavy on Going-to-the-Sun. Traveling this road is most satisfying at off-peak times—sunrise, sunset, early summer and autumn. It is generally plowed and passable from mid-June to mid-October.

Opportunities for backcountry hiking naturally abound in Glacier. Its approximately 50 glaciers, 200 lakes, alpine meadows and forests are a haven for fishermen, hikers and wildlife alike. Two rustic stone chalets (**Granite Park** and **Sperry**), reached on foot or horseback, offer overnight accommodations. They were built around 1914, by the Great Northern Railroad.

The Continental Divide is Glacier's backbone, crossed by Going-on-the-Sun at Logan Pass. This is the place for the spectacular vistas of the **Hanging Garden Trail**, which leads to vast alpine meadow. Columbian ground squirrels greet hikers at the trail head, which process past deformed trees known as *Krummholz* (from the German for "elfin timber" or "crooked wood") and across the meadow, ever-changing repertoire of glacier lilies, Indian paintbrush, red monkey flowers and mountain heath. Mountain goats can sometimes be sighted from here, as well as grizzlies who feed on the meadow's bulbs and roots. **The Highline Trail**, across the road from the Hanging Garden is a more challenging and potentially dangerous trail. It is not recommended for the faint-hearted.

Near the park's western exit (a section plowed year-round) is **McDonald Creek**, a final resting place for kokanee salmon who travel here in late autumn from Flathead Lake to spawn. This event attracts hundreds of bald eagles, which in turn attracts an ever-increasing number of bird-watchers who silently peer through binoculars as nature takes its course.

Glacier National Park, Montana.

SKIING THE ROCKIES

No self-respecting skier exists who has not—or does not plan to—ski the Rockies. Stretching across Colorado, Montana, New Mexico, Utah and Wyoming, these huge peaks are blanketed by 200-500 inches (508-1,270 cm) of snow every year.

The hard part is deciding where to ski. There are about 100 resorts in the Rockies offering whatever you're after. Here are a few of the finest.

Colorado

One of the original Rockies resorts, **Aspen** also operates neighboring **Buttermilk** and **Snowmass**. The Aspen area is known for après-ski with a vengeance. For more variety than you'll know what to do with, buy a four-area pass to Aspen's properties plus **Aspen Highlands**.

Breckenridge, **Copper**, and **Keystone** are neighbors in Dillon, Colorado, and it's no more than 30 minutes from

one to the next. (A special Ski-the-Summit lift ticket allows access to all three.) Breckenridge is an old mining town packed with an odd mix of renovated Victorian houses, western bars, quaint shops and discos. The ski area offers a trail network of impressive variety. Copper specializes in high-powered skiing and low-key nightlife. Keystone offers two base areas, a fine cross-country center and the challenging Arapahoe Basin, a huge treeless bowl, well-stocked with powder.

Vail is the largest single mountain skiing complex in the United States with 95 named trails. Every kind of skiing, service and activity is available.

Montana

Big Sky is certainly the best this state has to offer, with 11 novice runs, 17 intermediate and 11 expert. Another good choice is **Big Mountain** in Whitefish.

New Mexico

Southwest charm, alpine-style lodging and more than 1,000 acres (400 hectares) of skiing make **Taos** a must. Other good choices in the state are Angel Fire, Rio Costilla, Santa Fe and Sierra Blanca.

Utah

Schuss with a silver spoon in your mouth at **Deer Valley** in Park City where the skiing is easy and the slopes are groomed to within an inch of their life.

For reliable skiing through April, **Alta** is your best bet—they actually brag about having no snowmaking, their powder supply is so reliable. Utah powder is known as the lightest in the world, and you'll find plenty of it at **Snowbird**, renowed for bowls, bumps and a massive tram.

Wyoming

Jackson Hole in Teton Village has got it all: plenty of powder, good expert terrain, mild cruisers, a seven-mile (11-km) trail and no lines. And while your're in Wyoming, don't miss Grand Targhee in Alta.

ACROSS THE GREAT DIVIDE

As waters flow west of the Continental Divide toward the Pacific, so have the paths of civilization. The Nez Percé, the Kootenai, the Pend d'Oreille, the Flathead and other mountain tribes lived and hunted here in peace. Later the Blackfeet came from the plains across the Divide on horse-stealing raids, a journey that many have since followed.

The first whites to arrive were trappers and traders in the early part of the 19th Century, followed by prospectors in search of gold and silver. Homesteaders heading west conquered the Rockies and moved on, some settling in eastern Washington. With the coming of the railroad, the lumber industry found a permanent home in the forests west of the Divide.

As US Highway 2 leaves Glacier National Park heading west toward Kalispell and Libby, Montana, it immediately crosses the middle fork of the Flathead and meanders through the pristine, cathedral-like wilderness of **Flathead National Forest**. This mecca for backcountry enthusiasts includes nearly 1 million acres (.4 million hectares) of specially designated wilderness, accessible only on foot and in some areas on horseback. This is home of the much beloved **Bob Marshall Wilderness** referred to affectionately as "the Bob." It is a land of high mountains, virgin forests and alpine lakes.

U.S. 2 also passes through **Hungry Horse**, named for some freight horses that escaped and nearly starved to death before being discovered and nurtured back to health. Along the road you'll see out-croppings of a very particular brand of backwoods civilization. The **Pines Cafe and Museum of Mounted Fish** in **Columbia Falls** features not only "home cookin'," but also a display of 21 different species of mounted fish including five state records. As if this were not enough, a gigantic Ponderosa Pine towers through the center of the dining room.

The highway passes through **Kalis-**

pell, meaning "prairie above the lake," to **Pend d'Oreille**. This city was founded just before the turn of the century by the well-heeled rancher and banker Charles Conrad, and it remains the only city of any size in this corner of Montana. Michael Cimino's ill-fated 1980 film *Heaven's Gate* was shot on location here. The production was plagued by myriad problems, but the visual appeal of the surroundings was clearly not among them.

West of Kalispell, the **Kootenai National Forest** takes over where the Flathead leaves off. Along the highway toward **Libby**, evidence of the lumber industry's presence in this area becomes progressively more apparent. Timber has been big business here since 1892, when the Great Northern Railroad arrived. But as with all national forests, the Kootenai is a mixed-use area and within its boundaries (an area nearly three times the size of Rhode Island) are acres of undisturbed wilderness. It is the habitat of elk, moose, deer and Rocky Mountain bighorn sheep.

Left, a knowing grin in Cut Bank, Montana. Right, rolling northwestern farmland.

There is one unique way for outsiders to grasp the beauty of this place—and the **Libby Ranger Station** holds the key.

A system of observation towers, manned around the clock, were once the primary method of forest fire surveillance. As methods have become more sophisticated, these structures have been vacated. The Libby Ranger Station has opened their lookout atop **Big Creek Baldy Mountain** to the public. It is available on a reserve-ahead and pay-ahead basis. That being arranged, just drive into Libby and pick up directions and the key.

The Lookout Tower

State Highway 37 out of Libby leads to forestry service access roads, the last of which winds its way up to the foot of Big Creek Baldy Lookout. The last mile (two km) or so is extremely rough and steeply graded. The thrill of making it to the top, mingled with awe upon viewing the panorama that awaits, will take anyone's breath away. A rather tame mule deer has been known to greet visitors as they disembark. And it only gets better after climbing the steps of the 41-foot (12-meter) tower.

It is akin to being in a room that rests on a stationary cloud. The 225-square foot (20-meters square) space with unobstructed windows and an observation deck on all sides, contains items essential to survival and comfort and nothing more—save a firesighting device smack in the middle of the floor. Below, the tranquil beauty of the forest stretches for miles in all directions. The wind is more than a whistle up here, not muffled by the trees. It is a solitary, spiritual and romantic place to spend the night. From Libby, where the **Cabinet Mountains** can be seen from downtown, it is a short drive along US 2 to the Idaho border. The highway parallels the Kootenai River, passing near the lovely **Kootenai Falls** and through **Troy**, home of the largest silver mine in the United States.

State Line gas station presages the border between Montana and Idaho.

Lookout Tower, Kootenai, Montana.

Though the landscape is a continuum of mountains, running water and dense forest, the northern Idaho panhandle is a transitional area. The myths of the West are left behind here as the Pacific beckons. A casual survey of headgear reveals significantly fewer cowboy hats.

US 2 enters Boundary County (aptly named with borders along Montana, British Columbia and Washington) and join US 95 just above **Bonners Ferry**. At **Sandpoint**, on the shores of the great Pend d'Oreille, US 2 splits off to the west, while US 95 bridges the lake on its way southwest toward Coer d'Alene. From 1890 to 1910 three transcontinental railroad lines forged their way through this part of Idaho, creating a string of towns which dot the highway.

Before reaching Coer d'Alene, US 95 greets the interstate. It is worth backtracking east along I-90 a bit here, not only because the road hugs the banks of **Coer d'Alene Lake** for about 11 miles (17 km), but primarily because it leads to two unique and thoroughly dissimilar vestiges of 19th-century Idaho: the Old Mission and the Enaville Resort.

The **Coer d'Alene Mission of the Sacred Heart** stands atop a hill overlooking the main road (I-90), as it has since 1853. It is the oldest standing building in Idaho. Constructed of timber, mud and wooden pegs by Father Anthony Ravalli and the Coer d'Alene Indians, it is said to have risen,"...like a miracle in an almost total wilderness where even log houses were rare.

The "Black Robes"

Jesuits, Ravalli among them, came to this part of Idaho knowing that they would be welcomed by the Coer d'Alene, who had heard from neighboring tribes of the great powers of the "Black Robes." Truly a Renaissance man, Ravalli's European training is reflected in the mission's design, which is perhaps best described as Native American-Italianate. The spacious, cathedral-like interior is decorated with chandeliers made from tin cans, whitewashed newspaper painted with floral

Pieces of the past at the Enaville Resort.

motifs, carved pine crosses, a wooden altar painted to resemble marble and many other precious artifacts.

In 1877 the Coer d'Alene were forced to abandon their beloved mission for a reservation to the south, but they still consider it their mission today and return every August 15th to celebrate the Feast of the Assumption. Due to its location, the mission became a rendezvous point for mountain men, fur traders and "all sorts of riff-raff," in the words of the cavalrymen who were often called in to maintain peace. Today each July brings the Historic Skills Fair, a 20th-century rendezvous of crafts people, mountain men and Coer d'Alene Indians.

The Old Mission had no confessional until the late 1800s, presumably to serve white settlers, some of whom may have sinned at an establishment now called the **Enaville Resort**, located east of the mission along I-90 and north on Coer d'Alene River Road. It was built in 1880 as an overnight stop en route to gold and silver country. The Enaville

has had several names over the years including the Snakepit, Josie's and the Clark Hotel. Located strategically across from a lumberyard, a rail crossroad and the fork of the Coer d'Alene River, it has served as boomtown bar, hotel and house of ill repute.

Today the Enaville is a relaxing place to stop for a drink, have a bite to eat and meet the locals. Furnishings have piled up over the years and include many pieces hand-wrought by a mysterious Finlander known only as Mr. Egil. His materials were pine burls, antlers, horns and animal hides; his recompense room, board and free beer. Joe Breckenridge enjoyed a similar arrangement. A friend of artist Charles Russell, he painted copies of Russell's works in return for a "reasonable amount" of free beer. A couple of these canvases still grace the saloon's walls.

A short drive west on I-90 takes you out of Idaho and into eastern Washington, land of deserts, canyons, coulees, wheat fields and irrigated farmland—a sharp contrast to the densely forested

Speeding along a flat stretch in Idaho.

terrain of northern Idaho. Historically, the region was home to numerous Native American peoples, most of whom lived along the banks of the Columbia River. Their descendants, members of the Colville Confederated Tribes, live today on a reservation bordered on two sides by the Columbia River.

This was uninviting territory for early white explorers. The Grand Coulee itself presented a major obstacle, with few openings through which to pass. In the 1880s the first white settlers in the region faced enormous hardships. Their numbers remained relatively few until the completion of the **Grand Coulee Dam**. Built during the height of the Great Depression, the dam and the Columbia Basin (irrigation and electrification) Project changed the face of this region for all time.

Outside **Spokane**, US 2 travels across undulant, golden wheat fields toward the dam. Road signs become a bit confusing here, as the road approaches not only the Grand Coulee Dam, but the towns of Electric City, Grand Coulee, Grand Coulee Dam and Coulee City. At Wilbur, State 174 goes north to the town of Grand Coulee, where State 155 continues on to the dam. As they say, "You can't miss it."

A Dam Ahead of Its Time

The impact of the Grand Coulee Dam cannot be overestimated—economically or visually. Its aims, achievements and sheer size are all on a grand scale. Although it is over 50 years old, the design of the dam is of such stylistic integrity it still looks modern today.

The drive along State 155, from the dam to Coulee City and US 2, is surprisingly beautiful. The road skirts the lake on one side and the algae-clad coulee walls on the other. West of Coulee City along US 2, gently sloping fields of wheat, dotted with the occasional farm house, give the appearance of a vast desert. Layers of blue mountains appear in the distance like a mirage—the first of the coastal chains.

Near **Farmer**, the road is a wide open invitation to speed. An old Chevy cruises by, a pair of feet hanging out the back window. Crickets sing above the whir of the engine. Slow down to pass through the lovely town of **Douglas**. Farther along at **Waterville**, the price of Kool-Aid drops a penny as the sun sets for the day.

At **Orondo**, US 2 follows the Columbia River and branches off tracing its tributary, the Wenatchee. This is orchard country. Green patches of fertile land jut into the river and contrast with the golden hills. Stands selling apricots put out signs reading simply, "COTS."

Gradually the road climbs and enters the realm of tall timber, passing through **Leavenworth** a self-styled, pseudo-Bavarian ski town and gateway to the **Wenatchee National Forest**. The **Cascade Mountains** are now more than a figment on the horizon. Over the rushing south fork of the Skykomish River, and through the **Snoqualmie National Forest** and several small towns with names like Gold Bar and Startup, US 2 brings you just northeast of Seattle.

Grand Coulee Dam.

SEATTLE: YOUTHFUL PORT CITY

Once rejected by Hudson's Bay Company as location for a trading post, it is now a cosmopolitan port city, considered by many to be America's most livable. **Seattle** has come of age, but not without its share of growing pains.

Downtown Seattle was burned to the ground, rebuilt, raised one full story and regraded. It was abandoned and ultimately resuscitated by its citizens. All this in less than a century and a half.

Seattle is a young city, even by North American standards. One octogenarian Seattlite, walking purposefully between the stalls at the Pike Place market, refers to herself as a "pioneer." An inaccurate statement perhaps. Seattle's modern history began in 1851 with the arrival of the Denny party from New York: seven men, five women and 12 children. They set up camp and with a mixture of wit and optimism called it "New York *Alki*," meaning New York by-and-by. Within a year they relocated across Elliott Bay, to what is now Pioneer Square.

Although, the names of several Seattle pioneers are immortalized on street signs, there is at least one important omission: David Swinson "Doc" Maynard, a man who did as much for this city as anyone has ever done. Maynard arrived in 1852 and immediately became a driving force within the community. A physician by training, he was also a shrewd businessman, a philanthropist, a friend to the Indians, a bit of a drinker and a man with a vision. He imbued this town with his spirit and suggested its name, after Chief Sealth of the Duwamish Nation.

Chief Sealth was quite shrewd himself. It is said that he charged the settlers $16,000 for the use of his name, claiming that after his death he would roll over in his grave at every mention of it. The fee was compensation for future inconvenience.

Doc Maynard was known for giving things away, especially to those who might contribute to the progress and prosperity of Seattle. He gave away parcels of land—one went to Henry Yesler, who established a lumber mill on the waterfront at the base of a hill. Logs were slid down Mill Street, which became known as "Skid Road." Today it is Yesler Way.

Traveling along Yesler Way it soon becomes apparent that the north-south streets do not intersect as they ought to. The mismatched streets are the legacy of a quarrel between Denny and Maynard, who owned large tracts of land on either side of Yesler Way. Their quarrel was never settled, and the roads they built on opposite sides of Yesler Way never coincided.

In 1889 the citizens of this small lumber town had the opportunity to band solidly together or to set up shop elsewhere. Seattle was largely destroyed in what was thereafter called the "Great Fire of 1889." A flurry of rebuilding ensued before the embers had a chance to cool. Seattle emerged more elaborate, and more permanent. Raising the new streets remedied the rather unpleasant and unsanitary flooding which occurred whenever the tide came in. It also created "Underground Seattle," a maze of sidewalks and former first floors destined to a future devoid of commerce and light.

"GOLD! GOLD! GOLD! GOLD!"

Thus exclaimed the front page of *The Seattle Post-Intelligencer* on July 17, 1897, and the Klondike Gold Rush was underway. With the arrival of the steamship *Portland*, carrying 68 prospectors and more than two tons of gold, Seattle's ship had finally come in.

The catch phrase became, "Are you going?" And go they did, from around the world and around the corner. Seattle's own mayor resigned to seek his fortune in northwestern Canada. Seattle merchants were quick to realize that there was a fortune to be made by staying put and outfitting the stampeders. Just two weeks after the *Portland*

Seattle's Space Needle dominates the evening skyline.

dropped anchor, approximately $325,000 in goods had been sold with no end in sight. All this in a time of widespread economic depression. Seattle outdistanced the competition and became the premier outfitter for Klondike expeditions. It wasn't luck, and it wasn't simply a matter of being in the right place at the right time. Seattle promoted its way to prosperity along a path paved by the Klondike Gold Rush.

The scenario might have gone differently were it not for the efforts of one Erastus Brainerd. A journalist and somewhat of a huckster, he devoted a year of his life "selling" Seattle as the only place to outfit for the Klondike. Features to this effect appeared in newspapers around the world. He also arranged for people to write letters to the editor, singing Seattle's praises. His campaign was a resounding success. In an eight-month period Seattle merchants saw an estimated 25 million dollars in Klondike trade, emphatically more than just a flash in the pan. The great gold rush of the 1890s put Seattle on the map as a center for trade in the Northwest.

As the city grew, its population migrated northward. To accommodate this trend, Seattle underwent yet another facelift in the early part of the 20th Century. Its steep hills were leveled off in a number of regrades. It is still a city of hills, but they are negotiable.

The area that is now **Pioneer Square**, site of the first permanent settlement, the Great Fire and a bustling harbor was gradually abandoned. It became a district characterized by poverty and despair, not unlike the downtown, waterfront sections of other cities. During the Great Depression, Seattle's Skid Road entered the American vocabulary as "Skid Row."

Pioneer Square was left alone until the late 1960s, when it was slated for a program of demolition and rebuilding. In the wake of its very successful world's fair, Seattle was riding a wave of prosperity and confidence. The powers that be looked at their own skid row and saw it as a blight on their city's

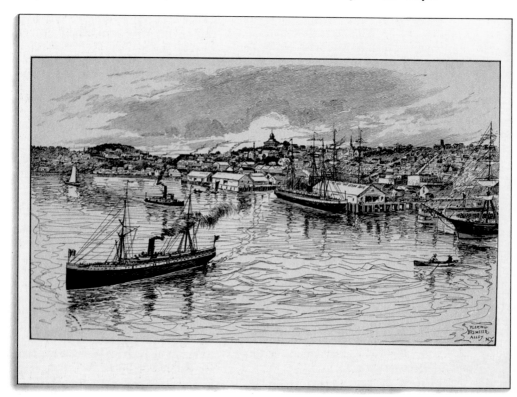

fair countenance, a blight to be eradicated. A passionate group of citizens felt there was a better solution, however, and fought to save the historic district. They were successful and Pioneer Square stands as a monument to Seattle pioneers past and present.

Pioneer Square, registered as a National Historic Site, is the heart of downtown. Hardly a sterile collection of restored buildings, it is a living and breathing community, reflecting various stages of Seattle's evolution. Historic landmarks and western-style bars are interspersed with upscale commercial ventures of all types. A considerable homeless and transient population is evident everywhere, as are the missions and shelters that serve them. This district is their traditional home; no effort has been made to drive them out. they coexist and share park benches with the gallery mavins, the cafe dwellers, the condo owners and the tourists.

Pioneer Square is a relatively small district, best explored on foot. A logical point to begin is cobblestoned **Pioneer Place** with its wrought iron pergola (ca 1910), a totem pole and bust of Chief Sealth. At Doc Maynard's Public House a tour of Seattle's "Underground" is available. Across the street from the Depression-era **Bread of Life Mission** is the **Elliot Bay Book Company**, a good example of what a bookstore should be. A cafe in the basement sponsors regular poetry readings. Less esoteric is the **J&M Cafe and Cardroom**, which conjures up visions of loggers and gamblers from another era.

Art, Music and Food

The city's largest concentration of galleries is found here. Notable among them is **Flury and Company**, representing the vintage photography of Edward S. Curtis, whose luminescent and dignified body of work documents the world of Native Americans. Downstairs from Flury and Company is **Bud's Jazz Records** where jazz buffs can happily pass the time of day; they even play requests!

Seattle Harbor then, left, and now.

The choice of eateries runs the gamut from chic to funky, but only one delivers the fare to your table on model trains. The **Iron Horse Restaurant** is billed as a place "the kids will love," but adults have been known to order that extra cup of coffee just to see the train come by one more time. It is a veritable museum of railroad memorabilia, displayed from floor to ceiling. Tracks run the perimeter of the room. A lower system delivers the food and an upper runs overhead all the live-long day.

A visit to the **Klondike Gold Rush National Historical Park** provides a fascinating introduction to this unique era in the history of the Pacific Northwest. Best of all are the nearly continuous showings of Charlie Chaplin's masterpiece *The Gold Rush.* For the pragmatic, gold panning demonstrations are available upon request.

Yesler Way leads down to the waterfront, where the *Portland* docked and unloaded its cargo of gold. This is first and foremost a working waterfront, now embellished by emporiums of all types, but mostly restaurants. The aroma of alder-smoked salmon, a Seattle specialty, fills the air.

Pike Place Market

Also downtown along the waterfront is the **Pike Place Market**, another labor of love taken on by Seattle's citizenry. Once threatened with dissolution, it has been restored and continues to operate, without interruption since 1907.

America's oldest farmers' market was started by locals who felt the middlemen were pocketing too large a share of their grocery money. It thrives today, providing Seattlites with an abundance of fresh produce at good prices, while sustaining the survival of small farms in western Washington. Chef Jacques Penin calls it "the best food market in the United States."

You will find more than fresh fruit and vegetables at Pike Place. It is a multilevel, multiethnic, multifarious place with a life of all its own and a pulse faster than the rest of the city. There are

Friend and ferret at Pike Place Market.

the fish markets with their fishmongers, real-life Eliza Doolittles selling fresh-cut dahlias and zinnias, street performers and an active community of craftspeople. The **Athenium Inn** ("...not a Greek restaurant," says the manager) has been in business since 1909 and features an old-fashioned soda fountain, a view of the bay and 150 varieties of beer (16 of them on tap). The **Read All About It Newsstand** advertises "Buy your papers from a human being instead of a machine" and offers an international selection of more than 150 newspapers and 1,000 magazines. There is a revival movie house located under the big clock, a tattoo parlor, a pawn shop, a Malay deli and a daily Alcoholics Anonymous meeting. Architect Fred Bassetti calls it "...a real place in a phony time."

Best known for its Space Needle and the Monorail that takes you there, **Seattle Center** is a 74-acre (30-hectare) "urban park" at the site of the 1962 World's Fair. It is a cultural conglomerate, home of Seattle's symphony, ballet,

opera and repertory theater companies. A big draw each summer is the **Pacific Northwest Festival** with its production of Wagner's entire "Ring Cycle"—the only such production outside of Germany. Other attractions include the **Pacific Science Center**, the **Seattle Art Museum** and an amusement park.

The **Space Needle** dominates the Center and the Seattle skyline. Not everyone is fond of this structure, but few are disappointed by the view from its observation deck. Majestic Mt. Rainier, the Olympic range to the west, the Cascades to the east and water all around. The Space Needle has also engendered a form of advertising perhaps unique to Seattle: commercial messages painted on the rooftops.

The people of Seattle are an outdoor-oriented, neighborhood-conscious lot. Their home and playground is blessed with a mild, maritime climate and enough water to satisfy all the sailors, fishermen, waterskiers, windsurfers and swimmers. The Cascade and Olympic Mountain ranges beckon climbers,

Mt. Rainer forms a permanent backdrop for the city of Seattle.

hikers, campers and other nature-lovers. But it isn't necessary to leave Seattle to get away from the hustle and bustle. There are over 5,000 acres (2,000 hectares) of parkland within the city limits. It is no wonder that Rand McNally's *Places Rated Almanac,* has chosen Seattle as number one in the recreation department since 1981.

A passion for parks goes back to the city's very beginnings. Several of today's parks were once the gathering places of native tribes. The land upon which Seattle Center sits was used for potlatches long before it was chosen for the World's Fair.

The Olmstead brothers (master landscape architects of New York City's Central Park fame) were consulted at the turn of the century concerning a master park plan for Seattle. Their inspiration for this city involved a system of neighborhood parks easily accessible by foot from every home. What was a good idea then, proved to be even better as the population grew.

Volunteer Park in **Capitol Hill** is a 44-acre (18-hectare) oasis designed by the Olmsteads. This neighborhood got its name when Seattle had hopes of becoming the state capital. The main building of the **Seattle Art Museum** is here, housing an outstanding collection of oriental art.

The **International District** is located east of Pioneer Square. Still called **Chinatown** by many locals, this pan-Asiatic community has drawn immigrants from all over Asia, most recently from Southeast Asia. Set high on a hill, **Kobe Terrace** is dedicated to the friendship between the people of Seattle and Kobe, Japan. It is loveliest in spring when the Mt. Fuji cherry trees are in full bloom (a gift from the people of Kobe).

The **Burke-Gilman Trail**, one of Seattle's newer parks, was dedicated in 1978. Created along the scenic path of an abandoned railroad spur, it extends from the top of Lake Union to the top of Lake Washington and is restricted to bicyclists, runners and walkers. With the general decline in the railroad industry, miles of forgotten tracks await libera-

Terraced gardens in the International District.

tion across the country. The trail has served as a model for other "rails to trails" projects. As with so many other Seattle projects, it was initiated by citizens—a positive response to disuse and abandonment. It seem as if Seattlites have perfected an ability to discover the silver lining in every cloud.

Condensation and Celebration

To many, the word Seattle is synonymous with rainy weather. Some theorize that natives have perpetuated the myth of abundant rainfall in order to discourage others from settling here.

Statistically, the total annual precipitation averages 34 inches (86 cm), less than many other major U.S. cities. It simply rains more frequently in Seattle. Much of the year is spent under a canopy of clouds when Mt. Rainier is visible only in the mind's eye.

But weather presents no obstacle to Seattle residents. They ignore it; they even laugh at it. With typical optimism they buy more sunglasses per capita

Seattle, party in the name of the sea.

than anywhere else in the nation! A craftsperson at the Pike Place Market does a lively business selling hand-screened sweatshirts inscribed with the words, *"The Rain in Spain Falls Mainly in Seattle."*

Bumbershoot, the largest annual arts festival in the Northwest is staged each Labor Day weekend. A cornucopia of musical events, art and food, it has the atmosphere of one large summer party. But without a doubt, Seattle's most important and probably most characteristic celebration is the annual Seafair.

Seafair is a month-long, midsummer extravaganza centered upon aquatic events, but providing plenty of entertainment for those landlubbers in the crowd. Seafair approaches its conclusion with the manic **Emerald City Unlimited Hydroplane Race** held on Lake Washington, as spectators line the shores and bridges, or float right on the lake. To top it all off, the Blue Angels fly in formation overhead, while all of Seattle takes its mind off the water and looks up to the sky.

THE OLYMPIC PENINSULA

Washington's **Olympic Peninsula**, this northwesternmost outcropping of the lower 48 states, is a remote, exotic and wildly beautiful region within easy reach of Seattle, Tacoma and Victoria, British Columbia. It is set apart from these places not merely by Puget Sound and the Strait of Juan de Fuca, but by its climate, its geology, the mystery of its peaks and forests and by the natural rhythms that guide the pace of life.

At the heart of it are the majestic **Olympic Mountains**, snow-streaked even in summer. Long the subject of myth, these mountains remained unexplored until the 1890s, when an expedition from Seattle set off in search of man-eating savages. Even the peninsula's Native Americans avoided venturing into the interior, fearing the wrath of mighty Thunderbird, who resided atop Mt. Olympus.

The Olympics are preserved and protected in a wilderness state as part of the **Olympic National Park**, which comprises 900,000 acres (365,000 hectares) of the peninsula, most of it inland but also including a 50-mile (80-km) strip of Pacific coastline. Only a few roads venture into the park, and these only peripherally. In fact, the park proper is surrounded by the **Olympic National Forest**, which makes it difficult to reach. Because the peninsula is largely under some form of federal jurisdiction, there is considerable conflict with the lumber industry.

The Olympic Peninsula sustains the rainforests of the Hoh, Quinault and Queets River valleys, the glacial peaks of the Olympics and the rugged Pacific coastline as well as lumber towns, fishing villages and nine American Indian reservations. Roosevelt elk, cougars and bald eagles reside here in greater concentrations than anywhere else.

Port Townsend sits expectantly on the peninsula's northeastern tip at the entrance to **Puget Sound**, approximately one hour's drive from Seattle. At **Edmonds**, due north of Seattle, a ferry crosses the short distance across the sound to **Kingston**, on the peninsula. From here it is a lovely drive to Port Townsend heading west and then north.

Charming **Port Gamble** calls itself "a permanent forest community, and so it is, an authentic lumber town reflecting a bygone era. Past here a bridge crosses the Hood Canal—the work of glaciers rather than men. At the town of **Discovery Bay**, (a good place to buy the fresh oysters, clams and herrings advertised on makeshift signs), State 20 veers off and up to Port Townsend.

Port Townsend, first settled in 1851, is the peninsula's oldest town. Sea captains and storekeepers from the East made their homes here. It was quick to become a boomtown, built up in anticipation of being linked with the Union Pacific Railroad and consequently becoming the major seaport of the Northwest. All this came to pass—but for Seattle, not Port Townsend. After the bust, they tore up the tracks, closed down the banks, and departed for more prosperous parts.

Left behind is an example of a Victorian seacoast town north of San Francisco. Declared a National Historic District, Port Townsend has become a haven for artists and headquarters of the **National School of Wooden Boatbuilding**, where a dying art is rescued.

US 101 loops around the peninsula like a misshapen horseshoe, open at the bottom. In the north it passes through Olympic National Park and on to the lumber towns of the "West End." The region between Discovery Bay and Port Angeles has been called the "banana belt," sitting as it does in the rain shadow of the Olympics. Farmers here see an average rainfall of only 17 inches (43 cm) compared with upwards of 140 inches (355 cm) on the other side of the mountains. Irrigated farms are a common sight along this part of US 101, as are Madrona trees, twisted and terracotta in color.

Towns along the way are small and distinctive. **Blyn** is gone before you can say "Little Brown Church of Blyn," its one and only landmark. **Sequim** (pronounced skwim) is a bigger town with a

A lumberjack stands by his work in the Olympic Peninsula.

sense of humor. (Thanks for "Sequim-ming".) Just north of here, on the Straits of Juan de Fuca (de Fuca thought this was the Northwest Passage) is **Dungeness**, of Dungeness crab fame.

Port Angeles is called the "big town." The plants of several major lumber companies are located here, and the smell of wood permeates the atmos-phere. From Port Angeles, the road traces Elwha Creek, enters the National Forest and winds down to crystalline Lake Crescent, within the National Park. From here the highway is lined with towering evergreens, and the road-side is carpeted with ferns.

Logging is a way of life in the penin-sula's "West End." US 101 passes through the towns of **Sappo** and **Forks**, the latter calling itself "the logging capital of the world." The evidence is everywhere: "clear-cut" hillsides, log-ging trucks and lumberjacks. Area res-taurants post signs forbidding the wear-ing of calk boots.

Most of the big timber is gone now or off-limits to lumber companies. Taking down the big ones, a hard day's work, is cause for celebration. One logger, wear-ing suspenders, his chain-saw slung over his shoulder, boasts, "I just took down an 11-footer!"

Primeval Forest

The temperate rain forests west of the Olympic Mountains contain some of the tallest timber in the world. Most accessible of these is the **Hoh River Valley**, located south of Forks and in-land on Hoh River Road. It is the em-bodiment of the "forest primeval" immortalized by Henry Wadsworth Longfellow. Most awe-inspiring are the ancient evergreens—western red cedar, Sitka spruce, Douglas fir and western hemlock—shrouded with club moss, filtered by light, surrounded by ferns and the sound of the river. It is an eerie, overgrown and magical place, barely touched by man—with one exception.

John "The Iron Man of Hoh" Huelsdonk came to the Hoh Valley from Iowa in 1891. Discouraged by all

Great silhouettes in the mist of the Pacific coastline.

124

who met him, he nevertheless poled his canoe up the wild river to make his home in the forest. What he could not carry by canoe, such as a cast iron stove, he strapped to his back. Hence the nickname and the birth of a legend. The Iron Man died and is buried in the forest he so loved, as is his wife.

The village of **La Push** on the **Quilayute Indian Reservation** is reached by way of La Push Road from Forks. Those who live here fish and those who visit come for the fishing. If La Push were not so unpretentious, it would surely proclaim itself the driftwood capital of the world. The beach is beautiful at night with a string of warming campfires and sea-stacks visible offshore in the mist.

You can't get any further northwest in the continental United States than **Neah Bay**. Forking off the Loop at Sappo, State 112 winds its way here along the strait. Vancouver Island is visible in the distance. Neah Bay is the ancestral and current home of the Makah National. Archaeological findings confirm their presence here since at least 1,000 B.C. Once renowned whale hunters who took to the sea in cedar canoes, they still live off the ocean, but the catch today is more likely to be salmon. Entering town, a sign proclaims: "Makah Nation—a treaty tribe since 1855." The Makah do not underestimate the importance of this treaty, which guarantees territorial and fishing rights, essential to their survival.

Neah Bay is a gateway to one of the nation's most splendid stretches of wilderness coastline. A network of gravel and dirt roads goes part of the distance, but to reach land's end it is necessary to do some hiking. Locals advise parking "at the old lady's" for the precarious trail down to **Shi-Shi Beach**.

The trail to **Cape Flattery** is shorter and less precarious. It descends an intricate stairway of tree roots through the forest, a clearing and a stand of huckleberry bushes before reaching the cliff's edge. Look out over Cape Flattery and know that you are standing as far northwest as possible in the coterminous US.

Mist settles in a valley of Olympic National Park.

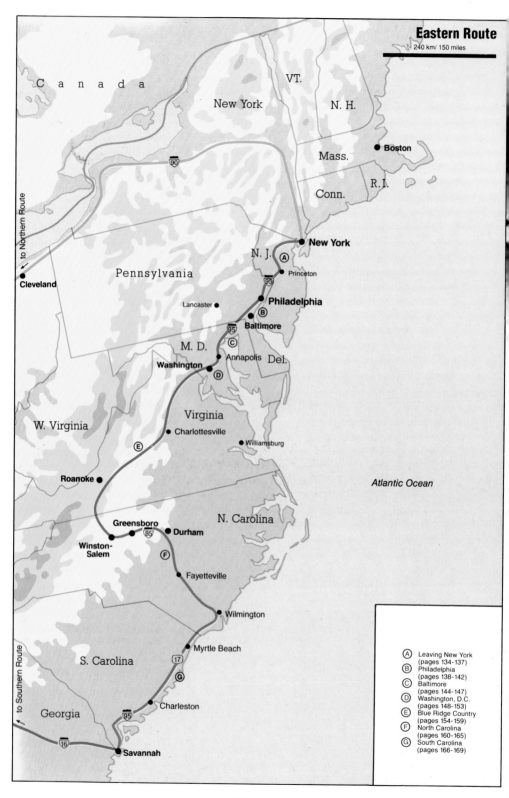

Canada

New York

VT.

N. H.

Mass.

● **Boston**

R. I.

Conn.

New York ●

to Northern Route

● **Cleveland**

Pennsylvania

N. J.

Ⓐ

Princeton

90

95

Lancaster ●

● **Philadelphia**

Ⓑ

95

Baltimore

M. D.

Ⓒ

Annapolis

Del.

Washington

Ⓓ

W. Virginia

Virginia

● Charlottesville

● Williamsburg

Ⓔ

Roanoke ●

Atlantic Ocean

N. Carolina

Greensboro

● **Durham**

85

Winston-Salem

Ⓕ

● Fayetteville

● Wilmington

S. Carolina

● Myrtle Beach

17

Ⓖ

● Charleston

to Southern Route

Georgia

95

16

● **Savannah**

THE SOUTHERN ROUTE

The southern route in *Crossing America* circles around three-quarters of the nation's periphery, forming a grand tour that reveals the astounding diversity of the United States: the old and new, rural and urban, open and crowded, wealthy and poor. The journey begins in the eastern seaboard cities, moves through the urban Southeast to ports along the Gulf of Mexico, through sprawling Texas and the natural splendor of the Southwest, and then shoots northward along the rugged Pacific Coast, through the occasional oceanside metropolis and by lakes, mountains, volcanoes and forests—areas untamed by mankind.

The settlement by Europeans of North America began at the east coast. So does the grand tour—in New York, the major port of entry into the country; Philadelphia, rich with colonial history; Baltimore, a vivid example of successful urban renovation; and Washington, D.C., home to the business of government as well as some of the country's greatest poverty.

South of D.C. comes rural relief. The tour cuts inland along magnificent roads into Virginia, through the majestic Blue Ridge Mountains and into tobacco-filled North Carolina. From here the tour moves coastward to the tacky-but-fun resort of Myrtle Beach and lovely Charleston with its elegant 18th-century homes.

At Savannah, Georgia, the grand tour cuts west through clay hills and pine forests into the cities of Macon and Atlanta before gliding into Alabama and the "American Riviera," the Gulf of Mexico coastline. The tour stops in the ports of Mobile and Biloxi and continues on to New Orleans, the most multifaceted and fascinating city in the South.

Next you'll enter the boggy bayou of Louisiana and then Texas, marked in the east by cities—Galveston, Houston, Austin—and in the west by cowtowns, empty plains and mountain ranges. Into New Mexico and Arizona, the grand tour traces a former Apache Indian trail by some of the most spectacular geography in the U.S.—including the ancient cliff dwellings of Montezuma Castle and the Grand Canyon.

The western leg of the grand tour begins at San Diego and moves rapidly to ultra-modern Los Angeles with its car culture, star society, trendy lifestyles and gorgeous beaches. Farther north the route joins the Pacific Coast Highway and skirts eroded cliffs that fall sharply into the ocean. On the way to Castroville, the road cuts through Los Padres National Forest and the seaside wilderness at Point Lobos and arcs through affluent Carmel.

The tour then proceeds to hilly San Francisco, a thriving city with unlimited, indefinable riches, and farther north you'll navigate an extraordinarily beautiful road marked by the Point Reyes seashore, Bodega Bay's secluded inlet, the violent Sonoma/Mendocino coast and grove after grove of giant redwood trees.

The route cuts inland before crossing into Oregon and encounters the sapphire-blue punchbowl of Crater Lake. Meeting the coast again at Newport, you'll pass the rugged peaks of the Oregon Coastal Range and visit an area once explored by the Lewis and Clark expedition.

The final leg of the grand tour cuts into the state of Washington and past snow-cloaked Mount St. Helens—resting since its violent 1980 eruption—and awesome Mount Rainier, whose gleaming dome remains in the rearview mirror for the duration of the journey into Seattle, where the great adventure comes to an end.

NEW YORK CITY AND ONWARD

New York City is a microcosm of the United States. If a certain product, culture, race, creed, religion, crime, luxury, social problem, trend, cuisine, look or lifestyle exits somewhere in this country, then surely it can be found—in some form—in New York.

New York has also been the American port of entry for innumerable tourists, adventurers and immigrants. A commercial, financial and industrial center, the "city that never sleeps" distributes people as well as merchandise to every section of the nation. Hence, the grand tour of America departs from here, the country's largest city.

The Immigrant Experience

The trans-American traveler who starts the journey in New York is following a pattern set two centuries ago, when the great influx of immigrants to the new promised land began. In the mid-19th Century, the flow reached fever pitch as Irish, Germans, Italians, Russians, Rumanians, Hungarians, Slovaks, Greeks, Poles and Turks began emigrating to the United States. Many of them settled in Manhattan's Lower East Side before moving on.

Most of the 8 million immigrants who entered the nation between 1855-1890 came through the Castle Garden station in southern Manhattan. But in 1890, immigration activity moved to **Ellis Island**, where between 1892 and 1954, 12 million more aliens entered the country.

More than any other American monument, the buildings at Ellis Island—along with the **Statue of Liberty**, which lies just to the south in New York Harbor—evoke powerfully and emotionally the immigrant experience. The buildings are being restored to their original state, and by 1992 Ellis Island will constitute a national park with a Museum of Immigration housing records of the period when millions passed through in eager anticipation of becoming Americans.

Manhattan, the most concentrated of New York's five boroughs, is bounded by the Hudson, Harlem, East Rivers and upper New York Bay. It is joined to the rest of the world by an extensive system of bridges and tunnels.

By far, the most picturesque and mythladen of off-island arteries is the **Brooklyn Bridge**. Its granite towers and steel cables have been the subject of more painting, etchings, photographs and writings than any other suspension bridge in the world. Hart Crane conceived it in his classic poem *The Bridge* as *the* dynamic emblem of America's westward march.

Unfortunately, however, the Brooklyn Bridge cannot figure in the grand tour; riding it out of Manhattan over the East River will put you in Brooklyn, the southwestern tip of another island, Long Island. To begin the eastern leg of the tour, you must experience one of the least pleasant ways of leaving New York: crawling through the **Lincoln Tunnel** into New Jersey.

The tunnel steers you onto the New

Preceding pages: Mabry Mill on the Blue Ridge Parkway, Virginia; above an Atlantic beach; Empire State Building lights up the Manhattan sky. Lady Liberty, left, a welcoming image. Right, Fifth Avenue, midtown Manhattan.

Jersey Turnpike (I-95), and at first New Jersey's nickname, the Garden State, seems a cruel joke. That is, if you base your opinion of the state on the tiny portion that abuts New York, where the big city's skyline immediately recedes into the haze of the industrial landscape. But further exploration of Jersey, past the factories, warehouses and landfills, reveals a diverse region of natural beauty and historical significance.

As you cut west onto I-280 toward the Oranges, the harsh landscape begins to soften. A luxurious greenery replaces the sparse scrub of the land by the turnpike, and the factories give way to churches and comfortable middle-class homes. Fifteen minutes out of New York City, small-town life begin to take the place of the urban crush.

Follow signs to State 508, which runs through the town of West Orange past the town hall with its prominent message board advertising events like the "West Orange Animal League Dog Wash." You will soon arrive at the **Edison National Monument.**

Cradle of Industry

The lab complex, sometimes described as "the cradle of American industry," is maintained by the National Park Service, which offers an excellent tour by well-informed guides. The tour begins in the chemistry lab, which is filled with antique burettes and beakers, and continues through the experimental machine shop in which Edison and his associates fabricated the parts necessary for the construction of products that have altered irrevocably the course of modern life: the light bulb, the phonograph and the motion picture camera, to name but three. A gorgeous wood library is on display, lined with thousands of leather-bound volumes in numerous languages. On the walls are several portraits of Edison as well as several placards inscribed with sayings of which he was fond: "There is no expedient to which a man will not resort in order to avoid the real labor of thinking": (Sir Joshua Reynolds) and the famous description of invention as "1

George Washington Bridge spanning the Hudson to New Jersey, left. Right, Edison's labcoat still hangs in his West Orange lab.

136

percent inspiration and 99 percent perspiration." Legend has it that Edison used to claim Reynolds quotation served as his 1 percent inspiration

Last on the tour is a walk by a reconstructed version of **Black Maria**, the world's first film studio, preceded by a screening of *The Great Train Robbery*, the first feature film produced at Edison Studios. You'll leave the complex filled with a powerful sense of wonder at the fecundity and range of Edison's artistic vision and technical prowess. Before leaving West Orange visit **Glenmount**, Edison's beautiful Victorian residence.

War Sites

Off I-287 is **Morristown**, where a constellation of Revolutionary War sites is to be found. At **230 Morris Street** stands the lovely colonial house that George Washington used as headquarters during the bitter winters of 1777 and 1780. Six miles (10 km) southwest of Morristown proper is **Jockey Hollow**, where the Revolution-

ary army encamped under Washington. Walk through **Wick House**, a restored 18th-century farmhouse rich with the smell of firewood. On weekends women and children dressed in colonial garb cook for display in the kitchen.

Continue south on US 202 toward Princeton to get the country flavor of the Garden State. The land is verdant and calming. You will soon arrive at **Princeton**, home of elegant **Princeton University**, which boasts one of the most beautiful campuses in the Northeast. The Gothic architectural style dominates, with a few modern structures thrown in. It has a fine collection of outdoor sculpture on campus.

Nassau Hall, the oldest building on campus, played host to the Continental Congress in 1783 when mutinous soldiers forced it to leave Philadelphia. Though its student body is far more varied than it was when author F. Scott Fitzgerald attended, Princeton remains a bastion of cloistered wealth, with preppie college kids browsing in the rich boutiques of Nassau Street.

Princeton University's venerable Nassau Hall.

PHILADELPHIA: BIRTHPLACE OF A NATION

On the whole, I'd rather be in Philadelphia.

—gravestone of W.C. Fields

At the time of the American Revolution, **Philadelphia** was the economic and political center of the fledgling United States. During the early years of the Republic, the nation's economic heart was transplanted north to New York City, while governmental power traveled south to the new city of Washington, D.C., leaving the "city of brotherly love" with an identity crisis.

Contemporary Philadelphia, the nation's fifth largest city, is for many Americans a mysterious place; it does not enjoy the media attention so liberally bestowed on its upstart brother cities to the north and south. But for tourists and historians it is — along with Boston — the revolutionary American city *par excellence*. To aficionados of music it is the home of the great Sun Ra and his Intergalactic Arkestra. For sports enthusiasts it is the home of the freewheeling 76'ers basketball team, the rough and tumble Flyers hockey squad and the gritty Eagles footballers. Philly's very diversity may contribute to its vague public image, but a leisurely few days in town can do much to dispel the mystery. All of W.C. Fields derogatory jokes aside, Philadelphia reveals itself to be a fascinating metropolis.

Situated at the intersection of the Schuylkill and Delaware Rivers, Philadelphia was founded in 1682 by the English Quaker William Penn, who had just received a parcel of land in the colonies from King Charles II in payment of a royal debt owed to Penn's father. Penn envisioned a colony in which the individual's right to freedom of religious expression would not be quashed in the name of majority interest or opinion. The heritage of Philly is one of pluralism; it is not surprising that it was here that representatives of the 13 colonies convened to sign the Declaration of Independence on July 4, 1776, thereby giving birth to the United States. Philly's ecumenical quality is today reflected in the ethnic diversity of its neighborhoods, from the Italian enclave of South Philadelphia to the German and Dutch area of Germantown and beyond.

Because they feel their city is undervalued in the popularity contest of American metropolises, Philadelphians are genuinely pleased to field questions about the history and culture of the town. Perhaps they will complain that there are not enough public trash cans or that Philly's pay telephones are few and far between, or that the city has yet to discover iced coffee, but these quibbles will be overruled by a quiet enthusiasm for the charms of the city.

Although Philadelphia has experienced an impressive flowering of fine restaurants since the mid-1970s opening of the haute cuisine Restaurant School, native Philadelphians wax more ethusiastic when they speak of their beloved cheese-steaks and soft pretzels. Real connoisseurs of traditional Philadelphia eats will suggest a breakfast order of scrapple, a Pennsylvania Dutch peppery pork specialty, or will insist on Italian Water Ice, a flavored summer cooler that seems conspicuously *declassé* in the age of sorbetto. Any trip to Philly would be incomplete without a thorough sampling of these low-budget local specialties, and a walk through the historic neighborhoods with a hoagie-packed stomach may be one of the best ways to experience simultaneously old and new Philadelphia.

A Nation is Born

At **Independence National Historic Park**, the main area of which extends from Second to Sixth Streets between Walnut and Chestnut, the extraordinary concatenation of events which led to the founding and empowering of the United States becomes palpable to the visitor. The Declaration of Independence and the Constitution were signed in elegant **Independence Hall**, where the **Liberty Bell**, the best known emblem of Philadelphia, once stood. For those especially thrilled by authenticity, the **Assembly Room**, which contains the inkstand used by the signers of the Declaration as well as the "rising sun" chair in which George Washington is said to have sat during the drafting of the Constitution, should not be missed. Nearby is **Congress Hall**, where the U.S. Congress convened during the hal-

Sampling one of Philly's famous soft pretzels.

cyon years of Philly's ascendancy as national capital, 1790-1800.

Chimes of Freedom

A block up from Independence Hall is the curious **Liberty Bell Pavilion**, a glass structure which has been home to the famous cracked bell since its 1975 removal from the exterior of Independence Hall. While the bell itself has an undeniable aura as a hallowed symbol of American liberty, the constriction caused by the hordes of eager tourists who cram the tiny building does much to deflate the potential exuberance. The Liberty Bell seems almost incarcerated here. Word has it that the building, which was originally designed to protect the bell from the ravages of Philly's weather, is not doing its job; the glass walls of the structure seem to amplify rather than to deflect the heat of the sun from the exposed bell.

Continuing down Market Street toward the Delaware River, you'll find **Franklin Court**, site of Ben Franklin's residence. The house itself — no longer extant—is commemorated by an evoca-

tive outline of its walls and shape made of ghost-like painted white steel beams. Here and there you can look through windows by your feet into the exhumed basement and sewage system of Franklin's home. The effect is eerie—an archeological dig for relics of a man dead not two centuries ago. Beneath the courtyard, a museum features multimedia displays and a film about Poor Ben's rich life as a colonial mover and shaker.

Christ Church, at Second Street just above Market, was built in 1695 and was the preferred house of worship for the men in the Continental Congress. Plaques mark the pews once used by George Washington, Ben Franklin and Betsy Ross. Nearby **Betsy Ross House,** furnished in 18th-century middle-class styles, is the place where the nation's first flag was stitched.

From Independence Hall, wend your way toward South Street via the cobblestone streets and garden paths of **Society Hill**, Philly's original residential district. The elegance of the 300-year-old Federalist-style homes might seem to indicate that the neighborhood's name refers to the rich families of colo-

Left, shining face at the annual Mummer's Parade. Right, cityskaters take a breather.

nial Philadelphia, but the area is actually named after the Free Society of Traders, a company formed by William Penn to develop this tract of land near the city's harbor.

In the late 1970s, Philadelphia's waterfront—like that of many other eastern seaboard cities—underwent considerable rehabilitation. **Penn's Landing**, between Market and Lombard Streets along the Delaware River, is where William Penn came ashore in 1682. Today the area features the **Port of History Museum**, several historic ships moored in the harbor and views of Camden across the river

Stroll down one block below Lombard to **South Street**, where you'll find a stimulating array of punk haberdashers, chic boutiques chock full of every kind of trendy curio and, on weekend nights, a high concentration of flashy urban cruisers. South Street's gentrification tale is by now well-known: a seedy downtown district becomes home to artists and culture hustlers because of low rents and a sense of urban immediacy. Entrepreneurs and developers follow and transform the neighborhood into a hip living, shopping and dining

district. This redevelopment, while adding life and commercial luster to a formerly dingy area, has also brought about the occasional crass condominium project complete with phony Georgian-style architecture. Still, South Street must now be reckoned among Philly's most vibrant areas.

City Hall, at the intersection of Broad and Market Streets, is the largest municipal building in the United States. The heavily ornamented structure is patterned loosely after the Louvre but resembles more Paris' Hôtel de Ville. The 37-foot (11-meter) high rooftop statue of William Penn is the tallest on top of any building in the world. Until recently, the Philadelphia skyline was protected by an ordinance which declared that no structure within the confines of the city could exceed the height of Penn's hat. Yet growing pressure from development concerns has altered that ordinance, and Philly's humble skyline is changing fast.

The **Benjamin Franklin Parkway**, built in the 1920s, was modeled after the Champs-Elysées in Paris. The broad road cuts diagonally through Philly's square grid from City Hall to the beginning of Fairmount Park, the largest municipal park in the country. On the parkway at 20th Street stop for a visit to the **Franklin Institute**, a science museum that also acts as a memorial to Franklin and contains many of his personal possessions. The museum's four floors of participatory exhibits relating to science and industry are sure to amuse and educate. In addition, the **Fels Planetarium**, a 1933 gift to the city from laundry-soap king Samuel Fels, has several shows daily.

Art in the City

Two blocks up is the **Rodin Museum**, featuring an excellent collection of casts and originals by the great French sculptor. Among them is "The Thinker," one of the most beloved statues in the world. At the end of the parkway stands the **Philadelphia Museum of Art**, one of the great American art museums. Among the best known works in the painting collection are Breughel's "Village Wedding," Picasso's "Three Musicians" and Duchamp's "The Bride Stripped Bare by Her Bachelors, Even," Aficionados of medieval art will be pleased to find an extraordinary col-

William Penn stands tall atop City Hall.

lection of art and artifacts from the Middle Ages.

At 33rd and Spruce Street, on the campus of the **University of Pennsylvania,** is the **University Museum,** which is renowned for its collections of artifacts from primitive and ancient human civilizations. Archaeological findings from places as diverse as Mesopotamia and Central America are on display.

After the hours spent walking the streets of Philly's historic districts and those spent inside the town's museums, the gorgeous greenery of **Fairmount Park** will serve to rejuvenate even the most exhausted traveler. In addition to the lush meadows and acres of woodland, the park features a horticultural center, a zoo, a Japanese house and tea garden and several historic houses along the banks of the Schuykill River. Bring a picnic lunch and plan to spend a full day taking in the pleasures of the park.

The Brandywine Valley

Thirty miles (48 km) southwest of Philly on US 1, in the heart of the Brandywine Valley, are the beautiful **Longwood Gardens**. Extensive and ex-

quisite, the gardens feature a staggering variety of greenery set in beautiful displays. In the conservatories you can see meticulous bonsai trees, orchids, roses and acacias of every variety. High-ceilinged rooms festooned with flowers of dazzling colors are used as concert halls in the summer. Stroll on the Flower Garden Walk to the Italian water garden which features a fountain of 600 jets of water. To the west are rose gardens, topiary gardens and an "idea garden" in which home plants and vegetables are grown along with such ingenious hybrids as the 5-on-1 apple tree that yields McIntosh, Lodi, Red Delicious, Yellow Delicious and Red Rome apples at different times of the year. There is even an alphabetical vegetable garden.

On the outskirts of nearby **Wilmington**, Delaware, the **Nemours Mansion**, the **Winterthur Museum and Gardens** and the **Hagley Museum** are testaments to the extraordinary wealth of the Dupont family. The mansions are filled with artifacts and furnishings from the colonial period. And the Hagley Museum features memorabilia from the early era of the Dupont family power.

Philadelphia's historic Elfreth's Alley.

AMISH COUNTRY

Lancaster County, 45 miles (76 km) west of Philadelphia, one of the nation's most developed cities, is home of one of the most old-fashioned, least assimilated immigrant groups in America: the Pennsylvania Dutch. The best known Pennsylvania Dutch people are the Amish, a small orthodox sect of Mennonites who have turned their back on the modern world. Their adherence to traditional customs such as wearing plain black clothing and driving horse-drawn buggies makes them recognizable.

The Mennonites are a Protestant sect that arose among Swiss Anabaptists and then seceded from the church in 1525 after rejecting its authority. They refuse to take oaths and hold the Bible as their sole rule of faith. The first Mennonites in the United States settled in Germantown, Pennsylvania in 1683. Twenty-six years later they settled the city of

Lancaster, still the center of Amish activities. The conservative Amish Church, under Jacob Amman, broke away from the main body of Mennonites in Europe in the late 17th Century and has been a separate—though related—sect ever since.

Lancaster County is one of the most beautiful and serene spots in the eastern United States. Most of what you see will be farms, for this region produces mostly tobacco, grains and livestock. But what is most special here is the soft light, which lends a kind of dreamy feeling to the neatly manicured fields and farm houses.

Make your first stop in Lancaster the **Pennsylvania Dutch Visitors Bureau Information Center**, 1799 Hempstead Road. And if you have the time, watch the 36-minute movie. *The Lancaster Experience*, which introduces you to the history and heritage of the region.

Two of the many recreated Amish homes and farms open to the public stand above the rest in quality, although both can get unbearably crowded. The **Amish Homestead**, 2034 Lincoln Highway East (US 30), Lancaster, offers tours of a 200-year-old house that is still occupied by an Amish family. A similar experience can be had just up the road at the **Amish Farm and House**, 2395 Lincoln Highway East, a replica of a 10-room Amish house. Some of the annual events you'll get a chance to watch here are sheep shearing in late April, tobacco planting in early June, wheat harvesting in early July, tobacco harvesting in late August, corn picking in November and tobacco stripping in December.

These heavily touristed places will provide you with information about the Amish people, but because they're so crowded, they may make you feel as if you're looking at caged animals in a zoo. Remember, though, that you're not. The Amish are human beings, and the best way to get to know them is to meet them. In general, they are friendly and will be more than willing to speak with you.

[The city of Lancaster, in Lancaster County, can be reached by heading west on US 30 from Philadelphia for about 45 miles (76 km).]

BORN-AGAIN BALTIMORE

In the years since the opening of its acclaimed **Harborplace** waterfront renovation, the number of tourists annually visiting **Baltimore,** Maryland, has more than tripled. Along with the brand new convention center, Harborplace has catalyzed Baltimore's economy by luring tourist dollars to a city once considered to be among the sorest on the eastern seaboard. The transformation of a decrepit harbor district into a glittering array of nouveau boutiques and eateries was the finest moment in a 30-year project of downton renovation that has made Baltimore into a model for urban redevelopment.

Baltimore was the first city in the United States to introduce the "urban homesteading" program in which residents of the city can buy rundown houses for one dollar with the provision that they renovate the property. Though its thriving housing projects were slowed by the Reagan administration's cutbacks, Baltimore's neighborhoods experienced a resurgence of activity during the city's renaissance in the late 1970s.

The Real Baltimore

Although the new national image of Baltimore has been determined largely by the successes of Harborplace and similar entrepreneurial schemes, locals will tell you that the real Baltimore is to be found in the city's ethnic neighborhoods. From **Little Italy** to **Little Lithuania,** the city's ethnic communities are filled with the sounds, smells and tastes of the proverbial "old country."

Each summer Baltimore features the "Showcase of Nations," a series of ethnic festivals with song, dance and food from such exotic places as Korea and the Ukraine. In addition to these festivals, there are innumerable special events such as the Crab Derby (a race for Maryland's famous shellfish), a typing contest for secretaries and a pistachio nut eating contest, all of which lend an air of small-town friendliness to big-city Baltimore.

The favorite food in Baltimore is undoubtedly the Maryland blue crab fresh from the waters of the Chesapeake Bay.

Try them the traditional way, steamed whole with lots of peppery spice. Ask a local to instruct you in the rarefied science of extracting the sweet meat from the claws and innards of this feisty crustacean, and be ready to make a mess while you learn. For those less-intrepid types unwilling to brave the whole crab, the crab cake or crab imperial, two specialties made from filleted backfin crabmeat, will do nicely. If possible, try to sample all three dishes.

The only rival to the blue crab in popularity is Baltimore's beloved baseball team, the Orioles, who have been pleasing the city's residents for years as one of the winningest major league teams. A visit to the O's nest, **Memorial Stadium,** on a hot summer night is as good a way to spend time in Baltimore as there is. Baseball addicts unlucky enough to be in Baltimore during the off-season can get a fix of the national pastime by visiting the **Babe Ruth Birthplace/Maryland Baseball Hall of Fame** at 216 Emory Street. The shrine is baseball fanaticism at its most remarkable and even features a "computer controlled, animated Ruthian figure that looks and sounds like the Bambino in his prime."

Enthusiasts of horse-racing will want to visit **Pimlico** which plays host every May to the Preakness, the second jewel in the equine triple crown. Baltimore is also known as the national capital for the game of lacrosse. Perennial power Johns Hopkins University is the site of the **Lacrosse Hall of Fame.**

Start your visit to Baltimore by seeing all of it from the **Top of the World** observation deck located on the 27th floor of the pentagonal **World Trade Center,** a building designed by I.M. Pei. In addition to the fine panorama, there is an exhibit which details the activities of the port of Baltimore plus a collection of picture displays on some of Baltimore's more famous residents, including writers H.L. Mencken and Edgar Allan Poe and former Baltimore Colts football star, Johnny Unitas.

One pier up at Pratt Street is the extraordinary **National Aquarium,** complete with an Amazon Rain Forest, a coral reef display and a 220,000 gallon open ocean tank. The building is a fascinating modern construction, the angles of which create an interior space of great surprise and mystery. Particularly fun for children are the flashlight

Highland-town resident among rows of marble steps.

fish and the nasty looking sharks that glide menacingly about the open ocean tank.

After a stroll around Harborplace, you might wish to take a cruise in the harbor, where you'll smell spice by the McCormack Spice factory, the sweetness of raw sugar by the Domino Sugar Plant and, finally, the odor of detergent near the Proctor and Gamble factory. For those wishing to navigate the harbor waters themselves, small motorized boats and manual pedal-boats are available for rental.

Seaside Sites

Fell's Point, Baltimore's first shipbuilding and maritime center, still maintains the charm of an old port town. Walk along the cobbled streets of the historic district where you can see more than 350 original colonial homes, many of which are in impeccable shape. Interspersed are old pubs, antique shops and restaurants that serve the fresh fare of the sea. Tugboats line the wharves of the harbor, and lobster trawlers can be seen cruising out to sea as they have done for nearly three centuries. Enjoy a stroll through the original wooden **Broadway Market** where you can purchase such foods as pickled pig's feet, blue crabs and whole grain bread made with honey.

The last, and the best-known attraction on the waterfront is **Fort McHenry**, protector of Baltimore's inner harbor. During the war of 1812 the fort withstood a 25-hour bombardment from the British fleet, prompting the young Francis Scott Key to open the lyrics of what was to become the U.S. National Anthem. What many don't know is that Key took his melody from an old drinking song. Restored to their pre-Civil War appearance, the fort's buildings offer exhibits chronicling its history.

Mount Vernon Place, designated a National Historic Landmark, features many of Baltimore's oldest and most elegant town houses, churches and cultural institutions. At the center of the district stands the **Washington Monument**, the *first* formal monument to George Washington, paid for by a public lottery. Climb the 228 stairs of this 178-foot (54-meter) white marble column for an unobstructed view of the city.

Baltimore's Hausner's Restaurant is a museum unto itself.

Be sure to see the **Walters Art Gallery**, a recreation of an Italian Renaissance Palazzo; the **Peabody Conservatory of Music**, a combination of French and English Renaissance styles containing thousands of books in five ornate iron balconies; and the **Maryland Historical Society**, which houses the original manuscript of Francis Key's "Star Spangled Banner."

Travel up Charles Street to **Johns Hopkins University,** which since its inception in the late 19th Century, has been a major conduit for the exchange of continental and American philosophy. Next door to the University is the **Baltimore Museum of Art**, designed by John Russell Pope who later designed the National Gallery of Art in Washington, D.C. The museum contains major works by Picasso and Matisse, art from Africa and a beautiful modern sculpture garden.

A Colonial Port Town

Leaving Baltimore, take I-95 south to I-695 east and on to State 2 south to **Annapolis**. Upon entering Annapolis you will cross over the **Severn River Bridge**, which affords a view of sailboats crisscrossing the stunning expanse of water on both sides of the river.

Annapolis sparkles in a way particular to towns built on and sustained by the sea. At dusk its elegant Georgian houses and winding narrow streets shimmer in the dying light of day. It is easy to see most of the town by walking. Start at the top of Annapolis where the **Maryland State House** sits. Here the Continental Congress ratified the Treaty of Paris, the document which officially put an end to the American War of Independence.

Wend your way toward the beautifully preserved 18th-century **Waterfront.** Stop in at **Chick 'n' Ruth's** deli on Main Street, for 50 years a favorite hangout of local politicians and midshipmen. In addition to the fine corned beef sandwiches you might want to try the "Geek," a concoction made with vanilla ice cream and covered with strawberry topping, marshmallow, wet nuts, whipped cream, jimmies and a cherry. Navy buffs will want to visit the **Naval Academy** and its museum at **Preble Hall**, which has exhibits on all aspects of maritime life.

A studious walk through the U.S. Naval Academy, Annapolis.

WASHINGTON D.C.

Washington is the quintessential paper-pushing town, home to innumerable white-collar government functionaries who dutifully perform the daily chores involved in running a nation. It is also the quintessential tourist town, with enough bright white monuments and museums to keep the industrious visitor scurrying about for months.

Designed by Pierre L'Enfant to rival in splendor the great capitals of Europe, Washington rose from its original mosquito-infested fen to take its place among the great cities of America. After struggling for decades to establish itself as a cultural center, Washington of late has become increasingly sophisticated. With the opening in the early 1970s of the **John F. Kennedy Center for the Performing Arts**, Washington's eminent position was solidified.

Yet underneath the spectacle lurks another Washington that is usually overlooked by tourists. Several blocks away from the splendid esplanades of **Capitol Hill**, the ghettos of the southeast and northeast districts are a sobering reminder of the country's disturbing combination of extraordinary wealth and great poverty. This is not the D.C. of tourbooks, nor is it the D.C. of governmental splendor. Rather, it is the Washington known by the longstanding residents of the town, four-fifths of whom are black.

Because so much of Washington depends on government, the city seems to experience an atmospheric shift with each presidential election. Though the bureaucracy itself remains fairly stable from election to election, the image of the nation's capital is to a large extent dependent on the image of the administration in power. Not surprisingly, since the 1978 election of Ronald Reagan, Washington has become more than ever a magnet for conservative young professionals looking for a rapid road to power and money.

This change is particularly evident in **Georgetown**, the most popular nightspot for the young urban professional (YUPPIE) cadre. Once a homey neighborhood with friendly sandwich shops, good record stores and hippies ambling about its beautiful side streets, Georgetown has been transformed into a glitzy collection of overpriced restaurants and discos that serve as the pick-up playground for the professional set.

The side streets off Wisconsin Avenue and M Street still offer the pedestrian an opportunity to view some of the oldest and more beautiful homes in D.C. and ought to be visited during the day, when a quiet walk can still be taken. For those bothered by Georgetown's cold hustle, the area around **Dupont Circle** offers an alternative for eating and nightclubbing. Those interested in contemporary pop music should try to see one of D.C.'s go-go bands. Go-Go is the name of Washington's most recent musical style which combines elements of New York City rap with the fuller instrumentation of soul music to create a foot-stomping barrage of dance rhythms. And given the city's geographical position near the Mason-Dixon line, it is not surprising that D.C. is a center for bluegrass music. WAMU, the American University radio station, specializes in bluegrass and other folk music. Finally, D.C. has a thriving punk and hardcore scene which directs a snarl toward the self-satisfied denizens of the city.

Capitol Hill

In Frank Capra's film *Mr. Smith Goes to Washington*, Jimmy Stewart portrays a country bumpkin who arrives wide-eyed in Washington after being elected to the House of Representatives. The **United States Capitol** is the first building he sees upon disembarking from his train at Union Station. As if drawn by a magnet, Stewart rushes out of the station to get a closer look at the building that has entranced him. This symbol of U.S. governmental authority continues to entrance visitors.

Along with the Statue of Liberty, the Capitol must rank as one of America's best-known landmarks. Free tours leave the Rotunda every 10 minutes and take you through the enormous building to the visitors' galleries of the Senate and the House. If you wish to enter the galleries on your own, request a free pass by writing your congressman or senator in advance. Should you wish to attend a committee meeting, check the *Washington Post* for schedules of daily congressional activities.

The evening glow of the Capitol dome, D.C.

The **Supreme Court Building** is one block in back of the Capitol and is open to the public; no reservations are necessary. The *Washington Post*'s "Court Calendar" will say whether the Court is in session on a given day. If you're lucky you'll be able to hear an argument being put forward to the nine justices.

Reading Rooms

Across from the Capitol at 1st Street and Independence Avenues stands the complex of three buildings which make up the **Library of Congress**. The oldest of these, the Thomas Jefferson building, is elaborately decorated with mosaic, sculptures and murals. The library is the most extensive in the world, with more than 80 million items in its collection. The reading rooms in the art deco John Adams building are a lovely place to repose with a book.

Located in the home once owned by the writer, former slave and black activist Frederick Douglass is the **Museum of African Art**, which houses a fascinating array of African objets d'art. The sculptures and masks in the collection will give you the sense of the extraordinary innovations of African traditional art.

A great number of Washington's tourist attractions are located on or around the **Mall**, which extends from the Capitol west to the Lincoln Memorial. This grassy expanse between Constitution and Independence Avenues is great for walking, picnicking and playing frisbee.

The numerous museums of the **Smithsonian Institution** are among the finest in the nation. The Smithsonian's red-bricked administrative center, known as the **Castle,** is located on Jefferson Drive. Stop by the visitor information center to pick up maps and brochures about the various museums.

The Smithsonian's **Freer Gallery of Art** at 12th Street and Jefferson Drive S.W. features a beautiful collection of Asian and Indian art and artifacts as well as several works by the American painter James McNeill Whistler exhibited in the Peacock Room. The circular **Hirshhorn Museum and Sculpture Garden** houses a collection of modern

Main Reading Room of the Library of Congress, Thomas Jefferson Building.

paintings and one of the finest collections of contemporary sculpture in the country.

Next door is the **National Air and Space Museum,** an infectiously exciting collection of airplanes, spacecraft and exhibits documenting our progressive conquest of the skies. Touch the moonrock, visit the Albert Einstein Spacearium for a simulation of space flight, and be sure to see at least one of the two films, *The Living Planet* and *To Fly,* which are shown on an enormous screen five stories high. The museum is always packed.

Across the Mall is the **National Gallery of Art** which offers an excellent collection of European painting and sculpture from the 13th Century to the present. The gallery's new **East Wing** is connected by an underground concourse. Designed by I.M. Pei, the building is a striking example of the way an intelligently conceived building can alter one's perception of the objects it contains. The acute angles and airy interior of the building create an unusual sensation of freedom. The East Wing is an extraordinary place to view

modern art.

The Smithsonian's **Museum of Natural History** includes exhibitions on everything from dinosaurs and minerals to American Indian culture and marine life. Next door, the **National Museum of American History** documents the country's technological and cultural achievements. Automobiles, women's high fasions, an 18th-century apothecary and one of Thomas Edison's phonographs are among its many exhibits.

Monuments Aplenty

Walk up the Mall to the **Washington Monument,** a 555-foot (169-meter) high marble pencil which suggests the fortitude of the nation's first president. The view of the city from the observation room is magnificent.

Separated from the Washington Monument by two reflecting pools is the **Lincoln Memorial,** designed by Henry Bacon. Abraham Lincoln's Gettysburg and Second Inaugural Addresses are carved into the marble walls of the monument's interior and cannot but inspire a sense of wonder for their rhetorical power. One century later, an-

A parade marches away from the Capitol.

other great American rhetorician, Martin Luther King, Jr., gave his "I Have a Dream" speech from the steps of the Memorial. Daniel Chester French's gigantic statue of the seated Lincoln dominates the Memorial's interior.

Down along the Tidal Basin is the **Jefferson Memorial**, a domed, circular structure with a statue of Thomas Jefferson smack dab in the middle of its interior and panels inscribed with excerpts from Jefferson's writings. And near the Lincoln Memorial you will find the black marble **Vietnam Veterans Memorial**, a V-shaped structure which seems to be sinking into the earth. The walls of this haunting memorial are inscribed with the names of the more than 58,000 Americans who died in the war as well as those of soldiers still missing. The stark, silent simplicity of the monument elicits shudders.

The President's House

Home to every president except George Washington, the **White House** is a symbol of American authority as well as an emblem of American government. Because the public tour is not very extensive and is usually preceded by an unfortunate two-hour wait, write your congressman in advance to arrange a "VIP tour." This way you'll get to see more than the few rooms covered by the public tour.

Nearby, on 17th Street between E Street and New York Avenue N.W. is the **Corcoran Gallery**, known for its collection of American art from the 18th Century to the present. The museum also houses the W.A. Clark collection of European paintings and sculpture and plays host to changing contemporary exhibits.

East of the White House at 511 10th Street N.W. is **Ford's Theatre,** where Abraham Lincoln was murdered by John Wilkes Booth on April 14, 1865. The **Lincoln Museum** is located in the theater's basement. There you can read the assassin's diary and see the pistol he used to kill Lincoln.

The **National Archives**, at 7th Street and Constitution Avenue N.W., houses the Declaration of Independence, the Constitution and the Bill of Rights, all of which can be seen in the

The Vietnam Veterans Memorial, a sobering statement on war.

Exhibition Hall. The documents seem to have an almost sacrosanct air about them. Connoisseurs of the profane will not want to miss listening to the voices of Richard Nixon and his cronies on the Watergate Tapes, which are now a part of the Archives Collection.

Named for a leader in law enforcement, the **J. Edgar Hoover F.B.I. Building** features exhibits detailing the history of crime and its prevention in the United States. There is a kind of rogues' gallery where one can see pictures and read accounts of the lives of such criminals as "Baby Face" Nelson, A1 Capone and John Dillinger. The tour concludes with a literal bang as F.B.I.-trained agents give a display of firearms.

The D.C. Vicinity

Cross Memorial Bridge into Arlingon to visit **Arlington National Cemetery**, where more than 175,000 Americans are buried, among them John and Robert Kennedy. The **Tomb of the Unkown Soldier**, an enormous marble block inscribed with the words, "Here rests in honored glory an American soldier known but to God," is moving in its simplicity, although the militaristic changing of the guard ceremony that takes place at the tomb every half hour may put you off.

Just a few miles south of Arlington, **Alexandria's Old Town** is a quieter version of Georgetown, with lovely 18th-century buildings recently restored and transformed into upscale boutiques and chic restaurants. Among the noteworthy sights is the **Torpedo Factory Art Center**, a crafts complex located in a renovated warehouse.

At the end of the George Washington Memorial Parkway is **Mount Vernon**, the splendid estate of George Washington. Mount Vernon is especially beautiful in spring, when its lush gardens and greenery are in bloom.

Take the parkway northwest to Canal Road toward **Great Falls**, the last falls of the Potomac before the river calms as it enters Washington. Walk along the **C & O Canal** towpath and turn off on one of the trails that leads toward the falls. The big rocks in the river afford a good vantage point from which to watch the turbulent waters of the falls and the graceful hawks hovering high above.

Changing
of the guard,
Tomb of the
Unknown
Soldier.

VIRGINIA'S BLUE RIDGE COUNTRY

Cities wear the traveler down with a constant barrage of sights and stimuli. After touring the eastern metropolises you will be ready for the leisurely splendor of the **Blue Ridge Mountains.**

Take the Key Bridge out of Washington, D.C., and follow signs for I-66 west. The road will take you to the town of Front Royal and Skyline Drive, which runs south along the eastern rampart of the Blue Ridge Mountains. A few miles west of Fairfax, Virginia, on I-66 is the Virginia Visitors' Center which offers hundreds of free brochures covering every facet of Virginia tourism. Stop in for schedules of current events and festivals at "Old Dominion."

Already the pace of life seems to slow as you drive along increasingly serpentine roads with vistas opening to reveal the majestic Blue Ridge Mountains looming in the distance. Cumulous clouds hover over the dark peaks and play with the sunlight, alternately illuminating and obscuring the trees of the countryside. Small waterfalls slide down the rock face along the road. Beautiful pink and purple crown vetch, dandelions and goldenrod grow wild on the hillsides.

Rolling down the road through the hills of Fauquier County, you begin to feel removed from the ugliness of modern civilization when **Front Royal** bursts upon you with its A & Ps, K-Marts and McDonald's crammed into a few town blocks. Drive through quickly and keep your eyes closed (all except the driver) for the scene is a shock to the senses.

Oh Shenandoah

Luckily, the shock doesn't last long before you reach the north entrance of **Shenandoah National Park,** where the 105-mile (169-km) **Skyline Drive** begins. Established in 1926 by an act of Congress, the park was an experiment in land reclamation. At the time, the region was overpopulated and the land was eroding, so president Franklin Roosevelt had the Civilian Conservation Corps build recreation facilities and complete the construction of the Skyline Drive in 1939. In the years since, the forests have revived and are once again densely overgrown with oak, hickory, pine and locust trees.

The cost to enter the park is $2 per car. A sign greets you: "You are southbound on the Skyline Drive." Four-and-a-half miles (seven km) down the road is Dickey Ridge Visitors' Center, open from April 1 to November 1. Here you can pick up maps of the park, books on local vegetation and animal life and information on camping and lodging. If the pioneer spirit of "roughing it alone" does not strike your fancy, there are informative hikes and talks on the natural life of the park led by park rangers.

The splendor of the Skyline Drive can be experienced from the car, but you will undoubtedly be tempted to bail out of your coupe to hike on the beautiful forest trails. If you don't plan to hike or fish, at least pack a meal to eat at one of the seven picnic locations.

Immediately upon entering the park the speed limit slows you down to 35 miles per hour (55 k.p.h.) and the lumbering pace of the cars sets the mood for a leisurely drive. Initially, the two-lane drive is a winding road covered with dense trees on both sides. As the road ascends, however, you begin to get magnificent glimpses of the **Shenandoah Valley** and **Shenandoah River** to the west. Stop at one of the many overlooks, get out of the car, and allow yourself to be enveloped by the majesty of the sight. Inhale the pure air, hear the birds chirp, and listen to the kind of quiet you hear only when you are far away from the working world. As you continue along in the car you'll see **Massanutten Mountain** between the north and south forks of the Shenandoah River. After about 10 miles (16 km), the road switches to an eastern view of the Piedmont country.

At mile 50.7 (kilometer 82) stop for a 1.5-mile (2-km) round-trip hike to **Dark Hollow Falls**, the waterfall closest to the drive. The water tumbles 70 feet (21 meters) over a greenstone face. Nearby Big Meadows is — along with Dickey Ridge — one of the two main visitors' centers in the park. For those wishing to stay overnight, the **Big Meadows Lodge and Campgrounds** are convenient.

Shenandoah
National
Park.

Charlottesville: Land of Jefferson

From the foot of Skyline Drive take I-64 east for 20 miles (32 km) to **Charlottesville**, site of the University of Virginia and home of Thomas Jefferson. It might be said that the well-known adage, "Every man is born either a Platonist or an Aristotelian" finds its American equivalent in the transformation, "Every American is born either a Jeffersonian or a Hamiltonian." The people of Charlottesville are fanatically Jeffersonian, and though the town is experiencing encroaching Hamiltonism in the form of syndicated restaurants and hotels, it has managed to retain a countrified splendor. Allow the calm pace of town and the sweet Appalachian air to lull you into a revelry of what it might have been like to be a landed gentleman in the gorgeous foothills of the Blue Ridge Mountains. It will not be difficult to understand Jefferson's agrarian idealism.

Jefferson designed the original buildings and campus of the **University of Virginia** in the 1820s and claimed late in life that it was of this achievement that he was most proud. The architecture is based on the European classical style adapted to local materials such as red brick and painted wood. Daily tours of the university leave the **Rotunda**, which is modeled after the Roman Pantheon. Looking out from the elevated walkway of the Rotunda, you will see the splendid swath of grass known as "**The Lawn**," which is bordered by columned pavilions. Originally these were the residences of all the students and professors of Jefferson's "academic village"; now they are inhabited by school officials and honors students. **"West Range"** is on McCormack Road where Edgar Allan Poe lived during his unsuccessful undergraduate tenure. The room is open to visitors.

Walk down University Avenue to **"The Corner,"** a collection of restaurants and shops catering to students, tourists and local residents. Charlottesville's preppie contingent ambles contentedly along University Avenue and will not fail to impress you with its clean-cut, brightly colored appearance. Farther downtown is the Mall, a shopping and entertainment center.

Even before you arrive at **Monticello**, the "little mountain" estate of Thomas

Rotunda building, University of Virginia.

156

COLONIAL WILLIAMSBURG

If the present year were 1775, most Americans would probably be living in Virginia, the largest and most populated of the English colonies. And those with a taste for cosmopolitan living probably would have occupied one of the numerous plantations surrounding the colonial capital, Williamsburg. It is not necessary to wonder what life there would have been like—it can be lived today, much as it was then, at **Colonial Williamsburg**, an ambitious recreation of the historic town. Colonial Williamsburg goes far beyond most historic reconstructions to revive not only the buildings, streets and gardens, but the very industries and lifeways of the nation's infancy.

Established in 1633 under the name Middle Plantation, Williamsburg (renamed for the reigning British monarch William III) inherited the colonial government from neighboring Jamestown in 1699. Stimulated by this close relationship to the mother country and by the area's wealth of natural resources, the town grew into an outpost of culture, fashion and festive living amid the harsh realities of the untamed American wilderness.

Most of the region's population was scattered among the surrounding tobacco plantations. The wealthy plantation owners maintained close ties with England, sending their sons there to be educated in the traditions of European manners and, more significantly, English liberty. The idea of English liberty, not to mention loyalty to the crown, however, underwent some revision at the local **College of William and Mary,** alma mater to such revolutionary heroes as Thomas Jefferson and John Marshall and still one of the most respected colleges in the Southeast.

After the nascent State government moved to Richmond in 1780, the city languished until 1926 when the Rev. W.A.R. Goodwin approached John D. Rockefeller, Jr. for the funds to save those historic buildings still standing and to rebuild several others. Using original blueprints and materials, Goodwin resurrected the entire town, from the **Congress** where George Mason, presenting his Declaration of Rights before the House of Burgesses, laid the foundation for the Constitution, to the **Raleigh Tavern** where George Washington plotted military strategy in the revolt against British rule.

The colonial capital of 2,000 residents has been repopulated with authentic representatives of the original Williamsburg community, all of whom carry on their daily business in the manner of the town's preindustrial past. The blacksmith pounds away at glowing iron as visitors look on. Clad in knee breeches and powdered wig, the cabinetmaker carves chair legs on a pedalled lathe according to 18th-century designs, and a colonial maid in bonnet and hooped skirt weaves linen at a 200-year-old loom. These craftspeople, along with bakers, printers, wigmakers, glass-blowers and a host of others, can be observed at their work.

[Colonial Williamsburg can be reached via I-64, about 40 miles (64 km) west of the junction with I-95.]

Jefferson, you will be familiar with its shape, for its image adorns the tails side of the U.S. nickel. Jefferson designed every aspect of this elegant residence, and the imprint of his fecund mind is everywhere apparent.

Try to arrive early, as the wait for the mandatory tour is known to extend up to two hours at midday. The tour takes you through the ground floor of the residence and then you're free to wander about the lovely grounds of the mansion. The house's gadgetry is particularly endearing, especially the seven-day clock by the entrance, the double writing machine in Jefferson's study and the dumbwaiter in the dining room. Ask about the home's extraordinary toilet system. In the library the walls are lined with leather-bound books, many of which were authored by the philosophers of the French Enlightenment who strongly influenced Jefferson. Jefferson died on July 4, 1826, exactly 50 years after the signing of the Declaration of Independence, of which he was the main author. His grave is visible as you leave the grounds to return to the parking lot.

Jefferson's good friend James Monroe, fifth president of the United States, lived nearby at **Ash Lawn**. Though not nearly as stately as Monticello, Monroe's residence has a friendly charm to it. As you drive back toward I-64 you will pass the **Michie Tavern**, a pre-Revolutionary watering hole which is now a museum filled with colonial furniture and artifacts.

The Road to Natural Bridge

From I-64 west take State 250 to Rockfish Gap, where the 459-mile (739-km) **Blue Ridge Parkway** begins. Cutting through the **George Washington National Forest,** the Parkway was—like Skyline Drive—cut into the side of the Blue Ridge Mountains. Because it is not a national park it is filled with farmland. If you're driving alone on this winding road, be sure not to allow the spectacular views to lure your eyes too far from the road or you'll find yourself tumbling down the side of a cliff. Trees carpet the surrounding mountains, which seem bluer and bluer as they recede in the distance. If anything, the views on the parkway are even more spectacular than those on Skyline Drive.

Early autumn in the Smokies.

At mile 61 (kilometer 98) take State 130 west to **Natural Bridge** and prepare yourself for some of the crassest come-ons in the grand tour. Billboards blare "See the Natural Bridge!" and offer to throw a wax museum and cavern into the bargain: "See all three Attractions for one low price!" At $7.95 the price is anything but low.

Cheesy Tourism

In order to get down to the Natural Bridge, which is an extraordinary 215-foot (66-meter) high rock formation, you are forced to pass through a knick-knack shop as big as a department store which is absolutely packed with junky tourist paraphernalia. Descend the stairs, walk past the electronic game room and begin the short walk down to the main attraction. The Monocan Indi-ans called it "The Bridge of God," and no doubt the enormous limestone arch must have been a place of great wonder in the past. But by the time you arrive there you may be so queasy from the patina of cheesy tourist exploitation that it becomes difficult to conjure up the requisite awe. The concern that

owns Natural Bridge has been good enough to assist in the creation of a sense of religious wonder by installing loudspeakers on high to broadcast re-cordings of churchbells.

Back on the parkway continue south toward North Carolina. Below **Roanoke** the road slithers gracefully through farmland. In early summer the hay is neatly rolled into picturesque bales. Wooden fences turned silver-gray by time intermittently line the road to keep the cows grazing languidly in their rich green pastures.

Just before the North Carolina bor-der you will pass through a stretch of farmer's markets which sell local pro-duce like peaches and cabbage at bar-gain prices. Interspersed among these roadside vendors are displays of inex-pensive plaster-cast statues (the kind you see occasionally on southern lawns) as well as reliquaries and religious curios of all sorts. The accent of the people in this area is very heavy, almost incomprehensible to the ear of a northerner. If you begin to feel you are in another country, you will be ready for the deeper South ahead.

Coal trains, Roanoke, Virginia.

SMOKIN' THROUGH NORTH CAROLINA

All that remains of the first-known settlement in present-day North Carolina is one word. That word—Croatan—has kept etymologists and philologists busy for centuries since it was found scraped into a tree in the vanished colony of Fort Raleigh on Roanoke Island. Nothing else was left of the "lost colony," which was founded in 1587.

Contemporary natives of North Carolina aren't concerned with such matters, however. Instead, they boast about the natural beauties and cultural traditions of the Tar Heel state. A construction worker from Gastonia suggests, "North Carolina must be the most beautiful place on earth. You got the mountains. You got the sea. You got everything. I wouldn't want to live anywhere else."

Though the mountains and sea are constants, the culture contained between is experiencing great change in an age of media standardization. A native mill worker claims, "In a half-century most of what is distinctively local with probably fade away."

Meanwhile, North Carolina's distinctive culture seems to be thriving, even as its citizens continue to believe in "God, motherhood and Jesse." After one of the dirtiest Senatorial campaigns in history (1984), the reactionary Jesse Helms retained an almost fanatical devotion among his supporters.

North Carolinians are just as proud of their local food. Bar-B-Q, which is made from pork shoulder smoked several days over hickory, is a beloved specialty. Tar Heelers thumb their noses at Texas Bar-B-Q, for in their estimation the cow has nothing on the porker when it comes to richness of taste. Boiled peanuts are an acquired taste for many, but should not be missed. The salty peanuts are served as a snack boiled in the shell and do not crunch so much as mush in the mouth. But perhaps the best North Carolina specialty is a breakfast consisting of fresh eggs fried over-easy, grits, a buttery biscuit, mouth-watering country ham and a large glass of milk. The ham is saltier and more delicious than anything you'll find up north. Some hearty locals like to eat their grits with red-eye gravy, made with coffee and other un-

likely ingredients. As to the coffee itself, it is usually weak, sometimes filmy, and generally the only disenchanting aspect of an otherwise stellar meal.

Tobacco Country

US 52 takes you over the border from the Blue Ridge Parkway into Mt. Airy and then on down to Winston-Salem. On the road you'll pass by a sign for "King and Tobaccoville." Take the exit and follow the back roads to **Bethania**, a town founded by Moravians who came to the New World to escape religious persecution. The road is lined with graceful weeping willows and leads past fields covered with tobacco plants.

State 67 east leads to **Winston-Salem**, home of the **R. J. Reynolds** tobacco factory, which produces more than 450 million cigarettes daily. The odor of tobacco wafts throughout the town, a constant reminder of the second largest industry in North Carolina (the first is textiles). The Reynolds plant is located, naturally, on Reynolds Boulevard and is open to visitors during the week.

Salem was founded by the Moravians in 1766. The name is derived from the

Tobacco hanging in Mikisch Tobacco Shop, left, and soaking up the Carolina sun, right.

Hebrew word shalom, meaning peace. In 1913 it was incorporated with its neighbor Winston. The old buildings of Salem gradually fell into disrepair, which led to the creation of a restoration project in the 1930s. The success of this effort can be seen in **Salem Old Town,** which is entered from the Old Salem Road near the center of town. Particularly interesting among the many sights of Salem Old Town are the **Mikisch Tobacco Shop**, thought to be the oldest tobacco shop still standing in America; the **Winkler Bakery**, a restored Moravian bakery that produces lovely bread Monday through Saturday; and the **Salem Tavern** with its nearby **Barn and Farm Museum**. **God's Acre,** the nearby Moravian graveyard, has 4,000 graves, many of which are graced with flat marble markers symbolizing the equality of the deceased.

Ten miles (16 km) southwest of Winston-Salem is **Tanglewood**, an 1152-acre (466-hectare) park left as a gift by the late William Reynolds. The park features a 36-hole golf course, tennis courts, swimming pools and horse stables. It is the site of an annual steeplechase run the second Saturday of May.

US 421 east leads through undistinguished country toward **Greensboro**, sometimes site of the ACC Basketball Tournament in which the great college teams of the southeast are pitted against one another. North Carolina is a basketball-crazy state and its Tar Heels (U.N.C.), Wolfpack (N.C. State), Blue Devils (Duke) and Demon Deacons (Wake Forest) continue to do the state proud.

The Research Triangle

Continue on to **Durham**, home of **Duke University**. Along with Chapel Hill and Raleigh, Durham is part of the **Research Triangle**, a liberal oasis in the middle of North Carolina which claims to have more Ph.D.s per 100,000 residents than any other area in the nation.

The Duke campus is ranked among the most beautiful in the South and is filled with Gothic and Georgian buildings. The Duke University Chapel houses the **Benjamin N. Duke Memorial Flentrop Organ,** a 5,000-pipe extravaganza. While in Durham stop in at **Bullock's** restaurant at the five corners in downtown for some excellent North Carolina cooking.

Duke University Chapel, left, and its enormous pipe organ, right.

ELVIS PRESLEY'S GRACELAND

Okay, so maybe Elvis Presley *did* wear diapers late in his life. So what? Since the great singer's demise in 1977 there have been innumerable exposés of his sad tragectory from show-biz God to mid-life wreck. Yet the poverbial airing of Elvis' dirty linen has not smudged his reputation one bit among his legion of fanatical admirers; rather, it has further entrenched the legend of Elvis Aaron Presley, the martyr who led the youth of America toward the promised land of rock-'n' roll and its various liberations. Nowhere can the phenomenon be better glimpsed than at **Graceland,** Elvis' Memphis residence which has been transformed into something of a mausoleum.

Located, of course, on Elvis Presley Boulevard, Graceland is easily accessible via car or bus from downtown Memphis, Tennessee [approximately 450 miles (720 km) west of Winston-Salem. N.C. on I-40]. Just across the

Elvis
Presley

street from the mansion you will find the ticket office complex. In the dusty overflow parking lot there are automobiles sporting license plates from a greater variety of states than at any other tourist attraction in the South.

Be sure to visit the extraordinary gift shop, where fellow travelers on the royal road to Graceland can be seen purchasing everything from velveteen paintings of Elvis in heaven, to dinnerware emblazoned with the image of the mansion, to bags of dirt which are officially certified to be taken from the yard of Graceland. A small pouch of dirt costs only $2.50 and is a bona fide bargain at that, for it comes in a special folder stamped with a gold seal. It makes an outstanding souvenir.

For only an extra couple of dollars you can climb aboard the *Lisa Marie,* Elvis' private full-size commercial airplane. In order to get to the aircraft it is necessary to pass through a short vestibule in which are displayed several flight logs, including a record of a remarkable trip to Denver for Elvis' favorite peanut butter and banana sandwiches (no kidding!). The gold-plated seatbelt buckles which adorn every seat on the plane, as well as the king-size bed, cannot fail to impress.

The guided tour of the house begins in the front hall, from which can be glimpsed two living rooms, the walls of which are decorated with original portraits of the King. Perhaps you will recognize these artworks because reproductions of them are on sale in the gift shop. The tour continues through the TV room, where Elvis had three full-size television sets installed next to each other, reputedly so that he could watch all three networks' coverage of football games simultaneously. The **"Jungle Room,"** the only room in the house to be decorated by Elvis himself, features colorful shag carpeting and carved wood furniture from the South Pacific.

Outside, past the pink Cadillac Elvis gave to his mother, is the gravesite where the faithful come to leave flowers and pay their final respects.

Graceland is one of the great American tourist sites, easily on a par with the White House and Mount Rushmore.

Nearby **Chapel Hill** is the home of the pleasant **University of North Carolina** campus. U.N.C. is said to have been the first state university chartered in the United States. Fans of astronomy will not want to miss the **Morehead Planetarium** located on E. Franklin Street.

Pottery Boom

Take US 15-501 (also known as the Jefferson Davis Highway) south past residential Chapel Hill toward **Sanford**. You'll see many advertisements for pottery shops, as this area of North Carolina is experiencing a pottery boom. The locally produced earthenware makes an excellent gift. At Sanford, change onto US 421, a road lined with fast-food shops. You are now on the way to Wilmington, the principal deep water port on the North Carolina coast.

By Sanford the road is hot and dusty in the summertime. The fields on the side of the highway are densely covered with tobacco plants. The occasional weeping willow or algae-covered pond do little to dispel the oppressive heat, but no doubt the road will make you long for the cool breeze of the coast.

At **Dunne**, take State 301 toward **Fayetteville**. The smaller road runs through farm country. Corn and tobacco fields extend for acres. There are innumerable small churches along the road, the majority of which are Baptist.

Take the 95 overpass at **Fayetteville** and continue south onto State 87, the scenic route to the coast. The peaceful, meditative road takes you away from fast-food culture deep into the heart of southeast Carolina. Twenty miles (32 km) south of Fayetteville is the tiny town of **Tar Heel**, consisting of **The Tar Heel Game Room**, a grill serving Bar-B-Q, an Exxon station, a general store and, of course, the omnipresent tobacco fields.

On to the Coast

By the time you reach **Elizabethtown**, you may be so tuckered out from driving that a swim will seem a tantalizing idea. Follow State 41 to **White Lake**, an oasis in the middle of the Cape Fear region. The placid lake is surrounded by private homes that serve as vacation residences for the inhabitants of southeastern North Carolina. On the eastern side of the lake is **Goldston's Beach**, a public beach with the requisite shops selling towels inscribed with slogans proclaiming the splendors of White Lake, as well as any number of suntan oils and bikini styles. The water is warm and soothing, and the sand beach will prove a haven for muscles weary of the routine of driving. The small amusement park nearby has pinball machines from the mid-'60s and old skee-ball games which lend an anachronistic air to the place, as if Goldston's beach had been spared the developments of 20 years.

Continue on to **Wilmington**, where you can visit the U.S.S. North Carolina Battleship Memorial. Nicknamed "The Showboat," the ship was commissioned in 1941 and was considered at the time to be the greatest fighting vessel the United States had ever produced. In town, many historic houses are to be seen, among them the **Zebulon Latimer House** at 126 South 3rd Street and the **Burgwin-Wright House** at 3rd and Market Streets. The southern grace of Wilmington's finer homes will pique your interest and prepare you for the more splendid homes of Charleston and Savannah to the south.

A Sanford potter arranges her mugs, left. Right, the U.S.S. North Carolina.

SOUTH CAROLINA'S COAST

On Dec. 20, 1860, South Carolina became the first state to secede from the Union. The policy of nullification initiated by John C. Calhoun to combat federal laws which were perceived as harmful to southern interests had not been enough to insure the existence of the southern economic order, built as it was on the institution of slavery. Knowing that its very way of life was threatened, South Carolina insisted on the right of the state to disavow the federal union and thereby plunged the nation into one of its bloodiest wars.

After the Civil War, the whites of South Carolina could not countenance the idea of granting the vote to newly freed blacks. This refusal resulted in the imposition of military rule in the ruined state. Opportunists from the North called Carpetbaggers and the southern "scalawags" contributed to the economic misery of the state. Reconstruction in South Carolina was a grisly time.

The sad state of affairs in South Carolina continued right up until World War II, when the economy began to switch from an agricultural base to a newly developing industrial base. Textiles, furniture and chemical industries began to flourish. In the succeeding years, the modern industry of tourism began to gather steam in South Carolina, and it has become the second largest producer of revenue in the state. Nowhere can the burgeoning tourist industry be better experienced than along the Carolina coast, from Myrtle Beach and the Grand Strand down to Charleston and beyond.

The Grand Strand

Take US 17 south from Wilmington over the South Carolina border and you will have entered the 55-mile (88-km) stretch of beach resort known as the **Grand Strand.** The first oddity you will notice over the border is the ubiquity of fireworks shops. South Carolina is the only eastern state to have legalized the sale of fireworks, and throughout the state they are big business. The stores are usually the size of a

Commercialism run rampant in Myrtle Beach.

166

large pharmacy and are packed with fizzlers, swizzlers, smokers, crackers and bangers of every conceivable sort. These paper and gunpowder products are most often imported from China and may well bring out the suppressed pyromaniac in you.

Myrtle Beach is the third most popular tourist resort on the east coast, after Disneyworld and Atlantic City. The extraordinary commercialization of the area may well overwhelm you, for all along the King's Highway (US 17) there are innumerable high-rise condo developments, miniature golf parks and honky-tonk beach shops dispensing the accoutrements of beach culture. There is a certain confusion in the development, the result of schemers who want to individualize their particular restaurant or shop from the thousands of similar enterprises along the Grand Strand. Take, for example, the **Black Forest German American Restaurant** which is set in a phony leaning tower of Pisa. "Willkommen to the Black Forest Restaurant." That's confusion. It's also quintessential Myrtle Beach.

The **Boardwalk**, with its amusement parks, jungle lagoon golfing, tribal village French fry stands and hordes of munching tourists, is not to be missed. For excitement try the **Corkscrew**, a harrowing rollercoaster which turns you upside down at oblique angles and makes you think death may be just over the next hump. Avoid the rip-off freak shows along the Boardwalk: you needn't go inside to find the weirdos.

As for swimming, you're best advised to eschew the crowded strand at Myrtle Beach in favor of the less spoiled beaches to the south. **Pawley's Island** has a particularly beautiful beach. There you can enjoy the warm waters and good body-surfing of the Carolina coast without the tumult of the throngs and relax in one of the hammocks for which the island is famous.

Historic Charleston

Located on the peninsula formed by the Cooper and the Ashley Rivers, **Charleston** was the first permanent settlement in the Carolinas. The prosperity of its early days is reflected in the elegant 18th-century homes that fill the residential area south of Broad Street.

Surfers under the boardwalk on Pawley's Island.

These homes are still owned primarily by the descendants of the rich families of old Charleston, many of whom made their fortunes on plantations or in the shipping industry. Allow yourself a few days to amble about the cobbled streets, taking in the many museums and monuments the city has to offer.

The palmetto-lined **Battery** faces the Charleston Harbor and is a good place to begin a walking tour of town. In **White Point Gardens** you can see gorgeous live oak trees with languid Spanish moss hanging from them. At 21 E. Battery is the **Edmondston-Alston House**, built around 1828 by a wealthy wharf owner. It is decorated in Greek Revival style and offers an unobstructed view of the harbor. This home, along with the **Nathaniel Russell House** at 51 Meeting Street is maintained by the Historic Charleston Foundation, a non-profit restoration agency founded in 1947. The Russell House is even more elegant, with an impressive flying staircase spiralling unsupported to the top floor of the building.

Informative tours given by the foundation explain the intricacies of design at each home as well as the histories and customs of some of the families that have lived in them. Be sure to sit on the joggling board in back of the Edmonston-Alston House. The board is 16 feet (five-meters) long and works as a kind of rocking chair. Once thought to have therapeutic properties in the cure of rheumatism, the joggling board is also said to prevent spinsterhood.

The Charleston Museum administers the **Heyward-Washington House** at 87 Church Street as well as the **Joseph Manigault House** at 350 Meeting Street, both of which are highly regarded architectural attractions. Throughout Charleston's historic district you can see classic examples of the "Charleston single house." They are the long, narrow homes with the side piazzas and marked West Indian influence. Perhaps the best way to see Charleston's historic homes is to visit the city in the early spring, when the annual Festival of Houses opens many private homes to the public.

At the **Old Slave Mart Museum** you can see, among other things, facsimiles of bills of sale used in the slave trade. "A prime gang of 25 negroes accustomed to the culture of Sea Island Cot-

A rosy light shed on Charleston homes.

ton and Rice," says a placard advertising the upcoming sale of 25 human beings into bondage. It is startling and sobering to consider that this heinous practice was in full swing just a century and a quarter ago. Perhaps when you leave the Slave Mart Museum you will look at the self-contented opulence of the south of Broad area with a more informed eye.

Charleston is chock full of historic churches. Two of the more interesting among them are the **Huguenot Church**, a Gothic structure built by French Protestants, and **St. Michael's Episcopal Church** with its 186-foot (57-meter) high steeple. Nearby **Fort Sumter**, site of the Confederate attack on Union forces that precipitated Civil War, is accessible from the Charleston Harbor. A 2½-hour tour leaves several times daily from the Municipal Marina.

In the vicinity of Charleston are located two plantations that are certainly worth a visit. The **Magnolia Plantation and Gardens** on Ashly River Road (State 61) has beautiful gardens, a children's petting zoo, an 18th-century herb garden and a 16th-century horticultural maze to tantalize you. At **Middleton Place** farther up the road you can see the oldest landscaped gardens in the country, the result of 10 years labor by 100 slaves.

On to Savannah

Follow US 17 through the low country toward Savannah. Turn on to State 174 for a ride through rich marsh country under a canopy of oaks. In 24 miles (39 km) you will arrive at **Edisto Island**, a seaside resort community which has not yet allowed untoward commercialism to spoil its rustic charm.

Farther south on US 17 is **Beaufort** (Bew-fort), the second oldest town in South Carolina. Indigo and rice cultivation brought wealth to Beaufort in the 18th Century, but now tourism is the primary business. Beaufort has many antebellum houses, but after a stay in Charleston they may not seem that unusual. Perhaps the best way to experience Beaufort is to enjoy the low country seafood specialties and the friendly talk of the local residents at any one of the town's many seafood restaurants before moving south into Georgia.

Stately white columns in Beaufort.

URBAN GEORGIA

Among all the states of the "Deep South," Georgia has been most successful in keeping pace with the North and West. The world becomes ever more aware of Georgia's capital and largest city, Atlanta—heart of the "New South."

Defining the "New South" is difficult, but the entrepreneurial flash and mannered gentility of Atlanta and its power-brokers have set the pace for the rest of this primarily agricultural region. Seen by many as clinging to its one era of glory—the Confederate Era of the American Civil War (1861-65)—the South had for decades set itself apart from its conquerors (the Federal Government, or Union), stubbornly maintaining its identity with the antebellum ways on the Cotton Belt.

To this day considered a backwater, the poor, underdeveloped and uneducated rural South makes only slow, painful progress. The cities of Georgia stand in marked contrast. Atlanta,

which rests on the broad Piedmont Plateau of north-central Georgia, is fast-paced, wealthy and diverse; Macon, on the "fall line" running from Augusta to Columbus and separating northern Georgia from the Coastal Plain, has begun to reinvest in its ever-more-sparkling downtown; Savannah, on the Savannah River and Atlantic Ocean, surrounds its stunning, antebellum city center with modern industry and shipping activity.

Much of Georgia remains rural, but less so every year. Lumber products, fruit, cattle and poultry continue to figure prominently in the economy, while banking, manufacturing, media, the military industry and tourism rise in and around the cities.

Throughout Georgia, you can expect hot days and pleasant nights from May through September, temperate comfort in April and October and cool to cold temperatures November through March. Georgia blooms most beautifully in the spring, which is ideal visiting season. Southern Georgia, on the Coastal Plain, is balmiest, often sweltering in summer. It is there that Georgia's escalating tempo is most tempered, and it is

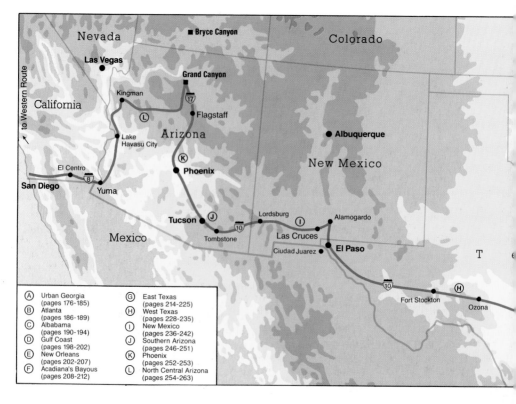

there that the grand tour of the South begins.

Savannah: Pride at the Precipice

Like Dublin, like Paris and San Francisco, Savannah is not so much a city as a region of the heart, a quality of grace and leisure which has almost vanished from urban life.

— Betsy Fancher

Savannah is a brilliant example of an idea rescued from the rubbish heap. The first permanent white settlement in the state, Savannah began as a planned utopia but very nearly lapsed into a blighted, polluted nightmare in the 20th Century.

Set slightly inland of the marshy mouth of the Savannah River, the city of Savannah is busy restoring its aesthetic glory and recapturing its pride. Having survived the devastating American Civil War and, later, industrial negligence if not outright rape, Savannah has set its sight on catching up to the "New South."

But the grace and leisure Savannah journalist Betsy Fancher ascribes to the city are uneradicable and captivating remnants of the "Old South." The tenor and splendor of Savannah are rooted in a proud lineage descending from the ideals of its founder.

Watchdog Colony

At the beginning of the 18th Century, present-day Georgia was settled only by Cherokee and Choctaw Indians. Nominally in the control of the British, the area was a buffer zone between Spanish Florida to the South and the British Carolinas to the North. Wary of Spanish expansionism, and to a lesser extent, the French presence to the west in Louisiana, the Crown granted a charter to General James Oglethorpe to set up a watchdog colony in Georgia.

Oglethorpe's motivations in establishing the colony went beyond colonial defense. Deeply moved by the plight of the unemployed and the imprisoned debtors in the homeland, he envisioned his colony—Savannah, in the territory named after charterer King George II—as a utopia where the hapless could fashion a secure economic and aesthetic prosperity. Along with 125 ragtag pioneers, Oglethorpe landed at the

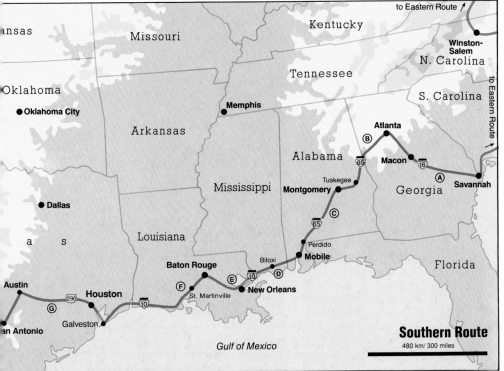

Southern Route
480 km/ 300 miles

mouth of the Savannah River on Feb. 12, 1733.

The Savannah utopia was painstakingly planned. Before setting out in the good ship *Ann*, Oglethorpe already had a city plan. Savannah was to be the first and best planned city in America. The idyllic outlay of squares and gardens was to be situated on Yamacraw (Creek) Indian land procurred from Chief Tomo-Chi-Chi, the "co-founder of Georgia."

Although Oglethorpe had ruled that the colony should be free of slavery, brandies and distilled liquors, lawyers and credit in alehouses, utopian ideals eventually gave way to socioeconomic pressures. The hard-bitten settlers laboring in the muggy, swamp-riddled lowlands of the new colony to establish a planned economy based on silk culture, wine and drugs soon grew embittered of their leader's ideals. All the while, the community diversified, attracting dreamers and outcasts from the Continent, most notably a substantial contingent of Spanish-Portuguese Jews.

The purity of Savannah's conception was eventually compromised, but its uto-pian spirit took form in the gradually realized city plan. And as far as the Crown was concerned, Savannah was a success. Spanish designs on the southern Atlantic colonies were put to an end with Oglethorpe's victory over the Latin pretenders at the Battle of Bloody Marsh on St. James Island in 1742.

Beautiful Obstacles

Unlike many major cities in the Deep South, Savannah was relatively undamaged by the Civil War despite its importance as a port and supply center. Savannah is where Federal General Sherman concluded his devastating "March to the Sea." (Sherman and his Union troops blazed a bitter trail through the South in 1864, leaving most of its cities in ruins.) Fortunately, because the city had already been evacuated, it was spared the usual burning to the ground.

Intact to this day, "Historic Savannah" is a picturesque grid of green squares and comfortable, well-developed streets. Betsy Fancher described the 24 central squares of downtown as "effective fortresses against the great enemies of the

Preceding pages: Arizona highway 89A; cacti near the Apache Trail; Helldorado Day, Tombstone. Left, William Sherman, a ruthless general. Right, port of Savannah.

178

20th Century: air pollution, high population density, tension and alienation." Most are surrounded by outstanding late 18th- and early 19th-century structures. The most universally applauded of these landmarks—and there are many, making Savannah the largest National Historic Landmark district in the United States—are the mansions of London architect William Jay. The **Owens-Thomas House** off Oglethorpe Square and the **Telfair Family Mansion** (now the city's Academy of Arts and Sciences) on Telfair Square are both superb examples of English Regency work in the Greek Revival style.

On or between squares, architectural marvels abound. Delicate ironwork adorns building after building, most of which are constructed of brick, stone and/or stucco. Interlaced with the older architecture are Victorian districts and, downtown, unspoiled representatives of 1950s and '60s department-store style.

Down by the River

Fronting the Savannah River downtown is the historic riverfront, an 11-block stretch of Bay and River Streets and Factors Walk. At Bay and Bull Streets is **City Hall**, a charming, almost anti-institutional structure boasting vaulted pillars, arched stone and flower boxes. Abutting City Hall to the east is a row of buildings. The elevated portion of **Factors Walk** is stilted over the cobblestone waterfront, including **Solomon's Lodge**, housed in the old Savannah Cotton Exchange (1886), an excellent brick structure. The Lodge had been organized by Oglethorpe in 1734 and is the "oldest continuously operating English constituted [Freemason's] lodge in the Western Hemisphere."

Beneath the pedestrian bridges that link Bay Street to Solomon's Lodge lies lower Factors Walk and, to its north, **River Street**. River Street, as you would expect, fronts the Savannah River; it's a charming cobblestone way inlaid with rails. For better or worse, River Street has been the focus of the tourist trade in Savannah, and its old brick buildings are inhabited by traders in antiques, art, trinkets of all sorts, food and drink.

Up and down the riverfront, signs of healthy port activity blend with preserved history, often incongruously.

Locals and visitors laze about, ride a reconstructed ferryboat or fish. As the sun sinks behind the blood-red horizon and the cool evening breeze cuts the heat, it's easy to understand the city's romantic spirit.

Navigating Savannah

Although Savannah's Streets are based on a fairly simple design, everything is easier in theory than in practice. The city is circled and sliced by a confusion of highways and interchanges, beguilingly marked. Getting in, you will find, is easier than getting out. Carry a good map.

Downtown, the squares impede linear travel. Traffic is pitched into an endless, if picturesque, counterclockwise merry-go-round every few blocks. Flow is regulated by stop and yield signs; skillful navigation is required and concentration necessarily diverted from the sights. For this reason, the driving tour is discouraged. Park your car, go by foot and enjoy it.

River Street is also better approached on foot; parking is, however, readily available right off the river. The cobblestones are rough on an automobile's suspension, and the two-way traffic usually conflicts murderously.

Outside the center of town, however, your car will be useful. It's worth your while to drive along **Forsyth Park** and south, where the less affluent neighborhoods sport vibrant street life and many architectural gems.

US routes 17 and 17-A allow access to Savannah from the north and west and drop you right near River Street, Bay Street (US 17) and the Visitors Center on West Broad Street. Traveling east on Bay Street eventually brings you to President Street Extension and US 80 east, which culminates on **Tybee Island** (locale of the popular Savannah Beach) and at **Fort Pulaski National Monument,** approximately 15 miles (24 km) outside of Savannah.

New Weaponry and New Ways

Separated from Savannah by marshland and splinters of the Savannah River, and from Tybee Island proper by a channel, **Cockspur Island** is the site of Fort Pulaski National Monument.

Activity on the waterfront.

Bridges leapfrog the marshes out to this outpost, which became the site of Fort Pulaski when the War of 1812 made the inadequacy of America's coastal defenses obvious. Built between 1829 and 1847, the fort was named after Count Casimir Pulaski, the Polish hero of the Revolutionary War mortally wounded at the bloody Battle of Savannah. The young Robert E. Lee, later the most famous general of the Confederate States of America, served as "acting assistant commisary of subsistence" (an engineer) at the fort soon after his graduation from West Point Military Academy.

When, in 1860, Georgia governor Joseph E. Brown organized a rebel force of 10,000 men, one of the first serious steps toward outright war had been taken. Early in 1861, Brown's men seized Fort Pulaski. In one of the most significant confrontations the "War between the States," Brigadier General Thomas W. Sherman and Captain Samuel F. DuPont commandeered an amphibious Union force that moved in to blockade the Savannah River and beseige the fort in late 1861.

The walls of Fort Pulaski speak of the Civil War.

It took the introduction of a new weapon, the rifled cannon, to breach the fort's mortar walls and bring Confederate Colonel Charles Olmstead and his 385 men to their knees. Olmstead surrendered with these words: "I yield my sword, but I trust I have not disgraced it."

Noble Surrender

When Confederate General Robert E. Lee surrendered to Federal General Ulysses S. Grant at Appomatox, thus ending the Civil War, the South yielded to the Union its sovereignty but not its spirit. But capitulation, even if noble, is never pretty; Fort Pulaski was transformed into a prison where hundreds of Confederate soldiers were kept in miserable conditions before the fort's abandonment. Only in 1933 did the National Park Service begin restoration of the fort. Today it is a national monument to a past which the South has never regained.

The Visitors Center houses a fine exhibit of old weapons, building materials, tools, utensils and artillery as well as notated and documented mementos

of the fort's history. As you venture out onto the trails and into the fort, beware of pests, especially mosquitos, and be prepared to encounter an occasional (harmless) snake in the spring and summer. When the water level drops on the rest of the island, you may also spot an alligator in the moat that rings Fort Pulaski.

Into the Heart

Interstate 16 is an almost purely functional roadway—a truckers' route from the port of Savannah to Macon, Georgia. The early stretch out of Savannah is featureless save for some remarkable, if eventually monotonous, pine to either side.

Relief comes in the last 60 miles (97 km) of the 160-mile (257-km) ribbon, when the road begins gradually scaling into the blue horizon. This is where you begin to encounter what the Federal Writers Project called "the rolling character of the land [which] makes for undulations in the roadways, the fields and the pine forests that border them. The clay hills are deeply gullied by erosion and their red color against the dark pines of the wooded regions creates a perpetually vivid landscape."

There is also some entertainment in dodging the ripped tires that litters I-16 and in riding the slipstream kicked up by the huge trucks muscling by. They leave you with dust on your windshield and the admonition, inevitably gracing their rears, to "Please Drive Safely!"

While guessing at what these behemoths haul, don't miss the two crucial service exits on this journey into agrarian Georgia: exits 23 (Metter) and 14 (Dublin). The "Geographical Center of Georgia," which seems to hold much interest locally, is accessible by exit 7.

Macon of a Renaissance

Pulling into **Macon** from the Second Street exit of I-16 affords none of the classic skyline views. The **Liberty Federal** and **Hilton Hotel** buildings, the tallest of four structures dominating the initial vista, are uncharacteristic eyesores on a restored city center.

Downtown Macon has twice pulled itself back from the brink of disaster, once by ruse and once by a sophisticated restoration plan. When in 1864

The Hay House, a preserved antebellum mansion.

General Sherman and his troops launched shots into Macon across the Ocmulgee River, they were met with return fire suggesting a substantial resistance force in the city. But the troops that turned Sherman and his torch down toward Savannah were not regular Confederate army, but old men and young children.

The marvelous antebellum mansions and civic buildings thus spared were later faced with greater threat than Union artillery: shopping malls. In the 1970s the onslaught began on US 80 in southwest Macon, when the first mall drained historic downtown of its major commercial attractions. The core of what had been an already neglected area was extruded; Macon was threatened with the "doughnut effect"—all extremity with no center.

Infusion of block grants leveraged by private funds helped Macon's central commercial district bootstrap itself back to respectability, while neighborhood groups and the Macon Heritage Foundation orchestrated restoration of the surrounding national landmarks.

The architecture that has been preserved and restored is incredibly diverse, yet thoroughly southern. As one resident puts it: "When people from outside the South come to find the 'Old South,' it's not in Atlanta, which is too new, nor is it in Savannah, which by virtue of its settlers and design is closer to a European city. The Old South is right here in Macon."

Cotton kings built lavish homes in the early Federal style with classical touches during the "cotton boom" of the early 19th Century. These were followed by structures in the Greek Temple style adapted to the climate. Over the years, waves of commercial expansion inspired forays into new styles for mansions and civic and commercial buildings. Italianate Revival, Second Empire, Victorian, Gothic Revival, Roman Revival and Academic Revival experiments carried through to the 1920s.

While exploring the city's expansive "Heritage Tour," you'll note the new upscale face of downtown, which now supports the light industry of greater-Macon with white-collar service companies and their attendant culture. Downtown is still no hotspot after-hours, but the nine-to-five activity sig-

"Jamming" Georgia-style.

nals the beginnings of an old city catching up to the times.

Mysterious Mounds

If you wish to step farther into the past than 1800, it's worth your while to take the short trip to the **Ocmulgee National Monument**, over the Ocmulgee River from downtown Macon via US 80. The monument conserves traces of the civilizations that populated the Macon Plateau from 8000 B.C.

The greater part of the exhibits in the Visitors Center and out on the trails reconstruct the life of the Mississippian Indians in the 10th to 13th centuries. At Ocmulgee, they painstakingly erected huge mounds of sand and clay, many for ceremonial purposes. Little is known about the mounds, but their very presence —and the exhibits examining archaeological interpretation—are fascinating.

More recent history of Macon is preserved at **Jarrell Plantation**, 18 miles (29 km) north of downtown on US 23 (Riverside Drive) and State 18. Set in a "country of red hills and stones," as Macon poet Sidney Lanier put it, Jarrell Plantation is still home to the descendants of a family that persevered through the rise and fall of the Georgia cotton industry. Many of the original structures still stand, including the first dwelling (1847), the mill complex, sugar boiler, smokehouse and blacksmith's workshop. The road that takes you up to the plantation is pure dirt and rock, but poses no peril when dry.

The Atlanta 285

Depending on your disposition, you may wish you'd stuck to dirt roads once you get to the "Atlanta 285." Whether you continue north on US 23 or follow I-75 all the way from Macon north to Atlanta, the journey is at least pleasant for a good while, about 75 miles (120 km). US 23 is noteworthy for its proximity to the Ocmulgee River, **Lake Juliette**, state parks, a wildlife refuge and campgrounds. The road twists into the peaceful town of **Jackson**, a warming respite from the open highway. From Jackson, you may either follow US 23 north or turn back to I-75 via State 16, which cuts through rolling farmland. Both US 23 and I-75 continue scaling to the highlands as the flora becomes more rich and the clay darkens.

The lull of simple highway cruising is cruelly shattered seven miles (11 km) south of Atlanta as you reach I-285, the **Atlanta ByPass.** I-285 rings the sprawling Atlanta metropolitan area, appearing (mistakenly) on the map as the quiet fringe outside the bustling city. But the eye of a hurricane is calmest, while its perimeter spins fastest.

The Atlanta ByPass is this city's answer to the Indianapolis 500, with its almost mythical, lawless road-rally in which southern gentlemen and ladies vent their frustrations on the way to and from their suburban homes. In the words of one southern Georgian, "If you do 55 in Atlanta the way they do up North, you'll get blown off the highway." Nowhere is this truer than on I-285. Average speed can reach 75 m.p.h. (120 k.p.h.); top speed goes up from there.

The hearty motorist will take to the bypass with relish; it can become almost addictive. You may find yourself circling the city for hours (rush hours are especially fun) in a trance. If the rush is not your preferred high, or if tailgating "semis" begin, to annoy, and well, if you can't stand the heat, get off the bypass.

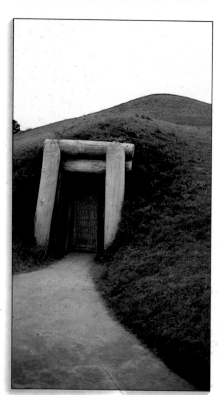

Ancient mound at Ocmulgee National Monument, left. Right, thumbs-up from a seasoned trucker in Mississippi.

184

ATLANTA

As Los Angeles is to the West, **Atlanta** is to the East. Occupying nearly the same latitude, these two cities embody novelty and incessant adaptation. But where Los Angeles "jes grew," Atlanta had to be burned first—90 percent of it by Federal Sherman in 1864. Like Macon, Atlanta was shaped by the cotton and railroad industries of the 19th Century, but there is little history preserved to remind us of its roots. Atlanta bounced back from disaster rapidly, using Reconstruction leverage to hoist even greater weight.

Today the sprawling, speeding state capital, Atlanta is impossible to consume in a short stay. From the Peachtree Center mall complex, to the aristocratic, removed, dogwood-shaded West Paces Ferry and Piedmont neighborhoods, to the Dr. Martin Luther King, Jr. Memorial on Auburn Avenue west of downtown, to famous restaurants and museums, Atlanta beguiles visitors with its plentitude.

But for a Small Taste...

No matter how long you stay in Atlanta, you will be able to enjoy many varieties of food. The restaurants here are given to superlatives, and two excellent representatives are **The Varsity** and **Aunt Fanny's Cabin**.

The Varsity, near the Georgia Institute of Technology, is self-proclaimed as "the world's largest drive-in." Curb service is actually available to only about a score of cars. The real "scene" unfolds inside this monument to the emblems of modern American culture—college football, television, Coca-Cola, fast food and automobiles.

Huge queues of burger-and-coke addicts from all classes wait at item-specific "stations" to order the best of deep-fried, grilled and steamed fare: cheeseburgers to chili dogs, french fries to peach-fried pie, milk shakes to the omnipresent Coca-Cola (which was invented in Atlanta). Once served, the hungry crowds migrate to small "dining rooms," each equipped with a television tuned to major network programming.

Aunt Fanny's Cabin, in Smyrna at the northwest edge of Atlanta, was founded in 1941 in the extant quarters of Aunt Fanny Williams, a slave born there in the 1850s. In the words of one Atlantan expatriate, "Aunt Fanny's serves the best fried chicken in the South"—and therefore, one assumes, in the world.

The original structure has been maintained and expanded with care and is furnished largely in original antiques. Here you can experience quintessential southern cooking: fried chicken and baked squash from the original recipes, turnip greens, corn muffins and biscuits, apple cobbler, "gen-u-wine Smithfield ham" and sweetened tea. An incredible 1,000 tons (1,016 metric tons) of chicken is consumed here *every month* in an ambience sustaining the famed Southern courtesy and character.

The High Museum of Art speaks much of Atlanta's dedication to being a "world-class city" (a distinction it long

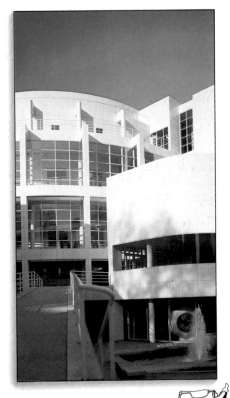

Left, home of Martin Luther King, Jr. Right, the High Museum of Art.

ago achieved when its airport became the second busiest). Located on Peachtree Street slightly north of downtown, the glossy, white, geometric structure encloses an atrium scaled by a 90-degree spiral section accessing each of the four exhibition floors.

The High Museum scrambles decorative art, African art, Renaissance temperas, modern conceptual canvases and more with a sly iconoclasm. The placement of Rodin's sculpture "The Shade" (1880) in the middle of contemporary conceptual works by Sol LeWitt and Frank Stella is one of many displays of an irreverent curatorial sensibility. The ultra-modern is flanked by 19th-century American paintings; to the side are 14th to 16th-century Italian works.

If fighting traffic and finding parking in downtown Atlanta leave you crying for escape, take a trip seven miles (11 km) east of I-285 on US 78 to **Stone Mountain Park**, a recreation complex including an ice rink, golf course, campground, waterslides, boating, fishing, tennis, wildlife trail, "Scenic Railroad" ride and reconstructed plantation. Unlike the Jarrell Plantation, Stone Mountain's plantation showcases buildings imported from points throughout the state.

The park sprawls about the central figure which gives it its name: **Stone Mountain**. The exposed portion of this granite giant occupies a volume of 7,533,751,000 cu feet and is thought to be almost 3 million years old. Its gestation period was long, as igneous rock struggled to push through the surface. Stone Mountain's thrust to the sky is a fine metaphor for the concrete explosion of modern Atlanta after its razing.

The mountain itself, smooth but for light pocks in the surface, is spectacle enough, but its focus has become a huge memorial carving 50 years in production depicting Confederate leaders Jefferson Davis, Robert E. Lee and "Stonewall" Jackson in their glory. The sculpture, which spreads 147 feet (45 meters) across and towers 400 feet (122 meters) above ground, was completed in 1972.

From downtown Atlanta, I-85 cuts a sure path southwest to the heart of Alabama. Through the rolling Piedmont highlands and into the heavily forested expanse of Georgia's neighbor, you can smell pine and admire the well-manicured grasses that line the highway.

Once you cross the **Chattahoochie River** and enter "Alabama the Beautiful," you'll note the disappearance of the many roadside invitations to gas up at Starvin' Marvin. Fortunately the Waffle Houses and Union 76 truck stops maintain a note of familiarity.

West Point Lake sits on the state line, engineered under the Flood Control Act of 1962. This enormous power source with a shoreline of 525 miles, (845 km) has been tailored as a resort area with 43 recreational areas for fishing, swimming, boating, hunting and general relaxation. The Alabama Visitors Center lies just over the state line on I-85. Its aggressive promotion of the state stands in contrast to Georgia's *laissez-faire* attitude. This distinction is certainly attributable to Alabama's image as a backwater state with little to offer the traveler or prospective settler.

Left, finger lickin' good chicken at Aunt Fanny's Cabin, Atlanta. Right, Stone Mountain confederate memorial.

ALABAMA: THE COTTON STATE

Alabama and much of the land to its west passed through several hands before it was taken over by the United States in the late 18th Century. Labyrinthine colonial struggles involving the Indian "Five Nations" (Cherokee, Seminole, Muscogee, Chickasaw and Choctaw) mark Alabama's early history, and its coat-of-arms displays the emblems of the five white nations which held its sovereign: France, Great Britain, the United States, the Confederacy and again the United States.

It is, of course, the last two of these regimes which have left the clearest stamp on Alabama, named for the Alabama River, itself named after an Indian tribe. This state has in particular clung to the brief pride and glory of the Confederate Era, memorialized at the state capital, Montgomery. Alabama rose to its economic apex during the cotton boom of the 19th Century. The state has seen better days, economically and socially; but its natural resources, hardworking citizenry and enduring pride refuse to admit decline.

After rolling through an initial forested area along I-85 westbound, you can turn off at exit 38 to **Tuskegee** via State 81 south and State 126 west. Tuskegee is the site of Booker T. Washington's **Tuskegee Normal and Industrial Institute**, one of the few institutions of higher learning for American blacks in the 19th Century.

In the words of the leading black intellectual, W.E.B. DuBois, Washington was "the greatest man the South produced since the Civil War." Politically deft and enormously inspired, Washington believed in cooperation with the ruling whites and in practical education to serve the needs of the black masses concentrated in the South. Washington's policy of avoiding confrontation made enemies among other educated blacks and "liberal whites." But he kept Tuskegee alive.

A film entitled *Up from Slavery* detailing the history of the institution and of Washington's struggle is presented at the **Carver Museum** on campus. The well-made documentary doesn't shy from presenting the controversies surrounding Washington and Tuskegee; for that alone, it is worthwhile seeing.

Carver Museum is housed in one of the many historic buildings preserved by Tuskegee and the National Park Service and is named after the famous black agricultural chemist George Washington Carver. Carver worked and taught on campus from 1896 until his retirement to "**The Oaks**" in Tuskegee, where he died in 1943. He had abandoned artistic aspirations to forge the pioneer science of industrial agriculture. His discoveries literally saved the southern economy from collapse after the boll weevil infestation of 1919 destroyed the cotton industry. In discovering 285 new uses for the peanut, 118 products that could be manufactured from surplus sweet potatoes and much more, a black man saved a region whose elite had oppressed and would continue to oppress his race, legally or illegally.

Back on I-85 south, you travel 41 miles (66 km) from Tuskegee to the boundary of **Montgomery**. Montgomery is a small, quiet downtown surrounded by wide outlying neighborhoods whose names smack of agricultural gentility: Old Acres, Pinedale, Pecan Grove, Open Acres, Spring Valley and Park Manor.

While the prairie muds are still rich and Montgomery bases its livelihood on government services, construction and manufacturing. Montgomery also benefits from the patronage of the U.S. Air Force, whose elite members are frequently assigned to **Maxwell Air Force Base** on the site of Wilbur and Orville Wright's flight school.

Although much of Montgomery is attractive, little is glamorous. By and large, no one in the city seems all that excited—except those who enthusiastically maintain and promote the city's "rich heritage." The **State Capitol** on Goat Hill and the surrounding historic sites are indeed rich.

More impressive than the lovely

Cotton field and processing plant.

State Capitol building are the two grand structures across Washington Street: the quiet **First White House of the Confederacy** and the imposing **Alabama Archives and History** building. The White House, moved next to the Archives from its original site at Bibb and Catoma Streets, was the home of Confederate president Jefferson Davis during Montgomery's stint as first capital of the Confederate States of America. This rebel nation was comprised of the 13 states and territories which seceded from the United States in 1860 and 1861 over the issue of states' rights—most importantly the right to maintain legal slavery. Davis has been eclipsed in history by Confederate General Robert E. Lee, but in the South he is still revered as an emblem of distinction and self-determination.

The great neo-classical Archives Building is a rich storehouse of American Indian arts, Confederate history and subsequent state development. From relics of the "first Alabamians," the Shell Mound Indians of the 10th century, to the Hank Williams Collection of great Alabamian country singer's clothing, the Archives pieces together the rich heritage that is "Dixie."

An underpublicized but significant memorial to recent civil rights struggles in the South is the **Dexter Avenue King Memorial Baptist Church** in downtown Montgomery at 454 Dexter Avenue. This is where Dr. Martin Luther King, Jr. began his non-violent protest of "Jim Crow" segregation. Before his assassination in 1968, King, an Atlantan, was the man most responsible for the civil rights legislation which finally, in the mid-1960s, criminalized racial discrimination in the United States. The church is notable for the mural "Montgomery to Memphis, 1955-1968," commemorating King's and blacks' struggles for dignity and equality.

The two most significant cultural events in Montgomery are **Jubilee**—a springtime community celebration held on the third weekend of May—and the **Alabama Shakespeare Festival** held in the winter and spring at the tailor-

The State Capitol in Montgomery.

made complex on the eastern border of the city. During the rest of the year, the zoo historic districts, riverboat ride and fine arts museum do nicely.

Another Alabama

I-85 into Montgomery dovetails into I-65 and continues south into the rural glades of southwestern Alabama. Along the way, the radio bands are striped with black contemporary music, pop, country, sermons and jazz.

Skid marks that swerve off to the shoulder suggest high-speed highway adventure. The soil deepens again to red where it had been sandy and gray in the "Black Belt" through the midsection of the state. Deeper exploration of rural Alabama is recommended, and US 31 is a good place to start. US 31 arcs through **Escambia** and **Baldwin counties**, grazing the northwesternmost edge of Florida near Atmore and Perdido. The land here is dotted with small green ponds and spread with groves of pine and oak. Cattle graze on the muddy soil, and farmhouses call forth images of peaceful backwaters.

Before reaching **Atmore**, you pass through **Canoe**, Alabama, where you might see a horse and buggy ride along one side of the road as a 100-car-long freight train whistles by on the other. Atmore is weary-palmed, open-fielded and railroad-tied. The Burger Bar fronting US 31 serves "catfish nuggets" and "taco salad." Churches are clearly indicated on the highway. A short diversion north on State 21 brings you past the Snappy-Wash, a local pawnshop, a welding shop and the Atmore Dragway before you arrive at the Best Western Motor Inn at junction I-65. Housed here is the famous **Good and Plenty Restaurant, Bakery and Gift Shop** run by Menonites transplanted from Pennsylvania. Religious books, cookies, breads and buffet lunch and dinner are served.

Continue on I-65 along a 13-mile (22-km) stretch before the next exit (exit 45) to **Perdido**. Just south of the highway, the fruit of Jim and Marianne Eddins' gumption and perseverance continues

On-stage on-guard at the Alabama Shakespeare Festival.

to thrive: **Perdido Vineyards.**

'Bama Wine

Winemaking in Alabama, once a great domestic industry, was effectively killed by Prohibition. Even afterward, Baptist leaders maintained that drinking, let alone manufacturing spirits was next to ungodliness. The Eddins family dared the opposition and began their muscadine vineyard in 1971, marketing the grapes to a Florida winemaker. When that arrangement fell through, the Perdido Vineyard began producing its own wine in 1979.

The muscadine varieties grown at Perdido—scuppernongs, higgins, nobles and magnolias—are from a tough vine indigenous to the southeastern US. Perdido's table wines, which may be sampled at the vineyard are mostly sweet wines with a few drier varietals, including an extra-dry white reminiscent of some California wines.

The Perdido venture met with initial hostility from the community, but its success and subsequent attention it brought to Baldwin County considerably warmed their reception. But as one disgruntled entrepreneur put it: "Sometimes you gotta get down on your hands and knees and pray for deliverance from the Christian businessmen."

Baldwin County is subject to a "pressure-cooker" climate, hot and prone to extremes of humidity. Nature has been hard on American farmers for centuries, but the environment was very attractive to a settlement of Greeks who came to the shores of Mobile Bay before the Second World War. Under the leadership of a Greek Orthodox priest named Malbis, the community established the lushest plantation in the county. When Malbis died in Nazi hands after he returned to Greece, the community carried out his plan to build an Orthodox Church in what is now the town of **Malbis**, between US 31 and I-10 four miles (six km) east of Mobile Bay. The church was constructed from materials imported from Greece and includes stunning tile work and stained glass.

Perdido Vineyards.

194

MARTIN LUTHER KING, JR.

The story of Rev. Martin Luther King, Jr. is that of the painful awakening of the American civil rights movement. Between his sudden rise to national prominence and his tragic death, King established an agenda of legislative reforms and an effective method for bringing it to fruition.

In 1957, 28-year-old King had just settled in as pastor of a small congregation in Montgomery, Alabama, when a minor racial incident thrust him into a position of leadership and responsibility. Mrs. Rosa Parks, a black seamstress, was riding near the front of the "blacks only" section on a bus when the driver asked her to relinquish her seat to a white man. Mrs. Parks, tired and in all likelihood fed up with Jim Crow, simply refused.

Her subsequent arrest prompted the formation of the Montgomery Improvement Association with King at its head. The group sponsored a boycott of the city-run bus line by the

black community which brought the buses to a halt and resulted in two major victories: a Supreme Court decision outlawing segregation on municipal buses, and the Civil Rights Act of 1957 establishing a Civil Rights Division of the Justice Department. In the process, King was arrested and his home bombed, but proved the power of nonviolent protest and sparked a movement that spread like a summer fire across the tinderbox of the American South.

In the months that followed, a series of nonviolent demonstrations escalated into violence as mobs of angry whites gathered to thwart the integration of public facilities. The struggle penetrated the national consciousness in early 1963 when King was invited to organize the fight for integration in Birmingham, Alabama. In his inaugural address, Governor George Wallace had called for "segregation now, segregation tomorrow, segregation forever!"

Time magazine responded by naming King Man of the Year for 1963. The Nobel Prize for Peace followed the next year.

National legislation continued to be enacted in the wake of King's activities, most significantly the Civil Rights Bill of 1964 authorizing the Attorney General to sue in cases of discrimination in schools, hiring practices and elections. But progress could not come quickly enough for many black leaders who advocated violent rebellion and broke with King. His support among more conservative black leaders also eroded as he attempted to forge an alliance of the civil rights and anti-Vietnam War movements. In April of 1968, amid an ambitious campaign in Washington to establish a minimum family income, King made an incidental detour to Memphis, Tennessee, in support of striking sanitation workers. There, an assassin's bullet brought his life to a sudden halt at the age of 39.

Behind him Martin Luther King left not only an extraordinary record of legislative achievements. His efforts on behalf of blacks have resulted in steadily increasing access to jobs, housing, education and representation in government.

THE GULF COAST: AMERICAN RIVIERA

The arcing coastline along the Gulf of Mexico from northwest Florida to southeast Texas can well lay claim to the title of "American Riviera." Not so much a Côte d'Azur as a Côte de Blanc, the Gulf Coast spreads its white sands along warm waters stocked with fine shrimp, oysters and other delicacies. Cities and counties along the coast sponsor annual "blessings of the shrimp fleet" within the first few weeks of June.

The excellent beaches of Gulf-Coast Alabama, Mississippi and Texas have attracted vacationers from the South and Midwest since the mid-19th Century. Tourism and fishing are certainly economic mainstays for all the beach communities, but they have been impinged upon by the growth of the oil industry which often drills and explores within sight of the sunbathers.

Whatever the ecological effects of oil retrieval may be, the petrochemical industry has been crucial to the survival of cities such as Mobile, Alabama. And it is still possible to retreat from progress by the impossibly blue waters of the Gulf states.

Mistaken for Alabama

Interstates 10 and 65 and US 90 (which picks up from US 31) all stilt the mouth of the Mobile River west from Baldwin County into the port of **Mobile**, Alabama. Mobile's strategic locale on river and gulf has made it the most contested area of Alabama in all of the state's twisted power struggles. The turmoil subsided after the Civil War, in which the Battle of Mobile ushered in the current federal government.

As a port, Mobile (Mo-BEEL) is the most diverse city in Alabama; the strains of its Continental heritage which persist in the architecture and lifestyle make the city genuinely atypical of the the state. In fact, the capsule history on one city map from 1984 begins: "It has been remarked by some observers of the 277-year-old city of Mobile that it was a mistake to include it within the state of Alabama."

Indeed, Mobile shares more in the culture of the cities and counties washed by the warm waters of the Gulf of Mexico than in the heritage of a land that outsiders regard as the most insular in the South.

Mobile is justifiably the most attractive destination for visitors to this "pass-through" state. Still dominated by the shipbuilding industry, Mobile's sea culture, stately brick and wood structures adorned with iron grill-work, fountained plazas and lush parks capture the hearts of wanderers arriving by ship or bus.

The flavor of Mobile comes through best in a stroll down lower **Government, Church** and **Dauphin Streets**, particularly where they cross South Georgia and South Ann Streets. The historic districts flourish with magnolia, azalea and oak, which thrive in the semi-tropical climate. Government Street (US 90) is shaded by an awning of live oaks downtown before opening into a mall-lined highway to the west.

On a sunny day, a trip to the beach is in order, back over the bay on I-10 to State

Preceding page: Louisiana's Oak Alley Plantation. Below, Fort Conde is dwarfed by modern buildings in Mobile.

198

59 south. Look for small, relatively undiscovered outposts such as **Little Lagoon**, which borders a game reserve on a small finger of land west of Gulf Shores.

At night, activity in Mobile centers around its many bars, where during the day you might observe a leisurely card game. There are also a few dance clubs, but the familiar chorus rings: "Not a lot goes on here." That is, besides shipbuilding and Mardis Gras. Mobile's pre-Lenten Carnival is actually much older (by 150 years) than the more celebrated edition in New Orleans.

King Coca-Cola

As US 90 pulls away from the Mobile Bay, it widens into its mall-motel-and-fast-food stretch. Upon reaching the town of **Theodore**, you'll spot a huge billboard directing you south on State 59 to **Bellingrath Gardens,** "The Garden For All Seasons."

All the hype—"Incomparable," "One of the World's MOST Beautiful Year-Round Gardens"—turns out to be pretty much true. Originally a semitropical jungle on the Isle-aux-Dies Riv-

er, the land was purchased by Walter Bellingrath. Mr and Mrs. Bellingrath landscaped 65 acres (26 hectares) of the 905-acre (366-hectare) plot, sculpting an evolving, living work of art to surround their magnificent riverfront home. Azaleas, roses, hibiscus, chenille, chrysanthemums, poinsettas, lilies, violets and dogwood are part of the "rapturous floral beauty" carefully maintained along with the home, chapel and exhibit of Boehm porcelain.

The Oriental-American Garden, honking geese, flamingos and teeming bayou will charm where the gift shop and restaurant depress. Renting a taped tour is an unnecessary distraction. The mapped walk is well-designed; but let yourself wander aimlessly, dream by the ponds and waterfalls, and loll about the gazebos.

US 90 is the "old highway" along the Gulf Coast from Florida to Louisiana, and it's recommended over the bald interstate. The going is generally slower, and traffic lights are more frequent in places. Nevertheless, US 90 offers a glimpse of town life in the deepest South.

The Bellingrath Gardens live up to their hype.

Out of Mobile and Theodore, US 90 passes through **St. Elmo**, where the colors of rust, green, violet and yellow patch the shoulders and line the railroad tracks which follow them. Five miles (eight km) westward, you arrive in **Grand Bay**, "home of the world's largest watermelon festival." At Grand Bay, State 188 swoops south into State 16 to **Bayou La Batre**, an oil, shipbuilding and shrimping town where the Blessing of the Shrimp Fleet in June and the Seafood Festival in late July are two of Mobile County's big attractions.

About five miles (eight km) outside Grand Bay, US 90 crosses into the state of Mississippi. The highway crawls through the towns of Pecan, Orange Grove and Kreole before skirting Pescagoula, one of the three major Mississippian anchors on the Gulf Coast (the two that follow are Biloxi and Gulfport).

Although the "old highway" is immediately announced as the "Scenic Beach Route to New Orleans," it takes about 27 miles (43 km) to get from state line to scenery. The roadway is streaked with inland commercial districts and malls, but subtle diversions and the final payoff at Biloxi make the initial stretch worthwhile.

A billboard puns that Jackson County is a "shipshape community" before you climb onto the drawbridge over the ship-dotted **Pescagoula River**. The land from Gautier to Biloxi is swampy, and the gray-blue skies are crystal clear. Another bridge delivers you into Harrison County, where you touch beach at a series of piers before entering the city of **Biloxi** (pronounced locally: Bluxi). Here US 90, called Beach Boulevard, is divided by palms, and the westbound lanes are shaded by great oaks tufted with Spanish Moss.

Storm-Beaten Resort

Biloxi was the second base of operations for the French government of the Louisiana Territory, following Mobile. Founded in 1699 across the Biloxi Bay from its present location, the city sits on a peninsula cut by two bays and the Gulf of Mexico, which provides a brilliant and popular beach.

Beach Boulevard is lined with stately old homes pillared and preserved despite

The windswept Beach Boulevard, Biloxi.

inclement conditions over the years. The most devastating attack launched by nature on Biloxi was Hurricane Camille in 1969, a vicious storm that ruined what had been a posh winter resort. In between the remaining historic structures have grown commercial enterprises: malls, fast-food restaurants, motels, a "teen nite-club," gas stations, a Waffle House, doughnut shop etc. Thus Beach Boulevard eclipses the business district proper, which is slim and concentrated in a two-block open mall quixotically called the **Vieux Marche**. The "Old Market" is most notable for its **Golden Fisherman** sculpture, shimmering with the quiet reflection of its fountain waters and commemorating the annual Shrimp Kings and Queens of Biloxi.

On the shore side of US 90, you can stop for a "po' boy" sandwich of fried oysters or shrimp and watch small boats float by before continuing west on the highway to Biloxi's most historic building: **Beauvoir**. Beauvoir is the Jefferson Davis Shrine, the last home of the Confederate president, now a showcase for many original furnishings and adjacent to a Confederate museum.

Farther west along the highway, you pass through Gulfport, Long Beach and Pass Christian, where piers stretch out into the gulf and the stately homes thin out. The beaches are still fine, and it's recommended you stop while you have the opportunity.

Soon, US 90 curves sharply away from the coast and crosses the St. Louis Bay, where a bridge terminates in **Bay St. Louis,** "Gateway to the Gulf Coast." With little warning, the road forks; State 609 takes the northwestern way toward I-10 and a National Aeronautics and Space Administration (NASA) test site; US 90 slides southwestward. Both bring you shortly to Louisiana and **Lake Pontchartrain.**

In the late afternoon, the skies over Lake Pontchartrain are gauzy and wide. Eight miles (13 km) of bridges form I-10 from shore to shore—from St. Tammany "Parish" (as counties are called in Louisiana) into Orleans Parish. As you cross you feel you're dipping and climbing through the water itself. Suddenly, New Orleans rises from the opposite shore. As you bob on a series of overpasses, downtown appears intermittently as an arc of skyscrapers amid a green lake of oak.

The Golden Fisherman throws his net at the "Old Market."

NEW ORLEANS: INTERNATIONAL GUMBO

A Seduction

Anchor of the Gulf Coast, "cradle of Jazz," tourist mecca, Mardi Gras capital, first defense of the Mississippi River: **New Orleans** is the most multifaceted city in the South.

New Orleans is a rich tapestry, deep and expansive yet well-defined by its watery borders. The humid, bayou-bound lands which surround New Orleans have been home to great colonial governments, great writers and musicians and great scoundrels since the city's founding in 1718 by the Sieurs d'Iberville and de Bienville.

New Orleans is most densely populated in the winter Carnival season. Average winter high temperature is a cool 67°F (19°C); in summer it's 91°F (33°C). Daily low temperatures average 20°F (11°C) below the highs. Aside from allowances for adequate accommodations and physical comfort, any time of year is good to visit New Orleans. Elegant, raw and seductive, it's one of America's most interesting and satisfying cities.

Cultural Blends

After Mobile and Biloxi, New Orleans was the last, and greatest, of all French territorial capitals in North America. Less than 50 years after its founding, the city that was etched out of swampland and barricaded against the mighty Mississippi River passed into the hands of the Spanish. From 1762 until 1803, when the United States acquired the vast Louisiana Territory, New Orleans developed a mixed-blood "Creole" aristocracy, in purest form a commingling of French and Spanish parentage, whose legitimate and semi-legitimate offspring were often partially black. "Creole" eventually came to mean "free persons of color."

Under Spanish rule, the city was a refuge and headquarters for French counterrevolutionaries and mercenaries of all nationalities. Along with Galveston, Texas, New Orleans served as a base of operations for the notorious pirate Jean Lafitte, who proved an ally of the United States during the War of 1812 with Britain.

New Orleans has never lost its sense of tradition nor its multicultural roots. Catholic Creole continentalism, American aggressiveness, African mystique and waterfront illicitness remain the woof and warp of this colorful city, which boasts America's most famous carnival: Mardi Gras. Since 1857, Mardi Gras has been the unbridled expression of New Orleans' spirit; at the private balls, in the wild parades, behind masks and under the glitter of costume jewelry, native and visitor join together to celebrate. With the advent of Lent, it's back to business as usual, which, at least in the French Quarter, is simply a muted version of same.

The Vieux Carré

The first stop for most everyone who comes to New Orleans is the **Vieux Carré** ("Old Square"), otherwise known as the **French Quarter**. The Vieux Carré rests on the Mississippi River between what are now Canal Street and Esplanade Avenue.

The seductive architecture of the Vieux Carré is a dense melange of brick, stucco and ironwork. Balconies are adorned with ferns and Mardi Gras beads.

The charming play of light and color that once incited Mark Twain's rapture has continued to make the most of time, like wine, or matronly grace. It does indeed strike the wide-eyed observer that these buildings, their exquisite harmony and display, only fit in this haunting locale. Only one building has survived the city's many changes—the **Ursuline Convent** (1750) at 1114 Chartres Street—but each of the French Quarter's streets has seen three names: French, Spanish and English. All are marked thus, with French and English names on the street signs and the Spanish names on tiles in streetcorner facades.

The heart of the French Quarter is artist-inhabited **Jackson Square**, the true "old square" fronted by the renowned **St. Louis Cathedral** (1794) and the **Pontalba Buildings**. Dating from 1849, the Pontalba Buildings are considered the oldest apartment buildings in the United States. Behind the 18th-

Young band member beats out a rhythm in the "cradle of jazz."

century cathedral on Pirate's Alley is the **Faulkner House.** Constructed in 1840 on the grounds of a former French colonial prison, this unassuming home is where William Faulkner wrote his first novel, *Soldiers Pay.*

By day and especially by night, the French Quarter is the culmination and expression of the Gulf heat. The sounds of jazz and Dixieland pop resound through the streets where they were invented—streets packed with clubs, restaurants, bars and glittery trinket shops. It is here that you find the most intense concentration of eateries serving Cajun, Creole and French cuisines. New Orleans' Vieux Carré has become a focus of the Gulf Coast cuisine which became an urban trend in the early 1980s, especially on the east and west coasts.

Round the Clock Circus

The main drag (in every sense) of the French Quarter is **Bourbon Street,** a pedestrian circus at all hours and in every season. Bourbon Street is San Francis-co's Broadway set in New York's West Village, a somehow elegant melange of T-shirt shops, sidewalk cafes, topless bars, cheap gift stores, a wax museum, glittery hotels, restaurants chintzy to chic, croissant cafes and cookie shops.

One block toward the Mississippi River and parallel to Bourbon runs **Royal Street,** the commercial center of the district. Royal is dominated by galleries and antique shops that are unable to suppress more pedestrian, if not always inferior, wares. The fare ranges from the sublime to schlock. Royal Street is practically an open-air mall.

The feel of Royal Street, tempered by its fascinating architecture, comes through in stronger form on **Decatur Street** along the riverfront where the old French Market has become a featureless shopping center. Barely a block away is the **Jackson Brewery,** New Orleans' answer to the specialty-shops-in-a-waterfront-structure motif. Like Faneuil Hall in Boston and Ghirardelli Square in San Francisco before it, Jackson Brewery has assumed an anonymity in the refurbishing that was to restore its character.

The Mississippi River means steamboats, here the "Natchez."

204

Miraculously, a few establishments have retained their character despite attention lavished by tourist guides. **The Old Absinthe House**, home of the "Absinthe Frappe," is one such outpost on Bourbon and Bienville Streets. A strictly local place by day, this survivor from 1826 boasts that "Thru these portals, pass the most beautiful women, in the world." Helmets and jerseys of pro football legends abound, the former hung on chains from the ceiling, the latter tacked to the beams. Colored beads and bras are draped from the chandeliers, old napkins and business cards yellow on the walls, and a pirate flag hangs over the octagonal bar. The tenacious conservatism of the Old Absinthe House is emblematic of an underlying resistance within the Vieux Carré to a seemingly unstoppable commercial whitewash.

Canadian Cajuns, Caribbeans and fringe Americans came to blend cultures, jazz has been the definitive sound since the early 20th Century. New Orleans' jazz found its apotheosis in Louis "Satchmo" Armstrong composer, singer and the most renowned trumpet player in the history of jazz music.

The blues are also commonly heard from the stages and the back alleys of the city. Late, great blues pianist Professor Longhair was for years the focus of the Gulf's particular strain of exhuberant melancholy.

Although the purest forms of jazz today are heard in venues such as **Preservation Hall**, a dilapidated wood and concrete structure with a basement-like interior, many cafes and restaurants have house bands that entertain as you delve into the menu fare.

Spanish ironwork on the balconies of St. Ann Street, French Quarter.

**Things We Do,
Eat and Drink**

In the hothouse where Spanish-French Creoles, Afro-Americans, French-

The brick-and-wood restaurants devoted to Creole and Cajun cuisine are everywhere in the Vieux Carré. The old standbys are po' boys, Creole gumbo, jambalaya and red beans and rice. A po' boy is, in the restricted definition, a sandwich of fried seafood on French

bread. Ideally, po' boy oysters will be light, dry and subtly textured. Gumbo is a muddy, peppery broth of crabmeat, shrimp, sausage, chicken and vegetables—the spicier the better. Jambalaya is a sticky rice dish with shrimp, sausage and chicken. Red beans and rice is self-descriptive, although it's sometimes dashed with green onions. All of the above are enhanced by a touch of Louisiana hot sauce, "the perfect hot sauce"—"One Drop Does It!"

Best with Creole food is a cold draught of Dixie beer, New Orleans' own brew. The definitive local liquor drinks are Sazerac and Ramos Gin Fizz. The chicory coffee here is also notable, and the home of that rich blend is the **Café du Monde** in the French Market at Decatur and St. Ann Streets. This sidewalk cafe also serves the sweet local speciality, *beignets*: squarish doughnut-like pastries heaped with powdered sugar.

The Greater Contour

Outside the Vieux Carré, New Orleans layers more of the Old South and New on a diminishing Continental contour. Elysian Fields Avenue, downstream from the French Quarter, is hardly the Champs Elysées, but then again, Decatur Street isn't the Boulevard St. Germain either.

The closest approximation of a Parisian *place* is **Lee Circle,** to which the St. Charles Streetcar rickets and groans from the intersection of Canal and Carondelet Streets. The St. Charles line is the last of the streetcar lines in New Orleans, which once included "Desire," made famous by playwright Tennessee Williams. The Desire line terminated in the district of the same name, an impoverished and desperate development.

Upstream from Canal is the business district, a closely-knit, big-city financial center smothering the old infrastructure. At St. Charles Avenue and Poydras Street rises **1 Shell Square**, a towering memento to the oil industry dominating the skyline. Near the financial district sits the **Louisiana Superdome**, a 170-foot (52-meter) high enclosed stadium, the largest of its kind in the world. The Superdome, which resem-

Bejeweled face at Mardi Gras, left. Right, a streetcar named St. Charles.

bles a toppled yo-yo, is home to New Orleans Saints professional football.

The St. Charles Streetcar wends its way through New Orleans' **Garden District**—a lush, placid and wealthy neighborhood where many grand antebellum houses stand proud. Stretching upstream from Jackson Avenue and riverward from St. Charles, the Garden District is rife with oak, azalea, palm and dogwood. Great baroque oaks shade and obscure the marvelous structures in Greek Revival, Renaissance and Victorian styles.

World's Longest Bridge

To the north of the city lies the vast Lake Pontchartrain, over which spans the amazing **Lake Pontchartrain Causeway**, "the world's longest bridge." The Causeway is a 24-mile (39-km) double stripe of highway propped above the surface of the lake. For miles, there is nothing to be seen on the horizon, and the camelback plunge into the void is akin to crossing the barren but subtle plains of Texas.

On the trip north over the causeway

The awesome spanse of the Lake Pontchartrain Causeway.

New Orleans: International Gumbo

to **Mandeville**, land first appears as a thin blue sliver on the horizon, an airy gray-blue strip melting off the murky waters into the sky. Gradually, the land becomes more distinct, broader and deeper in color until it becomes the interface of two great azure bodies: sea and sky. Returning, you will first see New Orleans as two large slabs anchoring the causeway. Then, to the east, the crescent of downtown rises like an island emerging from the lake, seemingly floating—as it very nearly does. New Orleans is built over a great water table, an underground lake that perpetually threatens to suck down the city's thoroughfares.

If you choose to cross the Lake Pontchartrain Causeway, it might be best to do so on your way out of the city and into the next leg of the grand tour. A round-trip across the lake may prove a bit overwhelming, and concentration tends to falter on the second stretch.

The Causeway touches land in Mandeville, where it becomes US 190. Four miles (six km) north of the lakeshore it interchanges with US 12, which runs 36 miles (58 km) west to the capital of Louisiana, Baton Rouge.

A Total Experience

Like San Francisco, New Orleans is a dream city where local reality and touristic fantasy interact uneasily. Both cities have grown—on money imported by business and tourism—into total environments, glitzing up natural resources and quaint antiquities to attract the conventioneers and vacationers who brace the economy.

Necessary to the appeal is a predictability that is alien to the indigenous cultures that started the whole thing. By edging out the unattractive elements and packaging tradition in a non-biodegradable wrapper, the great tourist destinations of America ossify culture in order to market it.

But New Orleans remains a great creative center because the frayed edges show and its inhabitants have the character to preserve tradition in a way that can never be formulated or controlled. Socially divided and politically arcane, New Orleans eludes native and tourist alike.

ACADIANA'S BAYOUS

As you follow the efficient I-10 out of New Orleans, you cut through the boggy, baroque bayou country on the southwest bank of Lake Pontchartrain in St. Charles and St. John the Baptist Parishes. The highway is stilted out of grass-fringed still water where the thin trunks that disappear into the mire mimic, when bare, the somber poles that hoist powerlines along I-10.

Bayous—narrow, sluggish rivers usually surrounded by wetlands—run in veins throughout southern Louisiana, or Acadiana. This expansive region of bayou country is named after the Acadians, Catholic French pilgrims driven out of Nova Scotia by the British in the late 18th Century. The Acadians settled the Louisiana lowlands, mostly Spanish dominion, where they were joined by Frenchmen fleeing the Republic.

The culture that arose in bayou country was called "Cajun" (a corruption of "Acadian"). In pure and intermixed forms, Cajun-French is still the backbone of this primarily rural area. Acadiana, stretching along the Gulf Coast to Texas and west from the Mississippi up to Avoyelles Parish, has been described as "South of the South," and, according to one promotion, its "Mediterranean-African roots and plantation past make it and New Orleans more akin to the societies of the French and Spanish West Indies than the American South."

I-10 meets the Mississippi River at the city of **Baton Rouge**, capital of Louisiana and the state's major port. The origins of the city's name, which is French for "red stick," are in dispute; however, it is generally agreed that the "stick" was a tree, red either from the blood of animals hung there by Indians or from the stripping of its bark. In the latter case, the tree may have been used to mark the boundary of Houma and Bayou Goula Indian land.

Although Baton Rouge abuts Acadiana, it has little to do with it, except in governing it and shipping its oil. The ambience is definitely "southern," and you'll notice, in comparison to New Orleans, a deepening of accent and of provincial ways. The rather quiet, laid-back tempo of the streets belies the intense industry and politicking which are at the city's foundation.

Sights to be seen in Baton Rouge are the old and new trappings of government. The **Old Capitol** building is a whimsical Gothic castle constructed in Spanish style (in 1849) on the edge of the Mississippi. The old governor's mansion stands in clean, neo-classical opposition; the mansion and the sky-scraping, art-deco, **New Capitol** (built in 1932 and resembling a small Empire State Building) were both erected during the regime of the legendary Huey Long, who reigned supreme over Louisiana through the Great Depression.

By all accounts a distasteful and corrupt man, Long nevertheless was an enlightened despot. He brooked no opposition in his semi-socialistic rule for the "common man." Highways, schools and hospitals were built; the unemployed put to work; the privileged

Left, Cajun woman on the bayous. Right, a natural gas rig, Atchafalaya Swamp.

heavily taxed. Gunned down in the state capitol in 1935 by a relative of a political foe, Long has been fondly remembered in the state he brought to maturity.

While huge sums of money are controlled from the State Capitol Complex, the city of Baton Rouge found its wealth in its port and petrochemical industries. The port, fourth most active in the nation, is the farthest inland of all deepwater ports serving the Gulf of Mexico, Baton Rouge is also at the heart of a massive energy industry that dominates southern Louisiana. To the outsider, Baton Rouge is largely impenetrable and culturally poor. But it's worth a stop to savor the Mississippi River breeze which cuts the unusually balmy air.

Back on I-10 west, you leave the Mississippi River behind and re-enter Acadiana at West Baton Rouge Parish. Entering Iberville Parish, you pass through Grosse Tete ("big head"), cross Bayou Maringouin and the curvaceous Bayou des Glaises before entering St. Martin's Parish at Whisky Bay. The sprawling swamplands around the Atchafalaya River, Lake Pelba, Lake Bigeux and Henderson Swamp are a fisherman's paradise, and the spectacle of mid-lake groves, tiny islands and waterlocked platforms is magical.

At exit 109, where State 328 leads to Breau Bridge, the grand tour deviates sharply from the comfortable but superficial freeway. There is some tough going ahead, so you might want to skip the adventure and stay on I-10. If so, join the tour again in Houston.

Petit Paris

If you're hungry and particularly interested in a taste of Cajun food and music, follow State 328 south of the interchange with I-10 to State 94 for a stop at **Mulate's Restaurant**, the "most authentic Cajun restaurant in Louisiana," and, according to locals, the best. Otherwise, or additionally, continue on State 328 to State 31, which becomes Main Street through quiet Breau Bridge. From there, it's 11 miles (18 km) to **St. Martinville** on Bayou Teche.

Energy and enterprise in Baton Rouge.

St. Martinville is one of the most unspoiled towns you will find in your travels in America. A former indigo plantation and Spanish holding, St. Martinville was populated by Acadians and Frenchmen in the late 18th and 19th centuries. The **St. Martin de Tours Catholic Church** was erected in 1765.

In the late 18th and early 19th centuries, the culture of St. Martinville was extremely rich; its inhabitants nicknamed it "Petit Paris." After its transformation to a minor port on the bayou, St. Martinville settled into its current form of small agrarian center, with visible Cajun and French roots. Locals are glad to recite half-remembered and half-invented histories in small cafes, which might serve Coca-Cola and catfish etouffe. The town is thoroughly infused with the legend of Evangeline (subject of a well-known Henry Wadsworth Longfellow poem), who allegedly walked from Nova Scotia to St. Martinville in search of her lover. The **Longfellow-Evangeline State Commemorative Area** preserves Acadian history

Unspoiled elegance in St. Martinville.

in the Acadian House Museum.

Out of St. Martinville south on State 31, you find your way to State 675, which plows through an only half-modernized rural area. Spanish moss begins to reappear on oaks, lending them a weepy feel. A sign by the side of the road reads: "Pigs for Sale."

State 675 tails out at State 14, which takes you west into Vermilion Parish and the parish seat, **Abbeville.** Abbeville is the site of the Louisiana Cattle Festival in October and the French Market Festival in August. It is an attractive town radiating from its original town square, which is an important crossroads and of immediate importance to the grand tour. At the town square, you have a choice of itineraries; the most comfortable tack is to continue on State 14 to Lake Charles, where I-210 swiftly returns to tried and true I-10. More adventurous travelers will turn south onto State 82 west, which runs down to the Gulf Coast on the least beaten but still paved paths.

All along State 82, the distinction

between land and water is hazy, although grazing cattle indicate solid ground. The closer you get to the gulf waters, the more you will see trees bent at an ever more acute angle. Whole groves bow to the winds which whip off the water. Wide bands of water line the shoulders of State 82 near **Intercoastal City**, marked by cattails and crossroads named "P-7-26" or "P-6-48" etc.

Intercoastal City anticipates the highway's leap over the **Intercoastal Waterway**, a mind-boggling canal that spans almost the entire length of the state. You pass the atypical Little Prairie, which is exactly that. Greens modulate brilliantly over the landscape. Through Pecan Grove and past the Rockefeller Wildlife Refuge, Vermilion cedes to Cameron Parish, but the sights are undifferentiated: little cemeteries, great oaks, huge insect-like vehicles, lodges, diners, gas stations and bogs. Under White Lake, the bogs assume a purple tint while black birds appear with greater frequency on the road, swooping from shoulder to shoulder and tempting disaster.

Grand Chenier announces its presence with a red, white and blue tower, followed by invitations to stop and "Have a Coke!" and then a few satellite dishes, churches, a sign noting "Ducks picked here," the forlorn elementary school and the great rolling reaches of Upper and Lower Mud Lake.

Then the hints of Cameron Parish today: first, in Grand Chenier, a small gas processing plant. Then, toward Oak Grove, a mysterious cluster of buildings labeled "Mobil." Out past Oak Grove, through Creole and Cameron to the eastern edge of Calcasieu Lake, other familiar names spring up by the roadway: Kerr-McGee, Transco Exploration Company.

Great triangular drills and exploration vessels hover over the inlet of the lake, where State 82 becomes a free ferry to the other side. Across the lake, a huge fence of poles stringing power lines speaks for the energy industry booming in the removed bayou country of Louisiana.

The Bayous are a way of life for, left, a graceful wading egret, and right, a couple fishing in Atchafalaya Swamp.

CAJUN CUISINE

Cajun cooking is hot. Of all the regional American styles of cooking to come to prominence in the food-conscious 1980s, none has been so enthusiastically received as the Cajun style. And with good reason, for the mouth-watering peppery concoctions of Cajun cooking are a welcome change from the bland fare served up at too many American restaurants. Cajun cooking is not afraid to offend; it wants to invigorate even the laziest palate.

The Cajuns originated in southern France and emigrated to Nova Scotia where they founded the colony of Acadia in the 1600s. There they lived until the British drove them out in the mid-1700s. The majority of the Acadians migrated to Louisiana, where they found a climate extremely well-suited to their traditional occupations of farming and fishing.

Cajun cooking has its roots in French cuisine, and continues to util-

ize many of the techniques of French cooking such as the preparation of various styles of roux (an oil and flour mixture which forms the base for several Cajun sauces), and pan-sautéing.

It is not all surprising that Louisiana should be the home of one of America's most innovative styles of cooking, for it is an area of extraordinary natural bounty. The subtropical climate is said to produce vegetables which are just a tad sweeter than those grown in rougher climes to the north. Creole tomatoes are lower in acid than their northern cousins and have a richer flavor. Okra and mirliton (a green pear-shaped vegetable often served deep-fried) are two of the more exotic vegetables often used in Cajun cooking. Most important are the peppers (Tabasco, cayenne, and bird's-eye to name but three) which have become the staple of Cajun seasoning.

Of course, the peppers are added to increase the "heat" of the dish, but it is a mistake to think that Cajun chefs are sadistically inclined to torture one's palate. Many of the peppers are sweeter than they are hot, and the idea is to combine them in a way which lights up rather than burns the tongue. More scientifically inclined analysts of the Cajun style will suggest that the peppers cause the mouth to water, thereby rinsing the palate clean in preparation for the reception of the next mouthful of food. In this way, they claim, one is actually able to better taste the food throughout the meal.

The greatest gift of nature to the Cajun chef in Louisiana is the extraordinary variety of fish and shellfish which teem in the brackish waters of the Bayou. Particularly interesting Cajun seafood dishes include *Cajun Popcorn* in which fresh crawfish are boiled in a spicy oil and served as an afternoon snack; the *Blackened Redfish,* perhaps the most renowned single Cajun dish, in which a filet of redfish is coated with a tangy mixture of peppers, thyme, oregano and garlic, dipped in butter, and then seared in an extraordinarily hot cast-iron skillet; and *Shrimp Etouffée,* a tangy combo prepared from roux, onions, celery and bell peppers.

EAST TEXAS: PORT, RESORT, CAPITAL

Few people who haven't been to, say, Idaho have a clear image of the state. But everyone has at least some picture of Texas. Tumbleweeds and cacti, oilfields, cowboy millionaires, humming border towns, cattle ranches: popular culture has disseminated a rugged, romantic vision of the largest coterminous state. The worldwide popularity of the television program *Dallas* is the latest manifestation of the fascination with this perpetual "boom" state.

But the familiar cultural snapshots both over and underestimate the sprawling diversity and vitality of Texas. This *is* where the West begins, but it is a West with no coherent definition. Risking simplicity, one can think of a passage through Texas as a microcosmic passage from East to West, with the turning point at San Antonio, the westernmost of Texas' great cities.

Within the compact urban triangle of Houston, Dallas-Fort Worth and San Antonio is centered the state's vast wealth and power. From Galveston through Houston to Austin, the grand tour arcs through the heart of East Texas—its resort, its port and the state capital.

Along the Gulf

Assuming you have followed the grand tour, you find yourself speeding over the first expanse of the incomprehensible stretch that is Texas on either I-10 west to Houston or State 82 west into Port Arthur. Those on I-10 should return to the Galveston tour, which immediately follows.

On State 82 into Port Arthur, you should interchange with State 87 south to Galveston. State 87 follows a line of extinct fortification installed to protect the Confederate shores of Texas against Federal invasion during the Civil War. The fort sites are marked by roadside historical markers which detail the action at that site.

For example, the marker at what was once Fort Manhasset notes the bravery of Dick Dowling and his 40-odd men in

All duded up at the Wichita Falls Rodeo.

214

repelling 22 Federal ships and gunboats at Sabine Pass. Removed to sea as a blockade, the Federal armada met an even more terrifying foe in the gulf storms that continue to ravage the coast. For two years in the early 1980s, State 87 was little more than a muddy slough after it was destroyed by a vicious squall. The road is open once again, and is almost always entirely passable.

State 87 cuts through the contradictions extending past the Louisiana border. Oil refineries abut wildlife reserves; outside Sabine Pass, great plains roll north of the highway, while The Gulf of Mexico roars ten yards (nine meters) to the south. The lonely waters attract large insects which pelt your windshield as you pass the "Breeze In Again Stop," which advertises:

STOP!
JUNK FOOD
TIRES.

You'll pass through tiny towns, such as **Crystal Beach** (pop. 776) where land developments are built for sale or rent.

Canal City, Pelican Points, Driftwood and Whispering Pines are such developments around **Gilchrist**. You can stop and fish from a pier. The sun seems to have got brighter and bigger; you smell resort in the air. Finally, 66 miles (106 km) southwest of Sabine Pass, the road ends at Port Bolivar, where you drive onto the platform that ferries you to **Galveston**.

Have You Ever Seen a Beach Before?

Galveston initially impresses with an air of southern California as you roll down Ferry Road (2nd Street) to Seawall Boulevard. The spacious streets, salmon coloration and regal palms have a West Coast feel that extends up Broadway (Avenue J) past Avenues O 1/2 and N 1/2. But farther downtown, the Victorian/neo-Classical aspect brings you back to the South; and along Seawall Boulevard, the feel is more Gulf Coast than Long Beach.

Galveston was a noted Texas seaport in the early 19th Century, but it flowered into a full-fledged and wealthy city in the local economic boom following

Sunset over the Gulf Coast waters.

the Civil War. Galveston became Texas' leading manufacturing center and, by 1899, the largest cotton port in the world. The great commercial houses of maritime and manufacturing firms along The Strand made that street "The Wall Street of the Southwest." Galveston had the first telephone system in Texas as well as the first newspaper, electric lights, golf course, brewery and Ford dealership. Galveston was also distinguished as the headquarters of pirate Jean Lafitte, whose name is also exploited in New Orleans, his other major base of operations.

Still an active shipping center, Galveston has become more involved with the resort industry, primarily for Houstonians, whose port has entirely overshadowed the island's. Galveston boasts 32 miles (51 km) of beach, the most popular stretch of which lies along Seawall Boulevard on the Gulf side of the island. The sands are somewhat grayish and the waters not as temperate as the southern Gulf Coast beaches, but the sand might as well be gold to those vacationing from Houston. Remarks one Galvestonian, "You'd think they'd never seen a beach before."

Old Wealth

Galveston's acclaimed **East End Historical District**, bounded roughly by Broadway, Mechanic Street, 19th Street and 11th Street, is where the Victorian homes stand, intermixed with a few pueblo-style buildings. The district layers neo-Classical, Renaissance and Italianate influences on the general Victorian style. Bungalows rest in the shade thrown by oleanders, oaks, maples and palms and are slightly raised from the ground out of respect for the gulf. A walk in this district, especially down Post Office and Church Streets, gives a glimpse of how the first rich Texans displayed their wealth. You'll have plenty of opportunities to see how the "nouveau riche" Texans do that in Houston.

Downtown, **The Strand** has undergone the familiar renovation-into-tourist-attraction, with the requisite galleries, cute shops and art-deco restaurants. The chamber of commerce is pleased, but not everyone else is. A

Ashton Villa, grand document of historic Galveston.

disgruntled employee in a tourist-oriented establishment claims that "the people who live in Galveston can't enjoy it." Further, "there's nothing for someone my age (early 20s) to do."

Renovation projects at least serve to preserve a few marvelous structures on The Strand and elsewhere. But a truer Galveston rises in the form of the **American National Insurance Company** eyesore at 19th Street between Mechanic and Market. This building is the legacy of William Lewis Moody, Jr., the company's founder and the founder of Galveston's City National Bank and many, many other enterprises in the early 20th Century. The **City National Bank** building (1921) on Market Street is, in contrast to the American National fiasco, a highly stylized, Latinate granite building now housing the Galveston County Historical Museum.

If you are interested in the antebellum ways of Galveston, stop to at least look at the **Ashton Villa**, Broadway at Tremont, on your way out of town. The 1859 Italianate structure in wood and iron is certainly one of the most beautiful buildings in Galveston,

and it will give you one last glimpse of the old before you continue northwest on Broadway and I-45 north to crowded, competitive Houston.

Houston: Space-Age City

It hasn't taken **Houston** long to become the fourth largest city in America. And tens upon tens of thousands of new residents storm the imaginary city limit each year—imaginary because Houston has long since pushed past its designated boundary, throwing up slabs of office complexes to all sides without rhyme or reason.

Houston is the definitive space-age city. It isn't that it's any more "modern" than New York, Los Angeles or Chicago, the only three American cities now larger. But even more than Los Angeles, Houston has taken its scant history as a blast-off point of no return. Growth is unbridled, boundaries unheeded, and the vast unexplored expanses of progress and money are the city's fixations.

The quintessential testament to Houston's ever-present frontierism is

Unflagging courage and hope; the figurehead of the preserved "Elissa."

the **Lyndon B. Johnson Space Center**, Earth-central for the spaceshot that landed the first man on the moon. You might well start here and then work your way into the depths of Houston proper. Johnson Space Center lies on NASA Road 1 off I-45 approximately 25 miles (40 km) south of Houston, that is, approximately 28 miles (45 km) north of Galveston. Moonrocks and spacecraft are on display, as are full-scale Space Shuttle trainers and the Mission Control Center you all, of course, remember from television.

When you pilot your ship along I-45 straight into downtown Houston, your first stop should be the companion piece to the L.B.J. Space Center: **Tranquility Park.** Named in reference to the July, 1969 Apollo moonshot, the park (at Bagby and Walker Streets) is a two-square-block landscaped monument to the United States' space program. Craters and mounds encircle the focal point of the park: five golden phalli cascading water in the image of takeoff. Relative to the downtown district surrounding the park, it is indeed tranquil. But its ultimate effect is to suggest a sense of Houston's takeoff

from the lazy Buffalo Bayou where it was established in 1836.

Other Tranquilities

Two blocks southwest from Tranquility Park, on the corner of Bagby and Lamar Street, is the entrance to **Sam Houston Park,** named, like the city, after the hero of the Texas Revolution. The park follows the bayou under the grumbling highways and interchanges which bound downtown Houston. On the downtown side are located a handful of historic buildings from Houston's barely remembered past. Here, Old Houston finds its small refuge from the skyscraping slivers jammed together within easy earshot and all that they represent. The park stretches out on the other side of the freeways, and here the deafening drone of crickets along the sandy banks of the Buffalo Bayou very nearly drowns out the blasts of traffic.

More deserving of the name "Tranquility" than the downtown park is the hushed **Rothko Chapel** in the **Museum District** at the southwest corner of the city. Set in a residential outpost at

Modern Tranquility Park.

218

Yupon and Sul Ross Streets, the chapel was created by American abstract-impressionist Mark Rothko as a place of nondenominational worship and meditation. Outside rises sculptor Barnett Newman's *Broken Obelisk*, dedicated to Dr. Martin Luther King, Jr. The obelisk is disturbingly moving yet reflective.

The unimposing brick octagon of the chapel houses 14 large Rothko canvases, five in solitary and nine in "triptychs." The source of light is a lone octagonal skylight centered with a black disc and surrounded by a tent-like duct. Four benches stand midway between the four long edges of the room and its center point, where a lone black mat props a small black cushion. The Rothkos are all textured pieces in black and blue with undertints of red. Holy books of many creeds are available to you, from Lao Tzu's *Tao Te Ching* to the *Holy Qur'an*, for your escape from the secular city.

A Wealth of Art and Worship

Houston's wealth, which has diversi-

fied from oil since the energy crises of the 1970s and 80s, has brought a wealth of art to the city. **The Museum of Fine Arts**, located at Main and Bissonet Streets a few minutes by car from the chapel, houses one of the finest and most diverse collections in any major city south or west of Philadelphia. The Matisse bronzes which turn their distinct backs to you as you enter the filtered light of the museum make their statement about Houston's attitude toward convention. But not the museum's attitude toward canonized art. The collection is strong in American painting, especially Remington, and the post-Impressionist period. (Van Gogh and his followers. Picasso and Braque, Rousseau, Kandinsky, the Pointillists, Kirchner, Cezanne, Gaugin, Miro and Gris are all here.) But the selections of pre-Columbian, Oceanic and Oriental arts are all superb, and the museum continues to experiment. Diversity is done tastefully here, with no chip on the shoulder.

Across the street is the corrugated **Contemporary Arts Museum**, dedicated since 1948 to current works and more

A striking contrast; Sam Houston Park hints at the past.

emblematic of Houston. Also nearby, at the entry to the recreational **Hermann Park**, is the hands-on **Museum of Natural Science**. The area is also rife with galleries and, interestingly enough, the worshiping places of Presbyterians, Methodists, Unitarians, Christian Scientists and Freemasons. The marvelous **Masonic Lodge** on Montrose a few blocks north of the Contemporary Arts Museum is the home of the oldest Freemason's order in Texas.

All the various forms of worship that are given reign in the Museum District represent a flip side to the gung ho capitalism rampant in the central areas of Houston. They represent a part of the city's cultural wealth that puts its material life in a clearer light.

What Riches They Are

Houston has not forgotten that it is part of Texas, although it's busily importing cosmopolitan flair. One still sees the patented ten-gallon hat and cowboy boots, even in the middle of downtown. Fashion that would be *faux-pas* material in the New York business world—for example, short sleeves and a tie—is all taken in stride in Houston.

Clubs and restaurants take loud, cow-poking fun in stride, and some make an attraction of it. The best-known bar in the greater Houston area is certainly **Gilley's Club** in Pasadena, run by Mickey Gilley, a country-and-western recording artist and cousin of Jerry Lee Lewis. Gilley's features big-name country music entertainment every Friday and Saturday, with Roger Miller, Conway Twitty and Tom T. Hall among the regulars. There's a live rodeo in Gilley's "arena" every Saturday, but on off-nights you can whip up a little dust of your own on the mechanical bull or on the dance floor.

Eating Tex-Mex

Along with nouveau-riche sophistication, Houston has imported outland cuisines, from Ethiopian to Polynesian; but the staple is still American—*i.e.* steak. And of course you'll find plenty of old-country Mexican cuisine that puts the so-called Mexican food found in cuisine-capitals New York and San Francisco to shame. Between Texan-

Texan holds onto his hat for a gander at a Houston skyscraper, left. Right, Mission Control, Johnson Space Center.

American and Mexican chow is Tex-Mex, a hybrid based on chili and steak, heavy on the peppers.

Another emblem of Houston's grandiose appreciation for what money can buy is the unbelievable **Astrodomain**, comprised of the Astrodome ("Eighth Wonder of the World" and enclosed-stadium home to Houston Oilers football and Houston Astros baseball), Astroworld (a 100-ride amusement park with what is reputed to be the best roller coaster in America), Astrohall (the world's largest one-level convention and exhibit facility), Astroarena show hall and Astro-Village shopping center. There are shopping centers all over Houston, serving as the foci of the scatter of neighborhoods and city centers. On sale are all the fabulously over-priced goods that new wealth adopts to show itself off.

Getting around from one skyline to another is fairly easy if you've got a good map; the freeway system, though tangled, is remarkably civilized and efficient. In fact, you may start to believe the city is actually smaller and more manageable than it really is—an unpleasant realization if you try to walk out of a neighborhood. Especially amazing after driving through the South will be the widespread, well-trained use of directional signals, at least on the freeways. At night, the sight of whole banks of flashing lights in a lane-to-lane ballet is almost breathtaking, as is the endless glitter of the skyscrapers that never seem to empty.

Wherever you go, note the triangular yellow signs that, in the South, advise motorists to "DRIVE SAFELY." Here they read: "Drive Friendly." The name "Texas," after all, is derived from "Tejas," a Spanish name given to indigenous Indians. "Tejas" means "friendly."

Ranch Country

Out of Houston off the I-610 bypass, State 290 west brings you quickly to the lush plains and gently rolling hills of the "ranch country" within the Houston-Dallas-San Antonio triangle. The dry purple grasses that surround State 290 in the early going gradually give way to

Urban cowboy rides the bull at Gilley's.

the wooded areas that couch the city of **Austin**, state capital and locale of the largest university campus in Texas.

Through Lee County toward Giddings, the "Drive Friendly" signs fade and the highway continues its twisted leaps from one odd patch of red to the next. Grazing cattle and hay bales usher you into Travis County and the limits of Austin. Austin sits in the middle of an agricultural paradise unique to the many Texan climates and terrains. Sheltered from the humid heat that sweeps in waves over Houston, green Austin and its forested environs are a pleasant ideal for ranching and recreation.

Austin Without Warning

Be prepared for the particularly nasty shunt from US 290 onto I-35/US 280/US 81. You arrive into Austin suddenly and without warning, but the highway goes about its business as if you knew perfectly well where you were going.

Unlike Houston, Austin is fairly well contained, although it's experiencing similarly phenomenal growth. Exit between Martin Luther King, Jr. Boulevard and 8th-3rd Streets from I-35 and you'll be in the middle of a walkable downtown. From First Street and the Colorado River up to 24th Street and the heart of the **University of Texas (UT)** at Austin along Guadalupe Avenue lies the visitor's Austin.

Texas' Cultural Capital

Austin, as one Houstonian said, is "becoming the Silicon Valley of Texas." Still the true cultural capital of the state, a distinction it's held since at least the 1960s when it was a "hippie" mecca, Austin has been drawing more and more high-tech and financial firms within its limits in the 1980s. Along with this mixed blessing comes the young urban professionals, and one need look no farther than 6th Street to see the impact of aggressive consumerism on the culture. Experiencing the same gentrification as San Francisco's Haight Street, formerly gay-dominated 6th Street is still a good place to bar-hop, but not nearly so much a community.

In the words of one local writer, "Obviously, Austin's booming. We know this every time we sit carbound

Stockyard compartments in Texas, left. Right, Dallas Cowboys coach Tom Landry.

222

DALLAS: MODERN BOOM TOWN

A city unique in the United States and in the world, **Dallas** was founded by John Neely Bryan in 1841 overlooking the hapless Trinity River. Bryan, an Indian trader, had somehow got the idea that the Trinity would render Dallas a major port. But the river, as a shipping lane, is a disaster. And Neely's nascent urban phenomenon might eventually have dried to dust in the prairie heat and blown away in a "twister" if not for the clever politicking and palm-greasing that, in the 1870s, landed a crucial railroad crossing close to the center of Dallas.

Perhaps because it never had a "reason" to be—at least, not a geographical one—Dallas has from the start been a place where shrewdness, endurance and survival are particularly valued. Never truly on the frontier, Dallas nevertheless evokes a frontier mentality: practical, absolutist and directed toward the future, its limitless horizon.

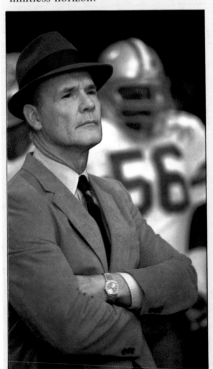

Pragmatic Dallas has little use for the past—indeed, it is almost terrified of it. "Making it" here and now is the collective pursuit, for it means a bigger, better, richer Dallas to come. And "making it" is pure business, a matter of cunning, calculation and efficiency.

The price to be paid is mere adequacy of local aesthetic achievement, although music, theater and art are widely patronized in Dallas. And the numerous visitors, whether conventioneers or tourists, often turn to the arts in a town where sightseeing is minimal. Theater finds its most prominent showcase at the **Dallas Theater Center** designed by Frank Lloyd Wright. The **Music Hall**, situated in State Fair Park (also home of the Cotton Bowl), hosts the Dallas Symphony Orchestra (spring) and the Dallas Civic Opera (fall). The **Dallas Museum of Art** is the major museum in the city.

The most exciting time to be in Dallas is the fall and early winter of each year. This is when "America's Team," the Dallas Cowboys, brings pro football fever back to its glorious pitch. For Dallasites, football is surely man's most sublime activity.

At one time, *Dallas* was the world's most avidly watched and widely disseminated television program. That it had little to do with "physical" Dallas is, at this point, immaterial. **South Fork Ranch** is not in Dallas; it's in Murphy, about 35 miles (56 km) east of the city. There are no large ranches anywhere near Dallas, nor are there (believe it or not) any oil wells. But South Fork is the most visited tourist destination anywhere *near* Dallas, unless you count "D/FW"— the Dallas-Fort Worth Regional Airport.

Authenticity is not what *Dallas* is about—its principal writer had not even been to Dallas before working on the series. But *Dallas* — or rather its centerpiece, "J.R." Ewing — embodies the pragmatic cunning which has made the city the quintessential 20th-century boom town.

[Dallas is located 245 miles (394 km) northwest of Houston on I-45 and 192 miles (309 km) north of Austin on I-35.]

waiting to make the turn we didn't used to have to wait to make. Every time we count the cranes above downtown . . . . Nothing can be done. The city's sold." Indeed, the shadow of the cranes working their way along Congress Avenue, the central north-south thoroughfare that leads to the capitol, is ominous. But one University of Texas student refused gloom: "There are still a lot of individualists here—people who refuse to change and just go their own way."

It would be unwise to underestimate Austin's staying power. At UT, with its 50,000 students, the counter-cultural element will always have its place, if an increasingly smaller one by percentage. The momentum of the local music scene does not look likely to dwindle too soon. And there are the legends that have persisted through worse than progress; for example, **Scholz Garten**. "The most historic restaurant and beer garten in Texas," Scholz Garten was established in 1866, 16 years before work began on the capitol building. Through various ownerships, additions, retractions, rowdies of all ages and storms of legislative dispute, Scholz has preserved

its original front room and unspoiled diversity. You can find good food here with unpretentious charm and heartfelt if stumbling music and dance on occasion. Try the chicken-fried steak, a Texas specialty.

The Lone Star of Texas

Scholz Garten is a few blocks from the **State Capitol** and the lower edges of UT, two major sources of business. The capitol itself is unmistakable; it's a red granite version of the nation's capitol in Washington, D.C. Its white, classical interior is focused on the great rotunda, commemorating the six governments the reigned supreme over Texas (Spain, France, Mexico, the Confederate States, the United States and, most proudly, the Republic of Texas). Above, at the apex of the dome, is the lone star that is the state's emblem: independence, self-determination and singularity.

Portraits of the state's governors ring the rotunda, and to all sides, wings lead to the offices of state legislators. "The Surrender of Santa Anna," a painting at ground level, captures the dramatic moment when Mexico's "Napoleon of the West" surrendered to Sam Houston, "Liberator of Texas" and commander-in-chief of its forces during the Texas Revolution against Mexico. Among the monuments to Texas' glory in that war and in the war between the states is found the quiet sculpture by Bill Bond, "150 Years of Texas," which commemorates Texas' sesquicentennial in 1986.

Despite its changing face, Austin retains much of its spirit. At heart, it's still got long hair and a beard, though it might also have a Mercedes and a kid. Austin is literate in styles and languages ancient and modern literary, legal and logical. It is one of those college towns that many graduates don't leave, and the UT campus is well-integrated into the city.

Austin also rocks, in a variety of forms. Nightclubs are plentiful, and on any given night, especially on weekends, you might have to choose between hard-edged country, "new music," ska, classical, blues, R & B or jazz. There's plenty of theatre and literary events. And good bookstores, record stores with an actual selection, cafes, fern bars and tiffany-glass restaurants intermix with funkier spots.

Left, a hatful of Texas pride. Right, University Tower, Austin.

224

WEST TEXAS

Of all the major cities in Texas, El Paso and San Antonio are the oldest, and the latter the most historic. It was in San Antonio that American Texas was born and nearly slaughtered by the Mexicans at the Alamo. El Paso began as the first Spanish mission in the state.

Stretching between San Antonio and El Paso is **Trans-Peco Texas**, a largely barren yet subtly beautiful, mountainous desert. There is a timeless quality to the landscape that stands in most marked contrast to the booming spectacle of the metropolitan east.

In the anchor cities, Hispanic culture has consistently revitalized itself, much more effectively than in Galveston, Houston or Austin. El Paso and sister city Juarez are bound as a Mexican/American metropolis, the gateway to the American Southwest.

The Alamo Remembered

A pleasant roll through mildly hilly and refreshingly varied plains country from Austin on I-35 south brings you, after approximately 80 miles (130 km), to colorful **San Antonio,** "Cradle of Texas Liberty." San Antonio was the Spanish capital of Texas before Mexico won its independence from Spain in 1821 and opened the territory to settlement by anyone who would develop the land.

After Stephen Austin led the first wave of southerners into the new land, the floodgates were open. Just before Austin's pilgrimage, there were 2,500 persons of European descent in Texas. By 1836, 30,000 Anglos, 5,000 blacks and 4,000 Mexicans populated the domain.

When Spaniards first came in the late 1680s to the San Antonio River valley which cradles modern San Antonio, they found there the Payaya Indians, hunters who supplemented their catches with the fruits of the pecan and mesquite trees and the prickly pear cactus. The Payayas cooperated readily with the Europeans, but the Apaches, who controlled the plains north of San Antonio, took more convincing. The roaming Comanches were always a threat.

Intent on securing their claims in the

area and on taming the heathens, the Spanish established a mission on the west bank of the San Antonio River in 1718. Mission San Antonio de Valero, later known as the **Alamo,** was relocated to the east bank and then closed down in 1793. Mexican troops were transferred to the old mission to protect the pueblo which had grown around the riverbanks. Renamed after *El Alamo* ("The cottonwood"), the Alamo became a crucial fortification.

Deathless Heroes

The dubious glory of the converted mission arises from an ill-conceived standoff with the forces of Mexican president General Antonio Lopez de Santa Ana in 1836. Mexico's 5,000 troops were met by 187 (or 186, depending on who you ask) American martyrs-to-be. In the words of memorializer Frank J. Davis, "All dead within one sanguinary hour; yet the heroes of the Alamo are deathless." "Remember the Alamo!" became the battle cry of Texans in the Texas Revolution that culminated in independence and the Republic of Texas in 1836.

Ever since, the Alamo and San Antonio have been tourist destinations. The plaque at city hall on **Plaza de Armas**, the site of Spain's Presidio de Bexar (located there in 1722), notes that in the Republic of Texas era (1836-45) the grounds had already become a busy market teeming with "noisy vendors of vegetables, fresh eggs, chili peppers and live chickens. Strolling guitarists, tourists and girls selling songbirds mingled with pickpockets . . . ."

Tourists still come to the site where subsequently a stone courthouse (known as the **Bat Cave**) and the current city hall were erected. The old market is still around, moved to **Market Square** and refurbished into a mall with a row of outdoor restaurants and shops, **El Mercato** (an enclosed trinket emporium) and the **Farmers Market**. It's still very popular.

But **Grand Central Tourist Station** is the Alamo. The plaque on its front door requests that you "Be quiet friend, here heroes died to blaze a trail for other men." The request is roundly ignored. The path to the pockmarked and grafitti-etched **Alamo Shrine** is well-beaten, and, friend, it's not quiet.

Because the taking of photographs in the shrine, originally the mission's chapel, is prohibited, most visitors raise their brief squall then retire to the lovely park shaded by everything from myrtles to the mescal bean tree, and then on to the gift shop. On sale are such reverent mementos as Alamo mugs, belts, patches, playing cards, pencils, plaques, postcards, dishware, license-plate frames, keychains, banners, bells, pins, coasters, caps, tote-bags and erasers. Plus, of course, Davy Crockett caps. Hillsman Crockett was one of the Alamo's 187–or 186–casualties.

It's an odd mixture of fetish and flash at the Alamo, but outside on **Alamo Square** the element of the sacred is abandoned completely. The easiest and best escape is to flee below street level, to the **Paseo del Rio** (River Walk). The *Paseo* is a legitimately lovely stone esplanade, shaded and at points completely serene. The *Paseo* is also shrewdly marketed as a dining and nightclub strip where you can indulge yourself while watching the smooth San Antonio River stream by. Out on the water, riverboats and creaky paddle-boats float by.

At the **Arneson River Theatre**, a stucco Spanish-style structure with stone arches suspending bells, grassy steps lead up from the *Paseo* to **La Villita** ("Little Town"), a reconstruction San Antonio's first settlement. La Villita is primarily an artists' showplace plentiful in galleries. Here as everywhere else you may see a number of servicemen; San Antonio remains an active military post with four air force bases and one army base.

Outside the Alamo, River Walk and *La Villita, downtown San Antonio* is dominated by the city's Mexican-American community, which lends the town its brash color and most of its cosmopolitan flavor. Several other nationalities have settled here in force, including Germans, Italians, Lebanese and Greeks. Cosmopolitan San Antonio is best experienced outside the well-trafficked areas, so get a map and forget the Alamo.

Miles, Mesas, Mountains

The longest unbroken stretch of the grand tour begins from downtown San

Paseo del Rio on the San Antonio

Antonio, where access to I-10 is easiest from Commence Street. Once on the freeway, you'll notice the highly developed areas of the city quickly drop off and give way to clusters of new developments and then a forested area near the **University of Texas at San Antonio** just outside the city.

From here on out, on the 564-mile (908-km) haul across the western expanse of Texas to El Paso at the state's westernmost edge, there will be no large cities. Nothing much more than a cowtown interrupts the tumble of plains, rock, mesas and mountain ranges. You should be prepared to rough it for at least the first half of the journey; there are few places on the highway to procure gas, food or lodging. From **Fort Stockton** (approximately 135 miles (220 km) from El Paso), where the great mountain ranges rise westward, the going gets much easier.

As tough as the drive can be, there is much in the way of natural beauty along the lonely highway. Once you enter Kendall County 25 miles (40 km) northwest of San Antonio you enter mesa country, where small, flat, rocky rises break the horizon, shaded green against the blue skies. Approaching **Comfort,** on the Kerr County line, you join the first rises that wax and wane through the farm and oil land.

Comfort is a cluster of farms and a haven for deer which on occasion venture out to the highway. A lovely pink begins flowering on the green fabric, later joined by fringes of yellow and violet. Between Comfort and **Welfare**, the rocky mounds grow higher, and toward **Kerville** the highway heads right through them.

After a brief stretch where the land levels out a bit and the low hillside pushes through groves and grazing land, I-10 slices through highlands in Kimball County near **Junction.** As you pass, "The City of Junction Welcomes You." Soon after is a great plunge through stone into the **Llano River Valley,** a bright, curvaceous lowland where black cattle munch grass unperturbed by the madness on the interstate. Here I-10 begins paralleling the Texas Pecos Trail, the pioneer path around the cactus and canteloupe country of southwest Texas.

The Alamo
Illuminated.

Scruff Land

After you cross the rocky Bear and Stark Creeks, the hills become barer and the median is stripped to rock and tufts of grass. Soon you're upon **Sonora,** where the caverns are named "The Most Beautiful in the World"—the first of many superlatives which abound in the naturally modest desert.

Out of Sonora, the land is relatively undramatic. The plains are scruffy and low, and a small lizard or large arachnid may scurry across the highway. In the heart of scruff land is **Ozona,** "The Biggest Little Town in the World." Outside this arid stretch, mesas and peaks are layered against the horizon, evening reflecting of hues gray, blue and green. As you push ahead, you cut through large slabs of rock into great valleys before reaching the Pecos River. Approaching Fort Stockton, Twelve Mile Mountain and Pikes Peak stand off to the south, and dead ahead the great rock walls appear cleanly cut into edges and arcs.

In the morning, the great ranges past Fort Stockton—the **Glass Mountains** and **Barrilla Mountains**—appear ghostly and obscured by light and mists. But later in the day, their browns, greens and grays emerge from the hazy blues. All different shades of cattle mingle in the sparse, sandy grasses to the south.

Hieroglyphic Mountains

Passing whole truck caravans camped at rest stops, you enter Reeves County, and I-10 neatly divides the sparse grazing land to the south from the more cultivated areas to the north, where the grass is greener yet still lined with yellow. The Apache Mountains rise in the distance, rougher now and almost hieroglyphic, marked by the waters that once submerged the plains. Past the rock-encased fields to the south are hidden the signs of a huge oil industry growing out from Fort Stockton down toward **Big Bend Park**.

The exposed cross-sections of the mesas are layered in white and gold, and streaked with horizontals and arcs. Through the tip of Jeff Davis County, knobby palms project at various angles from the median. At **Van Horn,** the vista is jagged; the small rises to the

Everything's done big in Texas.

232

side of the highway look slight in the context of the Apache and Van Horn ranges. The city of Van Horn comes as a virtual oasis after the desolate stretch which precedes it: gas, gift shops, fast-food restaurants and lodging spring up along the interstate. Past Van Horn, the mesas and mountains develop high rocky heads that rest on tufted shoulders. At **Allamore,** you enter the Mountain Time Zone and gain an hour amid the rocks. The highway runs parallel to a railway, and rust-colored freight cars rest by the roadside.

The truck-ridden road gets denser and the Mexican border gets nearer as I-10 pulls past "historical" **Sierra Blanca** and its 6,894-foot (2,101-meter) peak topped with a mysterious, ancient Indian "stonehenge." At **Esperanza,** you're a stone's throw from Mexico, and there I-10 pulls northwest along the border. To the south of the highway appear emerald stretches of grove, neat and geometric, and the deep greens roll on to **El Paso**.

Border Town

Where San Antonio has profited from redeveloping historic districts and monuments, the city of El Paso has failed. Of course, San Antonio is blessed with the bloody Alamo; nothing in El Paso is comparable as a marketable emblem.

Nevertheless, San Antonio has made exceptional efforts to upgrade and maintain its attractions while injecting romance into its riverfront. El Paso, on the other hand, has left the excitement and romance (well, excitement anyway) to its sister city *across* the riverfront. That city is **Ciudad Juárez**, and the river is the **Rio Grande**, separating the United States and Mexico.

El Paso, which spreads about the base of the Franklin Mountains, lies in the oldest European-settled area of Texas. In the 16th Century, Spaniards first crossing the Rio Grande to explore their territories in New Mexico headed along *El Paso del Norte*—the Pass of the North—which sent the river through a break in the mountain ranges. Soon *El Camino Real* was extended from south of Chihuahua City, Mexico, to what is now Santa Fe, New Mexico, by conquistador Juan de Oñate. In

A longhorn cattle drive.

1680, Franciscan missionaries built an adobe hut on *El Paso del Norte*, calling it Ysleta del Sur. The towns of Ysleta and El Paso sprang up about the mission; El Paso gradually assumed Ysleta but was itself split in two after the designation of the Rio Grande as the United States-Mexico border. The U.S. city remained El Paso and the Mexican city was dubbed Juárez.

El Paso's strategic location has made it a travelers' stop for centuries. The gold-rushing "forty-niners" passed through on their way to fortune in California. Refugees, desperados and tourists have all met here. Much of the commemorated history invokes gunfights, with the notorious Marshall Dallas Stoudenmire and John Wesley Hardin on many a winning end before finally "biting the dust."

And there's a lot of dust to bite. El Paso's climate is singularly dry, although rain is not unknown. But the rain just wets down the dust and refuse kicked up by the winds which herald it. Watering holes are few in the city proper, where downtown is underdeveloped and unremarkable.

Another Country

Over the Rio Grande, now split by a dry no-man's land relieved only by a few sad trees, Juárez is one of Mexico's largest cities. In its flavor, flash and gusto it eclipses slightly smaller El Paso. Juárez is accessible by car or foot; for car traffic the Stanton Street bridge handles southbound flow and the Avenido Benito Juárez/El Paso Street bridge northbound. Pedestrian traffic is two-way on both bridges. There is a small toll for both foot and auto passage, and, like everything else in Juárez, the price can vary wildly.

Avenido Benito Juárez is the main drag for visitors to Juárez. Its northern reaches are cluttered with dentists' offices; the southern reaches, toward Avenido 16 Septembre (the genuine main drag), with *dentistas'* offices. In between is a string of discotheques, liquor stores, bars, restaurants, curio shops and outlets for the leather goods and woven goods Americans haul back over the border along with the relatively cheap liquor. If you shop in Juárez, it's important that you apprise yourself of import restrictions!

Dusk over El Paso.

The streets of Juárez contrast markedly with those in the sister city. The lively, raw and open street life splashes off the tilework sidewalks where hard-luck types hawk cigarettes out of the carton. The fleshy, mottled tumble of the main streets peals where El Paso is silent. The residential areas are alive with birds and children in a block-to-block contrast of pretty homes and neglected rows. Huge cinemas rise beside baroque churches in the clogged streets where dry, dusty air and the lower standard of living breed the croaky, jumbled-English pitches of people trying to make a small living out of tourism. In Juárez it's just a version of what you'll see almost everywhere along the changing landscape of America; it's just closer to the bone. On the surface, it's a swindle, but if you challenge it, you won't get taken.

Back in the U.S.A.

Across the bridge on El Paso Street it's America, but Mexico hasn't ended. In fact, save for the ghost-town feeling, it's really the same city. The Mexican population of El Paso is large, and it's focused at the border. But the Latino presence is felt everywhere. It's said that English is spoken as widely as Spanish in Juárez; the statement is equally true in El Paso.

Because of its geographic and commercial situation, El Paso is an inexpensive city, but an unexciting one. Tourism is ultimately channeled to its environs and up to **Ranger Peak** in the Franklin Mountains. The **Tigua Indian Reservation**, a living pueblo of the oldest identifiable Indian tribe in Texas, is on the eastern edge of the city near the **El Paso Tourist Information Center**, an accommodating office off the Americas Avenue exit (exit 32) of I-10. The converted **Ysleta Mission** is in the Ysleta neighborhood in western El Paso, between Zaragosa and Old Pueblo Roads. **Fort Bliss**, site of the largest Air Defense School in the "free world" and home of the Fort Bliss Replica Museum, sits off the northeastern edge of the city. These attractions are all fine for those with particular interest, but are really somewhat prepackaged. Like El Paso, they are a matter more of convenience than necessity.

Beauty in simplicity of form: Tigua Indian Reservation.

NEW MEXICO: LAND OF ENCHANTMENT

New Mexico is one of the youngest states in the nation (47th admitted), but it has had one of the longest histories. At its northeastern edge, near Folsom, archaeologists have discovered spearheads at least 10,000 years old. In the late 16th Century, Spain's *El Camino Real* (now US 85) extended along the Rio Grande River from Mexico to Santa Fe, site of the oldest government building in the United States and the oldest capital.

From its beginnings here, New Mexico has attended to its somewhat mundane motto: *Crescit Eunde* ("It grows as it goes"). Railroading, agriculture and mining have thrived on the state's rocky surface, warm valleys and subterranean waters. From these often unforgiving yet transfixing lands, a new symbol for New Mexico's growth has shot to the heavens: the ballistic missile.

It Grows

New Mexico is sparsely populated by approximately 1.3 million people, roughly 11 per square mile (4.2 per square km). Among its notable residents have been sworn enemies Pat Garrett and Billy the Kid, "king of the innkeepers" Conrad Hilton, novelist D.H. Lawrence, artist Georgia O'Keeffe and firefighting legend Smokey the Bear.

New Mexico is known as "The Land of Enchantment," where natural beauty and the mysteries of its landscape have infected all its settlers, from prehistoric Indian tribes to generations of Hispanics to those who came to labor in topsecret laboratories during World War II.

The Road to Alamogordo

Exiting El Paso, US 54 east skirts the eastern slopes of the Frederick Mountains. Here it epitomizes the massservice, on-the-go highway; it might be wise to avail yourself of essential services before proceeding on the 83-mile (134-km) road to Alamogordo and the Tularosa Valley. Only at **Orogrande**, 46

miles (74 km) from El Paso, is gas or food available.

Outside El Paso, US 54 contracts to a two-lane undivided highway that cuts through undeveloped land and rockencased, dusty plains. Don't be deceived; these lands are no stranger to modern man, though they appear wholly undeveloped. As you ride the gorge between the Organ Mountains to the west and the Hueco Mountains to the east, you are passing through the **Fort Bliss Military Reservation**, home of the **McGregor Missile Range**. As soon as you exit Fort Bliss Reservation, you nick the edge of the **White Sands Missile Range**. Amid the towering green and rust-brown ranges, the U.S. government conducts much of its cuttingedge missile development and testing, the *raison-d'etre* for civilization in huge spanses of southern New Mexico.

The rich and secluded **Tularosa Valley**, lodged between the Sacramento and San Andreas mountain ranges, was chosen for secret weapons development during World War II. Then, "The Road to Alamogordo" was the path to a successful atomic bomb.

Concealed north of the stunning and colorful mountain slopes that herald **Alamogordo**, above the gypsum dunes of White Sands, is the **Trinity Site**, a sublime crater created in July, 1945, when the United States detonated the first atomic bomb. The public is barred from this sobering site except, normally, in early October (usually October 1). If you're in Alamogordo at that time, check with the chamber of commerce for the exact date of the tour.

No More Mañana

There is some evidence that Alamogordo was originally settled by pygmy Indians. A small but fascinating museum next to the visitors center in Alamogordo has on display artifacts of the alleged culture. The only certainty, however, is that Alamogordo was explored by ancestors of the Navajos and Apaches before the Spanish passed through, naming it for its great cottonwood trees and eventually settling on the Tularosa River at La Luz.

The locale of present-day Alamogordo was, however, left virtually untouched before two enterprising brothers from the East, C.B. and John A. Eddy, founded the city as a stop on

White Sands in the light of sunrise.

their railroad line. Seduced by the for- estland in the valley and its commercial potential as a rich source of lumber, the Eddys sold the railroad and settled down in Alamogordo to reap their riches from the indigenous resources.

Alamogordo grew as a trade center, but the development of the White Sands Proving Ground and nearby Holloman Air Force Base radically recast the con- tours of the city. In the words of one local historian, "No longer was it a sleepy, peaceful land of *manana*, but a hustling, bustling, fast-growing city."

Still a trade and manufacturing cen- ter, Alamogordo is dominated by the high-tech weaponry community. But Alamogordo also harbors, as its more notable visitor destination, a tribute to the peaceful uses of technology in the exploration of space. Although the logical extension of the NASA missions is the "Star Wars" defense program, the aggressive ends of space exploration are ignored at the **Space Center,** accessible by US 54.

The Space Center is a well-conceived museum of the international reach for the stars. Central to its exhibits are biographies of pioneers in space ex- ploration, from early dreamers to the moon-walking astronauts of NASA's Apollo missions. After admiring space shuttle models, a lunar TV camera and samples of foods brought aboard Apol- lo and Skylab missions (*e.g.* canned vanilla ice cream and dehydrated peach ambrosia), you can watch a video pre- sentation of highlights from the Apollo 11, 12 and 14 moon landings.

Blinding White of Gypsum

Aside from the Space Center, attrac- tions in Alamogordo proper are fairly few. But oases of natural beauty abound in its environs. US 82 to **Cloudcroft**, 19 miles (31 km) northeast of Alamogordo, is a noted scenic drive through **High Rolls Mountain Park**, a very popular skiing area. Just north of Cloudcroft is the southern edge of the **Mescalero-Apache Indian Reservation**, and it is best approached at Mescalero on US 70, 31 miles (50 km) from Alamogordo. **Oliver Lee State Park**, revered by mountain climbers and photo bugs, is back down US 54 west a few miles from Alamogordo.

Satellite technology near Alamogordo

But the most unique and spectacular of all is **White Sands National Monument**, 15 miles (24 km) southwest of Alamogordo on US 70-82. The monument is a stunning 144,458-acre (58,460-hectare) expanse of gypsum sand dunes carved out of the otherwise off-limits White Sands Missile Range.

As you approach White Sands, the glowing dunes rise from the base of the San Andreas Mountains as jets roar overhead. Upon arrival, you should perhaps stop at the information center (beat a quick path through the tacky gift shop) for some background on the formation of the dunes and on their stubborn inhabitants.

Gypsum is one of the most common compounds found on the Earth, but it is rarely seen on the surface because it dissolves readily in water. Surface sand is almost always composed of quartz. In the Tularosa Basin, however, the climate is dry enough and the winds strong enough to produce the rare, surreal dunes of powdered gypsum crystal.

White Sands will be breathtaking at any time of day, but will impress variously as the sun traces its path to the horizon. At midday, the sands are a beautiful, blinding pure white, reflecting so strongly they sting the naked eye. But as you clamber over the dunes, occasionally marked by the pawprints of nocturnal wanderers, you should periodically remove your sunglasses to fully appreciate the hallucinatory expanse.

Rainbow Dunes

As the afternoon cedes to evening, the sands begin to refract the light, breaking it down into a rainbow. The park is open until 10 p.m., and with care you might observe some of the 500 different animals that populate the dunes, from coyotes and roadruners to owls and skunks. There is also a sparse scattering of beautiful plant life, including the Hedgehog Cactus with its brilliant red flowers and the sunflower.

There is a planned drive through the dunes with spacious parking and picnicking areas. At the extreme of the paved "loop" through the heart of White Sands, the road surface is so thoroughly dusted with gypsum sand that it can be difficult to follow. The effect is disorienting and remarkable.

Winter view of Sierra Blanca, White Sands.

The Wild West

US 70-82 slowly but surely rises out of the Tularosa Valley as you continue west toward Las Cruces. Past the mottled peaks of the San Andreas Range, just above the Organ Mountains, the highway reaches its apex at the **San Augustine Pass,** 5,720 feet (1,743 meters) high and overlooking the valley which holds Organ and, beyond it, Las Cruces. Organ is 52 miles (84 km) from Alamogordo.

After taking the pass, you plunge down an exhilarating three-mile (five-km) slope into the beautiful low valley where greens and browns evolve through shades and mixtures below the pearly blue peaks in the distance. Once in the valley, nearly 2,000 feet (600 meters) below the San Augustine Pass, stiff crosswinds gust against your vehicle.

The route briefly engages **Las Cruces** before hooking into I-10 to Deming. Las Cruces is unremarkable, in fact, it's downright ugly; nevertheless, it does have some historic significance buried under the unrelenting landscape of shopping malls. Las Cruces inhabits the Mesilla Valley, which harbors what are believed to be traces of the oldest known structures in the United States, dating from the 4th through the 10th centuries. Las Cruces was first known to the white man as the burial ground of a caravan of travelers from Taos who were ambushed and slaughtered by the Apaches in 1830. The graves, marked with crosses, gave the site its name.

The village of **Mesilla**, a short drive from downtown Las Cruces on State 28 and State 292 (Motel Boulevard), has made greater efforts at historical preservation. There is a restored village plaza marking the site of the sealing of the 1854 Gadsden Purchase, which established the current boundaries of Mexico and the United States. Mesilla is also where the notorious outlaw Billy the Kid was tried and sentenced to hang for murder. The Kid escaped before his hanging, but subsequently met his maker at the hands of Pat Garrett. Garrett later became the sheriff of Dona Ana County, of which Las Cruces is the county seat.

Mesilla Plaza, dominated by its old gazebo, will give you some taste of the

Prickly sign of life in the City of Rocks.

240

Wild West. It's currently populated by crafts and curios merchants and the **Double Eagle Restaurant**, which dates from the early 19th Century. If you make a stop in Las Cruces, make it here.

Across the Great Divide

Once out of Las Cruces on I-10 west, you immediately cross over the Rio Grande River, which traces its way upstream to Albuquerque, past Santa Fe and into Colorado, where it originates. You're now in prime hitchhiking land, where beseeching thumbs point over the Continental Divide to Tucson, Phoenix and ultimately to the sprawling city of dreams, Los Angeles.

In Luna County, more and more specimens of the ostrich-like state plant, the yucca, crowd the roadside. These curious indigenous guardians of the desert watch travelers as they make their way westward. From here out to the Arizona state line, freeway exits are commonly marked with frontier-style outlets for supposedly characteristic goods. Behind false facades spring a trading post, "Wild West"

town or tepee where moccasins, cactus jelly and plant candy are available to the tourist.

Fifty-six miles (90 km) out of Las Cruces, you arrive at **Deming** which is encircled by four short mountain ranges: the **Florida Mountains** to the southeast, the **Little Floridas** to the east, the **Tres Hermanas** to the south and **Cooks Range** to the north. Cooks Range is the largest of these, and its highest point—Cooks Peak, about 8,400 feet (2,560 meters) in elevation—commands an impressive vista. The Cooks Range was once in the heart of Apache Indian lands and served as the ideal lookout.

Culture in and about Deming reaches back indefinitely but was first significantly marked by the Mimbres Indian tribe. The Mimbres, who settled the area in the 10th through 12th centuries, were a peaceful people noted for their exquisite pottery. Author J.W. Pewkes has claimed that "no Southwestern pottery, ancient or modern, surpasses that of the Mimbres; and its naturalistic figures are unexcelled in any pottery from prehistoric America."

Western front; movie set for *Silverado*.

Before there was Deming, there was New Chicago, an "end of the track" railroad town with a supply of water—crucial to locomotives—in the subterranean Mimbres River. Relocated 10 miles (16 km) west of its present site, Deming was of great strategic importance to railroad magnate Charles Crocker, who joined his Southern Pacific line to the Santa Fe Railroad at the site, renaming it after his wife's family, the Demings. Early settlers included soldiers, professionals, merchants and a large population of gunmen who dominated local affairs until the town was "cleaned up" in 1883.

A Tamed Frontier

There's a fine museum of local history and Mimbres crafts located in central Deming in the former **National Guard Armory** (1916). One exhibit recreates frontier life, which, in the words of one guide, was "as you can see just by looking around, not easy here. This wasn't a luxury place." Today, Deming is certainly pleasant enough, an easygoing, temperate city of about 10,000 where everybody seems to know everyone else, folks drive and walk slowly, and shade trees throw up their defenses against the sun.

Deming has become popular as a retirement settlement because of its dry climate, 98 percent sunshine and relatively mild temperatures. Its tourist image is summarized by the billboard that announces your arrival in town: "Welcome to Deming: Pure Water and Fast Ducks." The pure water flows in the sheltered **Mimbres River**; the fast ducks compete in the Great American Duck Race held here every August.

Deming is also a popular stopover for mineral collectors, lapidaries, rockhounds and "pebble pubs." Twelve miles (19 km) south of the city on State 11, which eventually leads into Mexico, is **Rock Hound State Park**, 250 accommodating acres (100 hectares) of mineral gems that are yours for the taking. If your passion is quartz crystals or "thunder eggs" (spherulite), Rock Hound is a must. North of Deming is the **City of Rocks**, 30 miles (48 km) via US 180 and State 61, an element-forged stone metropolis.

As you continue on I-10 west toward **Lordsburg**, you enter Grant County at the Continental Divide. After forging the mountainous line, you achieve the city of Lordsburg in approximately 32 miles (51 km). Lordsburg, the largest settlement in Hidalgo County, sits a pretty 4,258 feet (1,298 km) above sea level at the northern edge of the Pyramid Mountains. From Motel Drive, paralleling the Southern Pacific railroad tracks, there's a fair view of the valley to the north. The train tracks themselves tell the story of modern Lordsburg, which eventually eclipsed neighboring town **Shakespeare**. Shakespeare had been a stop on the great Butterfield Stagecoach Line run by the post office from Saint Louis, Missouri, to San Francisco, California, at the time Charles Crocker laid his rails.

This Town's Got Ghosts

Today, Shakespeare is a "ghost town," preserved in its state of decay after being abandoned for more profitable pastures. (Aside from the glaring Motel Drive, you might think Lordsburg is the ghost town.) Shakespeare, a short 1.5-mile (2.4-km) drive south on Main Street from Lordsburg, is the genuine item, although it *is* inhabited. Residents and owners Rita and Janaloo Hill open up the town only once a month—on the second Sunday—to conduct anecdote-peppered tours at 10 a.m. and 2 p.m. Preserved in Shakespeare, which has served as a location for Hollywood films, is the **Stratford Hotel.** Several notable characters were known to grace its dining room, including an escapee from Silver City jail: William Bonney, a.k.a. Billy the Kid.

Near Shakespeare is the **Shakespeare Cemetery**, an active burial ground located very near the original item. According to its hand-painted sign, Shakespeare's "Boot Hill" was the oldest of the "Pioneer Cemetery's" [sic] in southwestern New Mexico and southeastern Arizona. Here were buried the famous outlaws Sandy King (convicted of being "a damned nuisance" and hung by a vigilante commitee) and Russian Bill (who had stolen a horse, not because he needed it, but because "he wanted to show how tough he was").

BRYCE CANYON

The Paiute Indians called it *Unka timpe wa wince pock ich,* or "Red-rocks-standing-like-men-in-a-bowl-shaped-canyon." Maurice Howe dubbed it "a sunset petrified." And the pioneer cattleman after whom **Bryce Canyon National Park** is named referred to it as "a hell of a place to lose a cow."

Bryce's 36,000-plus acres of exotic, intricately carved red, pink and cream-colored rock formations have been sculpted from the Paunsaugunt Plateau of southern Utah. Eons of water and ice knifing through silt and limestone created this natural museum of sculpture and architectural fancies: 14 amphitheatres densely populated with fantastical stone turrets, spires, temples and minarets.

A partial list of the myriad formations that fill the canyon reads like a map of Disneyland attractions. Fairyland, Queen's Garden, Fairy Castle and The Cathedral are all located at

the northern end of the park where trails wind around the ruddy sculptures of Thor's Hammer, The Pope, The Temple of Osiris and Silent City—the city of stone. (Legend has it that a great Indian spirit, discontent with the evil on earth, gathered all the wicked people to this area and turned them to stone.) Open stands of ponderosa pines dot the canyon floor; the rangers will swear that its bark smells like something between Harvey's Bristol Cream and butter-scotch.

Bryce's **Rim Road** is a cool contrast from the fiery brilliance of the canyon's lower regions. Stretching from Rainbow Point at the park's southern end to Fairyland Point in the north, this paved byway weaves through forests of cedar and fir to spectacular vistas of Aqua Canyon, Natural Bridge and the Pink Cliffs of the Paunsaugunt Plateau. The ride is ideal for those who have only a few hours to spend at Bryce, and at many spots along the road, the many trails leading into the canyon are only a short walk away.

The park offers a variety of guided walks and talks. Saddleback trail rides to the bottom of the canyon, nature hikes, nightly slide presentations in an open-air theatre and flying bat watches are just a few of the activities to choose from. Not to be missed is the **Moonlit Navajo Loop Trail Walk.** On alternate evenings after dusk a ranger will lead a dozen visitors down twisting switchbacks and through eerie "hoodoo" (a Park Service word for one of those sculpted monoliths) moonshadows to a few log benches on the canyon floor. Once there, hikers are treated to Paiute Indian legends of the moon and the great spirit Coyote who once ruled over the area. The tour ends with a leisurely hike to the rim accompanied by live Renaissance music—harp and recorder echoing from a niche in the canyon wall.

Bryce Canyon National Park is located 26 miles (42 km) southeast of Panguitch and 18 miles (29 km) north of Hatch. It is easily reached from the south via US 89. At Bryce Junction, seven miles (11 km) south of Panguitch on US 89, turn east onto State 12 and drive for 17 miles (27 km) to the park entrance.

SOUTHERN ARIZONA

The name Arizona conjures in the mind of the English-speaker one image: arid. Yes, water is extremely precious here—"Arizona's most precious resource, next to its people"—but the name Arizona has nothing to do with lack of water. It may be derived from the Pima Indian word for "little spring place," or perhaps from an Aztec expression meaning "silver-bearing." On the grounds of accuracy, the latter rings truer; Arizona's first industry was silver mining.

But there *are* "little spring places" in Arizona, and just about every climatic, topographic and ecological variant known to America. From its ponderosa pine forests and saguaro-studded deserts to modern cities and unspoiled reservations, Arizona exquisite has made the most of its natural gifts.

Arizona would have gone nowhere, however, without irrigation and air conditioning. Technology has conquered the desert, although a great deal of arid and remains untouched. Though beautiful, the desert can be unbearable in the summer. Winter is "the season" in most of Arizona, particularly the south and west.

Stone Spirits

Just over the New Mexico/Arizona state line on I-10 is **Chiricahua National Monument**. Once the Chiricahua Apaches' land, the monument is accessible from I-10 west of Lordsburg by only one paved route: State 186 east from Wilcox Business Loop 10, and then State 181 north. There is a rough-and-tumble "back way" into Chiricahua, which follows US 80 west from I-10 exit 5 in New Mexico, then winds into the rock-strewn mountains past Portal and east of the monument. The "back way" is beautiful but harrowing.

Taking the first course, you'll make brisk time on the sparsely trafficked I-10 west of Lordsburg, toward Gary,

Road Forks and the Arizona state line. After the exit to **Gary**, the fields ahead glow a milky green that, as you approach, separates into dusty-green grasses, chaparral and off-white sand. This low, dry area is susceptible to dust storms.

For Hikers and Campers

After veering off I-10 into **Wilcox** on the business loop, you catch State 186 east through a residential area that soon drops away. From there, the road soars and twists magnificently, etching right into the mountains through the yucca-scattered plains. Entering ranch country, you turn off onto State 181 and pull up in four miles (six km) at the entrance to Chiricahua National Monument. The entire trip from Lordsburg measures about 110 miles (177 km).

Although Chiricahua is a bit off the beaten track, it is magnificent and completely worth the effort. Ideal for hiking, camping and scenic drives, the landscape at Chiricahua was and is formed by two predominant natural factors: volcanic activity some 15 million

years ago and precipitous leaps in elevation which layer many different forms of plant life and harbor various species of animals.

Lush Highlands

At an average altitude of 5,400 feet (1,646 meters), the Chiricahua highlands stand in marked contrast to the yellowed, dusty plains and gorges below. Benefitting from about twice as much rainfall, the Chiricahua provides a rich environment for harbor juniper, fir, piñon, yucca, oak, pine, cypress and sycamore along the dips and ridges.

The vegetation is refreshing and quite beautiful, but what stands out at Chiricahua are the ancient, eerie volcanic formations. These brooding rocks are vaulted in human-like forms and in forests of slender fingers. As you follow the well-built trails—to Echo Park, Inspiration Point, Punch & Judy or Duck on a Rock—you feel an amazing presence in the gestures advanced by the rocks and "lifeless" trees, a silent spirit aloof from the gaping mortals.

There are two ways to continue on from Chiricahua to Tombstone, Arizona. The easiest route is to backtrack to Wilcox, pick up I-10 to Benson and then follow I-80 all the way to Tombstone. A slightly more difficult but direct route is to continue south on State 181 to U.S. 666, which has the added advantage of passing the rattlesnake crafts, saloons and crumbling buildings on the main drag of an old copper-mining town called **Gleeson.** Just outside of town on the opposite side of a curvy hillside, **Tombstone** can be seen shining in the distance.

The Wild, Wild West

Tombstone was whimsically named by founder Edward Schieffelin after he was advised his mad hunt for silver would culminate in exactly that, his tombstone. The most famous of "Wild West" mining towns, Tombstone did indeed sit in the heart of lands rich in silver. Its dizzying growth and wealth in the 1880s attracted more than its share of troublemakers.

The quintessential frontier "showdown" unfolded at Tombstone's **O.K. Corral:** the Earps (with Doc Holiday)

Geronimo, once leader of the Apache Indians.

vs. the Clanton and McLowrey brothers. The latter group were at the fore of a "cowboy" gang that allegedly engineered a series of stagecoach robberies. The Earps, who were no angels either, represented "establishment" Tombstone. Political and personal clashes culminated in the legendary, bloody shootout at the O.K. Corral on Oct 26, 1881, leaving three men dead.

The O.K. Corral stands preserved, and other landmarks have been refurbished or recreated. The old studio of Wild West photographer Camillus Fly showcases some of his best work, including shots of the fierce, then pathetic, Apache chief Geronimo. In the multimedia presentation of the Tombstone story, narrated by Vincent Price, film dramatization is interwoven with a sort of puppet-show diorama. At the O.K. Corral, the grounds where the bloody showdown transpired are set with life-size models of the principles. In preserving the legends of its past, Tombstone employs fabricated icons, emphasizing the purely imaginary value of romantic lawlessness and the wildness of the West.

Fast-Growing Tucson

As you cross Country Club Road on I-10 west, you enter the city of **Tucson,** 43 miles (69 km) from Benson. Tuscon's roots in 18th-century Hispanic culture has not prevented it from embracing the future. In recent years, it has become a regional center of high-tech industries. Tucson casually mixes the new with the remnants of its 18th-century settlement by the Spanish.

Exiting from I-10 at Congress/Broadway leads you directly into the narrow heart of downtown Tucson, bordered by Granada on the east and Church on the west. Once contained within the adobe walls of a Spanish *presidio*, this delightfully spacious area is now dotted with artisans' shops, cafes, several good shade trees and some interesting architecture.

To the south is the Civic Center which, along with the University of Arizona campus farther west, forms one of the two main hubs of scattered Tucson. The **Civic Center** is itself very much like a campus with its centralized plazas, grassy walks and compact audi-

O.K. Corral today; plasticizing the past.

toriums. The old **Pima County Court-house,** a Spanish-Southwestern architural mix with columns, arches and tilework, is the most attractive building. The nearby **City Hall,** however, is a concrete eyesore. A bridge from the Governmental Center over Congress Street leads you to **La Placita Village,** an adobe mall that is one of the nicest complexes of its type. Below this is the **Community Center,** Tucson's arts and entertainment showplace, which, with its landscaped gardens and pavilions, lends a touch of the old ivy to downtown.

Vying with the palms and indigenous Arizona flora are the unusually designed traffic lights native only to central Tucson. In their shadow, visitors lounge by poolside at the **Holiday Inn** on Pemmington. When it grows dark, some drive up to **Sentinal Peak** across I-10 to admire the twinkle and the remaining strains of pink in the sunset. There's something in the clarity and color of the Tucson sky, in the airy pueblo-style architecture, that draws Tucson out of the desert and closer to the coast beckoning from the west.

The Apache Trail

Out of the urban "oasis" slowly spreading its man-made way along the paved tentacles of the high ways, US 89 north leads from Tucson to Pinal County. Once there, it becomes the splendiferous or "splendiflorous," **Pinal Pioneer Parkway.** Much of the nearly 100 miles (160 km) from Tucson to **Apache Junction** outside Phoenix on this route is lush with native vegetation, from the prickly pear and saguaro cacti to the catclaw and mesquite tree.

Starts at Apache Junction, now State 88. **Apache Trail** formerly the Apache Indians' track through the Salt River Valley. The modern road was built in 1905 to provide access to the pioneering **Roosevelt Dam** which would channel the lifeblood to Phoenix. When President Teddy Roosevelt dedicated the dam in 1911, he said: "The Apache Trail combines the grandeur of the Alps, the glory of the Rockies and the magnificence of the Grand Canyon."
The incredibly beautiful drive on the Apache Trail follows out of Apache Junction across Superstition Road,

San Xavier de Bac Mission, Tucson.

250

Tepee Road and Tomahawk Road with the first clear glimpses of the **Superstition Mountains**. Various legends are connected to the peaks which the Spanish called "Mountains of Foam" because of their effusive volcanic ridges. Apaches, who were once the terror of the mountains, shun it as a place of evil spirits. In the late 19th Century, Dutchman Jacob Walz struck a huge gold lode in the Superstitions; no one else was able to find the "Lost Dutchman Mine," and anyone who followed Walz on his expeditions there was never seen again. The Superstition Mountains have taken the lives of the overly curious ever since.

The Apache Trail cuts into **Tonto National Forest**, where vistas and foot trails skirt the highway. The fun really begins when the roadway takes its winding and narrow way into the highlands. Drivers beware: you'll have to keep your eyes more to the road than the alpine rises, glorious vistas and lush canyons. Saguaros and mesquite, dry riverbeds, odd rocks, and wave upon wave of mountain ridges follow a scenic overlook of the **Canyon River.** When

The Apache Trail, once exactly that, is now State 88.

you descend into the valley, pull up and drip down, because the blue waters are irresistable.

Two Feet from Hell

The Trail is well-paved for the 18 miles (29 km) up to **Tortilla Flat,** a required stop for lovers of desert lore and witty western character. The essence of Tortilla Flat is sold in two forms: a postcard reading "Tortilla Flat/Pop. 6/30 Miles from Water/2 Feet from Hell!"; and the hokey cans of Jack Rabbit Milk, "a balanced diet for unbalanced people." One of the six residents remarks: "Oh, it works wonders. Especially that vitamin P."

A hotel, post office, cafe/restaurant, gift shop, riding stable, curio shop, a legend and a marvelous view—Tortilla Flat is a great place to stop for "the best chili in the West" and a "Howdy" from "the friendliest town in America." Admire the hundreds of dollar-bills tacked under business cards on the ceiling and walls of the cafe before you exit back to the sun-drenched desert.

PHOENIX: VALLEY OF THE SUN

From Apache Junction, US 60, in conjunction with the superhighway I-360, takes you the 42 miles (68 km) to **Phoenix**. Entering: Valley of the Sun. Phoenix may not have had any real *ashes* to rise from, but it did have the often merciless, scorching, arid heat of the Salt River Valley to overcome. And it has done so, courtesy of modern technology.

The name Phoenix refers to the ruins of a former Indian settlement discovered there by Jack Swilling in 1867. Inspired by evidence that Indians had tamed the land with irrigation, Swilling decided the desert valley deserved another go. Phoenix hasn't looked back since.

Hot in the City

Beware Phoenix: the average high temperature June through August is 103 degrees Fahrenheit (39 Celsius); May and September aren't much better.

Peak tourist season is winter, when the high averages 70 degrees Fahrenheit (21 Celsius) and the resorts are in full swing.

Phoenix is a large, active and young city (average age is under 30). But its culture accommodates all tastes and degrees of "maturity," while it is an increasingly popular retirement locale. Phoenix shows off Arizona's western sun, sprawl and unique pace. The vast expanse of city is cut down to size by the fast-paced boulevards, but there's still no way to see it all on a short trip.

Almost everyone's number one year-round attraction is the **Heard Museum of Anthropology and Primitive Art.** This superbly designed and organized museum greets you with its quiet courtyard and orange trees surrounded by two floors of exhibit rooms. The collection features thousands of catalogued artifacts, including African sculpture, Native American basketry and rugs, Kachina dolls and jewelry. There are also outstanding exhibitions of contemporary Native American art. Heard Museum is located at 22 East Monte Vista Road near Central Avenue.

Easy access to Phoenix.

252

The downtown area is worth exploring just to get a feel for enterprising Phoenix. It's a strictly nine-to-five business district containing the city's relatively small skyline. Most of the unremarkable skyscrapers are with the possible exception of the **Valley Bank Center** at 1st Street and Van Buren, the tallest building in the state of Arizona.

Van Buren, the tallest building in the state of Arizona.   ·

Little forays into the baroque and the bizzare stand out: the Spanish-style, Spanish-language **Palace** movie theatre at Adams and 2nd Street, the **Phoenix City Hall** at 2nd and Washington, and the **Luhrs Tower** at 1st and Jefferson, a peeling yet interesting "post-Art Deco" marble and stucco building with green trim.

Another star attraction is the **Desert Botanical Garden** in Papago Park, on the Galvin Parkway off McDowell Road. Best visited in the early spring, the garden displays plants from the world's deserts, including half the known cactus species. Cacti are just where this amazing showplace begins, but they tower over it. The exotic power of these gardens cannot fail to impress; the landscaping is superb from the weird boojum tree, the stately saguaro cactus and the primitive pereskia cacti to the advanced mammillarias, ancient Joshua, healing aloe and nutritious velvet mesquite, you will find an exhaustive living catalog of plant life adapted to the passionate extremities of the desert.

There's plenty to do after hours in Phoenix, and there are plenty of ways to find out what. The two major newspapers are one source: the *Arizona Republic* and the *Phoenix Gazette*. The thick, "alternative" *New Times* is another, as is the less hip *City Life*. And there's always the local *Key* and *Where* magazines, plus the *Visitors Guide*, all three oriented exclusively to tourists and available either in hotels or at the Visitors Bureau.

Rock, country, blues, jazz and "DJ-dance" music are all here, from alternative to lounge varieties. Theatre, film, sports, dance classical music are to be found here as well. Nothing in Phoenix is centralized, so know where things are happening before you venture out into the limitless metropolis.

A view of valley sprawl from South Mountain Park.

NORTH CENTRAL ARIZONA

Through the Desert

Arizona north of Phoenix is blessed with some of the most spectacular geography in the United States, including the ancient cliff dwellings of Montezuma Castle, the lush Coconino National Forest, the foreboding San Francisco Mountains and the wondrous Grand Canyon. The region also boasts the city of Flagstaff—the crossroads of northern Arizona—and the transplanted London Bridge. Before ending at San Diego, the southern leg of the grand tour winds through the arid desert and into the "Golden State" of California.

On metro-connector I-17 beyond Phoenix, you enter a scenic stretch of highway. Past the exit to Carefree Highway (go if you must) lies a beautiful valley ruled by saguaros around **Black Canyon City.** After Bumblebee and Crown King, the road passes canyons and desert plateaus before dipping down a winding six-mile (10-km) downgrade into **Verde Valley,** which, true to its name, is a lovely patch of green framed by silver plateaus.

Eighty-eight miles (142 km) north of Phoenix at exit 289 is the **Montezuma Castle National Monument.** Don't expect Aztec ruins here. When pioneers first saw the "castle," they mistook it for a palace built by Aztec refugees as a "retreat" for their emperor. Montezuma Castle is actually a five-story, 20-room cliff dwelling erected by the Sinagua Indians (Indians "without water") in the early 12th Century. It's been remarkably preserved; the official claim is that Montezuma Castle is "one of the best-preserved cliff dwellings in the American Southwest," if not the best. And for good reason; renovation began in 1897 and the government has seen to it that as few human beings as possible get inside to spoil the work.

The Sinaguas migrated to the Verde Valley from Wupatki in north-central Arizona beginning in the mid-12th Century. They were preceded by the Hohokam, the original Phoenicians, who had sophisticated irrigation techniques with which they transformed Verde Valley into an agricultural mecca. They had all the tribes talking, and the local population swelled until about A.D. 1400. Soon after, the area was deserted, and nobody really knows why. You'll be tirelessly reminded of this fact as you tour the site; it's that bit of mystery which is the Castle's particular romance.

Birthday Celebration

As you drive the 50-mile (80-km) stretch of I-17 north of Montezuma Castle to Flagstaff, you enter one of the most spectacular of the great forests, **Coconino National Forest.** Set on the lofty Coconino Plateau at an average elevation of about 7,000 feet (2,100 meters), the forest has all the qualities of a northern pine forest, complete, in its higher reaches, with towering, ashen aspen.

Although in today's America some folks still go to extremes when celebrating the country's birthday, a group of pioneers camped in the heart of Coconino Forest in the summer of 1876 really did it in style. All they had were Old Glory and nature's bounty, but in true American spirit they made do resourcefully. Stripping down the tallest pine they could find to bare wood, they ran the flag up their makeshift pole to ring in the United States' second century.

The pole quickly became known to travelers heading for San Francisco through the Coconino, and the name "Flagstaff" was born. Blessed by passing railroad tracks, the area developed into a city, and modern-day **Flagstaff** is still very much with us though the pole is gone.

Arizona Crossroads

Flagstaff lies at the northern terminus of I-17, is cut by I-40 and is the turning point of loopy US 180 arcing from the north. It is the great crossroads of northern Arizona, and it's very heavily traveled. Flagstaff is ringed with a bounty of monuments, resorts, oddities and forestland and thus pulls in uncountable hikers, tourists, naturalists, skiers and seekers.

Streaming through Business Loop 40 is the lifeblood of Flagstaff, and that

The Grand Canyon.

route pulses mightily. Tourism may be Flagstaff's font, but a quick drive through the neighborhoods reveals other springs where the sweet-voiced natives sip. One very formidable presence in the city is **Northern Arizona University**, with a student body approximately 13,000 strong.

The Main Event

Some 81 miles (130 km) north of Flagstaff is a better reason for stopping through: that giant among America's natural wonders, the most sublime and humbling hole in the ground, the Grand Canyon.

You set out for this spectacle on US 180 west from Loop 40 in Flagstaff. Before you appears the towering black **San Francisco Mountains,** containing **Humphrey's Peak,** at 12,760 feet (3,862 meters) the highest point in Arizona. Hiking and camping there are of course popular, but the main event is skiing, when the high peaks catch the precious snows present in Arizona only in the winter and at insane altitudes. The skiing area on Humphrey's "little" brother, **Mount Agassiz,** elevation 11,600 feet (3,536 meters), is known as the Snow Ball. Off season, the ski lift becomes a sightseer's lift, and from the pinnacle all the area's wonders, including the Grand Canyon, spread before you.

Be careful up there; there's a "ball" to be had, but you might disturb the long-term tenants. The peaks are the dwelling place of the Hopi Indians' Kachina gods, who are known to come out every spring to listen for the ceremonial chants of their people. The Hopi no longer live on the Coconino Plateau, but their Kachina dances still strike up in the reservation, 40 miles (64 km) northeast at its closest point. The dances are performed sporadically from early winter to early summer. Also at home in the peaks are the Havasupi Indians' "cloud spirits."

The San Francisco Peaks are seven miles (11 km) northwest on US 180. The Snow Ball is then seven miles (11 km) east on a turnoff that claims to be "cinder" but is obscured by dirt and stone. The tortured surface and large chunks of rock will shudder your car all the way up to the liftoff point. You'll shudder more when you get to the top.

The Great Gorge

The Grand Canyon is the world's No. 1 example of what can happen in the absence of erosion control.
—Arizona lorist and cartoonist Reg Manning

Exactly how the **Grand Canyon** got started is another mystery wallpapered with some good theories. It is accepted, however, that the depths of the canyon were and are continually deepened by two contrary movements. The first is the gorge erosion carried on by the Colorado River, which probably started the whole mess. The "Mighty Colorado" which travels the 277-mile (466-km) length of the Grand Canyon is actually a sort of liquid sandpaper, so choked is it with rock dust. Slowly but perceptibly the river digs and widens the gorge as the second movement proceeds. The ancient rock around the river continues to push skyward, lifting the rim of the canyon. Meanwhile, rains and snow help erode the canyon walls, creating new contours and unveiling more color.

San Francisco Mountains; haven for gods and spirits.

Much can be said about the geophysics of the Grand Canyon. One of its most significant and amazing properties is its vast range of climates and "life zones." The first serious scientific explorer of this grand pit, C. Hart Merriam, noted in 1889 that as you travel from the Canyon floor to the top of the San Francisco Peaks, you find climates, plants and animals you would have to travel from the Mexican desert to the Canadian arctic to find at low elevation. And the rock itself—rising 5,700 feet (1,737 meters) from floor to north rim—records the geologic history of the area from about 2 billion years ago to about 200 million years ago.

The Grand Canyon is one of America's most precious resources, and the quick facts can only provide some framework for understanding its significance. And then there's the human side of the Canyon, the unscientific business of life in and tourism to what President Theodore Roosevelt called "the one great sight every American should see."

You Are Not Alone

In the summertime, anywhere from 11,000 to 12,000 individuals *a day* pay their respects to America's Wonder. Their reasons are sound. Very little can be written to impart the experience of the Grand Canyon; it is limitless, uncontainable, ineffable.

While a picture might be worth a thousand words, or a million, and although some beautiful photographs have been taken of the Canyon, no picture comes close to capturing the humbling, awesome power of that gaping maw. Your first view of the ethereal depths, the valley of color and majestic, impossibly formal ridges, the play of light modulating over, the surfaces of rock and the serpentine Colorado so far below, will stay with you forever.

At first, the image might waiver. It's all so jarring and immense, and there are the numerous distractions of other pilgrims. When you step away from the rim and are confronted with the overflow of humanity who have brought their small parochialisms, egotisms, loves, children, cameras, anxieties, hungers, expectations, passions, indifferences, attention spans and

The Canyon's shapes and surfaces change in every light.

vacation wages to mount at the great ly *seen* the Grand Canyon flickers.

There is much to do in the **Grand Canyon National Park** other than gape. You can fly the canyon, hike it, raft through its gorge, camp in it, talk to rangers about it, ride a mule across it. Everything except day hikes, talking to rangers and gaping will require forethought and contacting the park. The Backcountry Reservations Office is happy to help with permits and tips for long hikes through the Canyon. Be prepared, though; it's 21 miles (34 km) from rim to rim on foot, and most of that is uphill.

From the South Rim of the Grand Canyon, there's only one way out and that's the one way in. You have two choices on State 64: to bear east to **Cameron** and the **Painted Desert** in the Navajo reservation, or to bear south toward **Williams**. The grand tour follows the latter course.

If you've got the urge to stop, do so at Williams, just past the interchange with I-40, 57 miles (92 km) from Grand Canyon Village. Williams is commonly known as the "Gateway to the Grand Canyon," as it channels eastbound passengers on I-40 back up State 64. As such, it is, as you might expect, clearly marked by the tourist industry. Williams is milder than Flagstaff, much quieter and more attractive. It's set at the base of **Bill Williams Mountain** and clambers up the hillside like a European village. In season, Williams is a popular skiers' resort.

Out of Williams, jump on I-40 west, toward Los Angeles. Today, I-40 is the major access route for Californians to the Grand Canyon and the other northern Arizona attractions, but it started out as a camel trail, or rather, a camel "test site." In the late 1850s, the US Army tested the foreign beast's ability to negotiate the rough terrain of northern Arizona that was so inhospitable to horses and mules. Though the camels produced amazingly high scores, trouble appropriating funds and the outbreak of Civil War put them out of a job. They were also known to cause stampedes and to smell very bad. The camels were set free and soon became a nuisance until camel hunting enjoyed a brief but effective fad.

Kingman, about 115 miles (185 km) from Williams on I-40, is the Mojave

Mountain Lion Petroglyph, Painted Desert.

County seat and supports a local county newspaper. But by far, the most extensive "local" papers are the Los Angeles *Times*, the Las Vegas *Review-Journal* and the Phoenix *Arizona Republic*. This fact tells the story of Kingman, at least as itinerants know it. Unofficially, Kingman is the "Gateway to Las Vegas," the jump-off point from I-40 to US 93 north and the last major stop in Arizona.

Kingman is also full of launching pads to closer area attractions: **Hoover Dam** and recreational **Lake Mead**; mining "ghost towns" near survivor Chloride, Arizona; **Hualapai Mountain Park**; and, to the south, **Lake Havasu** and **Lake Havasu City**. In the local culture department, Kingman hosts the **Mojave Museum of History and the Arts**, housing exhibits of memorabilia, Indian culture, crafts and northeast Arizona history. And there's **Locomotive Park**, a monument to the Santa Fe line which gave Kingman its birth in 1883.

A Little Bit of London

Out of Kingman on I-40 westbound, you cross the Holy Moses Wash, pass the exits to Yucca and admire the compacted, toothy ridges to either side of the road. At exit 9, latch on to State 95 south, to Lake Havasu City, Lake Havasu State Park and the **London Bridge**. Yes, the London Bridge.

About 20 miles (32 km) south of the interchange, the smoky desert landscape yields to human development and the first glimpse of Lake Havasu, its brilliant blue gradually stretching southward. Lake Havasu, backed up behind the Parker Dam to the south, irrigates vast stretches of Southern California, including Los Angeles. As the lake had been planned and created, Lake Havasu City grew by its side as a planned resort.

Robert P. McColloch, Sr., the city's founder in 1964, will go down in history not for fathering a quite nice boating and fishing resort in the middle of relentless desert, but for negotiating the purchase of one of London's distinctive landmarks: the London Bridge. The bridge was moved block by block from the Thames to a Lake Havasu canal and dedicated in 1971 by the Right Honorable the Lord Mayor of London, Alderman Sir Peter Studd, G.B.E., M.A.,

London Bridge, Lake Havasu.

D.Sc. and the Honorable Jack Williams, Governor of Arizona precipice—the sensation of having real period. The incongruity of the bridge is slightly ameliorated by some nice landscaping, but it's still double-take material.

London Bridge English Village is located at the foot of the bridge in Lake Havasu City. There are Tudor-style "shoppes," restaurants and attractions, from Piccadilly Circus International Bazaar to Piccadilly Target Game to Piccadilly Ice Cream Parlor (in an old double-decker bus). There's a tiny replica of Big Ben and a London telephone booth. It's all jolly fun. You can rent any number of water-treading vehicles and make your way under the bridge and out into the crystalline lake.

Ferocious Heat

Or you can bring your own craft to **Parker**, 42 miles (68 km) south of Lake Havasu City on State 95. Parker lies just inside the Colorado River Indian Reservation and is also a "trading post." Have your fun now, because after Parker, the highway cuts inland and the water's gone with a vengeance.

If you're cruising along in your air-conditioned chariot and getting off for a bite or a drink in **Quartzsite**, 36 miles (58 km) south of Parker, you're in for a rude daytime awakening. The heat mellows out a bit in winter, but in summer, watch out. The ferocious desert heat is stunning, and as you continue southward into even lower elevations, it only gets worse.

Quartzsite in summer is not much to see. As one chagrinned resident claims, "Oh, a few things go on here in the winter, but absolutely nothing in the summer. Everybody gets the hell out of here." The "few things" that mark Quartzsite as a visitor stop in the winter are the Pow Wow in January and February and the year-round monument to "Hi Jolly," a.k.a. Hadji Ali, the camel driver left jobless when the U.S. Army abandoned its camel initiative. The Pow Wow is a sort of mineralists' convention, a huge, open-air "flea market" for seekers and sellers of rocks and stones of various values and forms. It is reported that approximately 750,000 conventioneers stop by the Pow Wow every winter.

Unless you're in Quartzsite for one of

Depiction of early Mojave dancers.

LAS VEGAS:
GLITTER GULCH

No, this is not a good town for psychedelic drugs. Reality itself is too twisted.

Dr. Hunter S. Thompson, *Fear and Loathing in Las Vegas*

Each year 12 million visitors to **Las Vegas** empty their pockets of $4.2 billion in a time-honored homage to frivolity, greed and gluttony—not to mention plain old fun. But for a long time after the Nevada state government legalized gambling in 1931, Las Vegas remained a sleepy desert town, only dimly aware of the tremendous forces legalization had set into motion. It took a visionary underworld hit man, Bugsy Siegel, to set free this seething neon dragon that spits not fire, but coins, even as it consumes them ravenously. In 1946, Siegel's **Flamingo Hotel,** sparing no expense in mob finances for its plush interior and sporting a flashing pink neon facade as dazzling today as it was then, set a new

standard for sheer swank among the town's gaming parlors.

From a high roller's point of view, Las Vegas is divided into two parts: the **Strip,** and downtown or **Glitter Gulch.** As far as gambling goes, either way you lose, but downtown casinos are said to afford better odds. Conventional wisdom has it that the safest way to experience Las Vegas is to set yourself a loss limit, and to stick to it. It doesn't take a genius to see that if every gambler follows this simple rule, the casinos stand to make quite a pile of greenbacks regardless of how big any one wins. Unfortunately, no one has come up with a better strategy.

The best way to do Vegas is simply to *enjoy* it, win, lose or draw. There's nothing quite like the Strip at night, ablaze with electric light and self-indulgence. Guests at the **MGM Grand Hotel** need not even step past the plush lobby: it could take weeks to make proper use of its casino, movie theatre, two stages, six restaurants, four cocktail lounges, two swimming pools, 10 tennis courts, jai alai courts, health spa and indoor shopping mall. Then again, for those easily bored it might be worth a stroll to **Cesar's Palace,** if only to be served amid opulent Roman decor by waitresses clad in flowing harem garb. Or on toward the immense flashing clown that marks **Circus-Circus,** where you can stuff quarters into the slots while acrobats swing overhead.

One of the town's greatest virtues is that it respects anyone's money, whether it comes in large or small quantities. While meals at the better restaurants can be costly, the casinos provide remarkably inexpensive (if barely edible) all-you-can-eat buffets to keep gamblers' engines stoked. Cocktail lounges featuring free live (or, more precisely, not quite dead) entertainment and cheap drinks adjoin ritzy theatres that host the likes of Liberace and Wayne Newton.

Las Vegas is about five hours' drive from central Los Angeles. The Santa Monica Freeway (I-10) leads eastward across L.A., meeting I-15 beyond Rancho Cucamonga. I-15 leads directly to Vegas, 226 miles (364 km) to the northeast.

those two reasons, your stay will certainly be short. Bite the bullet and continue on, now on US 95 south to **Yuma**.

The Devil's Road

When Padre Eusebio Kino, the most tireless of all Spanish missionaries to the American Southwest, opened a trail in 1699 from Sonoita. Mexico to what is now Yuma, he called the trail *El Camino del Diablo*—the Devil's Road. It seemingly led straight into the inferno. Yuma smolders to this day, but it's been tamed by the air conditioner into a city fit for human beings to inhabit and visit.

Set below the junction of the Gila and Colorado Rivers, Yuma has been a popular interchange since the California Gold Rush of 1849 and beyond. At the site of the only natural ford on the southern trail to the Pacific, enterprising Yumans got their start ferrying starry-eyed miners into gold country. Then, in 1858, gold was discovered to the east of Yuma, and the city blossomed as a port, where ore was transported by steamboat down the Colorado and into the Gulf of California.

Yuma Today

But the mines dried up and the river was dammed, so Yuma settled back into an agricultural center with help from irrigation technology. But it's still a crossroads, where I-8 from San Diego meets US 95, replete with an international airport. In the winter, it's heavily trafficked by seekers of the sun that is so relentless in summer. In the spring, Yuma is the training site for the San Diego Padres professional baseball team.

Of note for visitors to Yuma is "**Old Yuma**," the downtown heritage district near the riverbank. Also of note is the **Yuma Territorial Prison State Historical Park** not far from downtown. The remaining structures of the old prison, which was closed in 1909, are on display—its guard house, courtyards, cell blocks and notorious "Dark Cell" for solitary confinement.

One building of the prison has been converted into a fascinating museum of prison construction, life and lore. Prisoner portraits make great reading and weave a sharp picture of the lawless side of existence in the Arizona Territory at the turn of the century. Beside the pri-

Arid land near Yuma.

262

son exhibits are displays of Indian crafts, from Yuma beadwork and Hopi pottery to Apache and Maricopa basketry.

Larcenists, adulterers, manslaughterers, outright murderers, rapists and criminals "against nature" all found a home here by the Colorado. You can rest assured the cells weren't air-conditioned, so Yuma Prison must have been a fate so dreaded that at least a few desperados thought twice before pulling the trigger.

Eureka!: California

Over the Colorado River, rich fields herald the invisible passage into California, third largest and most populous state in the nation. As you follow I-8 to the coast, where the Pacific laps on the forever-sunny beaches, the myth of California gradually fulfills itself. But first there is the desert.

It is in lower Imperial County just inside this magnificent state that you will see the sand dunes elusive in the Arizona deserts. The quartz dust fringing the highway is well-anchored with bush and chaparral, appearing deceptively solid beneath the low clouds that rise like smoke on the horizon. Islands of irrigated green are dotted with palms, spelling "oasis" after the arid 58-mile (93-km) tumble from Yuma to just outside **El Centro**, supposedly the largest city below sea level in the Western Hemisphere. El Centro is situated within a ring of canals fed by the New and Alamo Rivers, principally the **All-American Canal**. To the west of El Centro, strong winds kick up a dusty haze around the palms and the fields, some fallow, some fecund.

On toward **Ocotillo**, 28 miles (45 km) west on I-8 from El Centro, you approach mountain ranges sweeping down from the northwest and at first obscured by the dust. Down into the valley where the highway skirts Ocotillo, you are swiped by strengthening winds and will begin to see clearly your objective. A 10-mile stretch into the rocky face of the range lies ahead, welcoming you with a strip of white-hot sand. At Mountain Spring you enter San Diego County and pull south to skirt the Mexican border. The interstate scales thousands of feet in just a few miles, past In-Ko-Pah Road and up to the turnoff to **Jacumba** on the border. The rocky rises are beautifully colored in modulations of white, red and blue.

San Diego Revealed

Near **Live Oak Springs**, 27 miles (43 km) west of Ocotillo, the winds die down and the rises level off. I-8 soon swoops to green valleys and into the **Cleveland National Forest**, winding through Pine Valley and Alpine. **El Cajon**, 43 miles (69 km) beyond Live Oak Springs, is a nicely landscaped city with leafy ridges on its westward horizon; it is the first major eastern outpost of the San Diego metropolitan area. **La Mesa** follows, set picturesquely in the hills which rise at the western outskirts of El Cajon.

Past La Mesa, the congested traffic on I-8 announces urban concentration; the overpass of I-15 is the portal to San Diego. As the interstate pushes out to the Pacific beaches, the shoulders open up onto shopping malls and high-rise hotels. To the south, buildings arched by trees on glimmer lazily the slopes. The city of San Diego is concealed behind them.

Poster from the Gold Rush days.

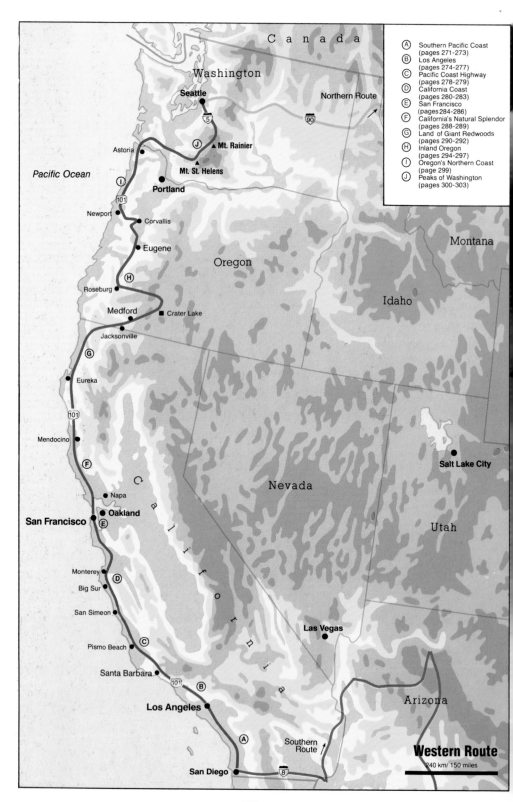

Canada

Washington

Northern Route

Seattle

Mt. Rainier

Mt. St. Helens

Astoria

Pacific Ocean

Portland

Newport

Corvallis

Eugene

Oregon

Montana

Roseburg

Idaho

Medford

Crater Lake

Jacksonville

Eureka

Salt Lake City

Mendocino

Nevada

Napa

Oakland

San Francisco

Utah

Monterey

Big Sur

San Simeon

Las Vegas

Pismo Beach

Santa Barbara

Arizona

Los Angeles

Southern Route

San Diego

Western Route

240 km/ 150 miles

THE SOUTHERN PACIFIC COAST

San Diego is the kernel of modern California, the historic seed from which the Golden State has blossomed. The city's geography also sets the tone for the rest of the state—a jumble of high desert and forested hills bordered by the Pacific Ocean.

In 1769, Spain's King Charles III dispatched 90 men from Baja to beat English and Russian settlers to the colonial punch on America's western shore. By the time the expedition made its first stop at the San Diego Bay's natural harbor, storms and scurvy had reduced its ranks to a mere 30 men. Among them were Father Junípero Serra and Gaspar Portola, who proceeded to found a string of missions and fortresses along the coast. Many of their settlements, including San Diego, have become California's major coastal centers.

Forays into San Diego's environs yield such delights as the spartan old mining town of **Julian, Lake Cuyamaca's** lush backcountry, and **Santa Ysabel's** best kept secret—the **Dudley Bakery. Tijuana**, Mexico, is a tempting excursion (admittedly less so following outbreaks of border violence), though seasoned border hoppers prefer **Tecate** or **Ensenada**. These areas, irresistible playgrounds for native and tourist alike, surround a growing city that combines the pleasures of a major metropolis with the spirit of a resort town.

Spirit of the Sea

Nowhere is this spirit livelier than in **La Jolla** (pronounced "La-Hoy-Ya"). This seaside community hosts the renowned **Scripps Institute of Oceanography** as well as San Diego's most picturesque homes. La Jolla is best known, however, for the caves carved into its coastal bluffs, a paradise for both skin divers and cliff divers. Nearby **Black's Beach** was once legally—and is now illegally—a nude beach. Hang gliders, launched from the cliffs above, float overhead against the empty sky.

The bayside skyline, a curious juxtaposition of glass monoliths, art deco palaces and Moorish towers, serves as a reminder that San Diego is California's

second largest city. The city's original commercial district, the **Gaslamp Quarter**, has been recolonized by artists and renovated to recall San Diego's days as a whaling port.

An unparalleled view of the entire city is available from **Cabrillo Point** at the southern tip of **Point Loma**. Loma's peninsula shelters the bay from the ocean, whose probing waves have carved its seaward bluffs into evocative formations at **Sunset Cliffs**. From an overlook among the serene, scrub covered dunes, you can spot gray whales swimming to breeding waters along the Baja Peninsula from late November through February.

The wildlife is on view year-round at the innovative **San Diego Zoo.** Not only does the zoo specialize in rare specimens it houses them in cageless environments, separated from spectators only by moats. Transportation between habitats is accomplished via moving sidewalks and an aerial tramway. The zoo dominates **Balboa Park's** 1,400 acres (566 hectares), but there is more to see. The park satisfies museum-lovers of all persuasions; its buildings

house excellent collections in the fields of aerospace technology, natural history, arts, sports, astronomy and anthropology.

Heaven on Earth

Another gorgeous patch of greenery in the city is dedicated to San Diego's history. **Presidio Park** features ongoing excavations of the original fortress and a museum dedicated to Father Serra's missionary work. **Mission San Diego de Alcala** itself can be seen as far as six miles (10 km) east in **Mission Valley.** However, the serene character of this and the region's other 20 missions offers no hint of the ghastly side effects of saving heathen souls. In the words of historian Carey MacWilliams: "With the best of theological intentions in the world, the Franciscan *padres* eliminated Indians with the effectiveness of Nazis operating concentration camps. The Franciscans baptized 53,600 adult Indians and buried 37,000."

Having assured the Indians a place in heaven, the new Californians were free to realize their individual visions of heaven on earth. As David Gebhard and Robert Winter point out in their classic study *Architecture in Los Angeles,* "the Southland provided a place that, given water, fertilizer, toil and imagination, could be transformed into almost anything that the human mind could conceive." It appears that human minds were wracked with fever dreams in **Orange County,** for this pastoral territory between San Diego and Los Angeles has been transformed into a bewildering array of fantasy parks.

Disney's World

Luckily the standards were set by the fertile imagination of Walt Disney. **Disneyland** still ranks as the most fanciful, romantic, sanitary and all 'round fun amusement park in the world.

Disney's example has been followed—albeit on a more modest scale—at **Knott's Berry Farm, Lion Country Safari, Alligator Farm, Movie World,** the **Movieland Wax Museum** and the **Palace of Living Art.** These attractions are perhaps the best preparation for the greatest expression of Southern California's passion for fabrication, the city of Los Angeles.

Left, Regal Tiger of Sumatra, resident of San Diego Wild Animal Park. Right, welcome fit for a king at Disneyland.

LOS ANGELES: MODERN CITY

A number of thoroughly modern and essentially American trends have been born in the sprawling metropolis of **Los Angeles.** Here the frontier spirit lingers amid the nation's highest standard of living, producing a self-oriented society noted for its hedonism. The American West's ample space has encouraged L.A. to ramble across an area greater than that of Manhattan, Boston, Cleveland, Milwaukee, Pittsburgh and San Francisco combined. The resulting dependence on automobiles, along with the city's obsession with the media, denotes an unusually wholehearted embrace of modern technology and mass culture.

That L.A. is the cultural capital of the West Coast is lost on most easterners, whose view of the word "culture" has been formed by New York's Museum of Modern Art and Broadway. But the city does boast its share of outstanding museums, including the **Museum of Natural History** in **Exposition Park** and San Marino's **Huntington Library and Art Gallery,** which displays Shakespeare's original manuscripts.

Nor are the performing arts neglected. Downtown's **Music Center** and the **Hollywood Bowl** form the hub of classical music and dance. However, nightclubs featuring popular music and jazz are not as plentiful as might be expected. They compete with L.A.'s favorite pastime—prime time television, and with its best known export—the Hollywood movie.

In addition, Los Angeles can stake some claim as a center of intellectual culture, housing two major universities in the **University of Southern California** (USC) and the picturesque **University of California** campus (UCLA).

What Los Angeles produces—and what America voraciously consumes—are lifestyles. The concept involves a concatenation of cultural details—hairstyle, homestead, vehicle make, model and color, musical taste and a myriad of others—into the ultimate *gasamthkunstwerk*. The bronzed, hulking surfer and the aerobicized Jane Fonda Workout jockette are among the city's more enduring creations.

To accommodate this diversity of life-styles, the city has built the world's most extensive system of freeways. That the network connecting L.A.'s disparate communities was conceived in the 1930s and built largely after 1950 is an indication of just how young the city is. L.A. history doesn't really begin until the early 20th Century when three events sealed the city's fate.

The discovery of oil at the turn of the century turned into a boom by the 1920s, giving the city a solid economic base. Secondly, the acquisition of the Owens Valley in northern California assured an adequate water supply for future growth. And most significantly, a cadre of renegade film directors came west from Chicago to escape Thomas Edison's charges of patent infringement. In the phenomenal expansion that ensued, the metropolitan area's growth was checked only by the natural boundaries of mountains, desert and ocean.

At the same time, the freeway has nurtured L.A.'s legendary love affair with the automobile. Angelinos wear cars like clothing, reflecting their character and position. The motor vehicle has touched every facet of L.A. life, including religion—Sunday drivers can even attend the **Drive-In Church,** "a 22-acre (nine-hectare) shopping center for God" in Garden Grove.

Driving is generally unavoidable in L.A. The downtown area, a manhattanesque assortment of concrete skyscrapers, is popular with tourists because it's the only part of town (save **Westwood** and the beaches) best explored on foot. L.A.'s versions of **Chinatown** and **Little Tokyo** are here—the former surprisingly unpretentious, the latter essentially an ultramodern shopping mall. The historic area surrounding **Olvera Street** is crowded with Mexican vendors selling colorful piñatas and sombreros.

Hooray for Hollywood

The most fondly remembered period in the city's history is the heyday of **Hollywood.** The Hollywood mystique pervades Los Angeles (though the studios have long since moved to **Burbank** and elsewhere). There is a distinctive thrill in fitting your sneakers to Marilyn Monroe's stiletto heel prints at **Mann's Chinese Theater** or scanning the north-

L.A.'s freeways and highways.

ern hills for the famed Hollywood sign. Even natives are thrilled to witness the filming of a television show or motion picture, a common sight on the city's streets. And while tourists wait patiently at **Barney's Beanery** or take the **Universal Studios** tour in hopes of sighting a favorite star, locals are just as thrilled to catch a celebrity at the supermarket.

Here national television amounts to local programming. The shows are shot here; their writers, directors and actors live here. It is here that American standards for physical beauty, both female and male, are forged; where the "normal" American family is formulated; where men and women fall in love while eyeing each other from separate cars at a stoplight.

This preoccupation with appearances is central to the Los Angeles ethos. Its historical roots can be seen in the beach community of **Venice.** When entrepreneur Abbot Kinney proposed his center of high culture in 1905, it was to be a replica of the Italian city, replete with canals and festive gondolas. The plan proved financially unviable; soon high culture yielded to amusement park rides, and eventually most of the canals were filled in.

Today Venice is a colorful haven for artists, roller skating break dancers and mohawked punks who crowd the commercialized boardwalk. Fenced enclosures along the beach feature oiled body builders who pump iron for spectators in the adjoining bleachers. Geese inhabit the decayed canal banks, honking in solitude as if to mock Kinney's dashed dream.

Surfside Subcultures

Along the outsider's conception of L.A. as a smoggy maze of freeways stands the shimmering image of an oceanside tropical paradise. The beach lifestyle of endless surfing and bikini-clad blondes has been canonized by the popular media in song (e.g. *"Surfin' U.S.A.* by the Beach Boys) and a generation of beach party films. And as in most cases where L.A. is concerned, the reality outstrips the image beyond all imagination. The women are tanned and gorgeous, the men are strapping hulks. Furthermore, the life of sun and

L.A. by night.

fun divides, by geography, into a number of surfside subcultures.

Malibu, farthest north, has recently become the new center of Los Angeles wealth. The quiet seashore homes of such stars as Johnny Carson, Dustin Hoffman and Larry Hagman are visible only from the back, where they look quite ordinary. The inhabitants have been known to cultivate dense shrubbery around signs that mark access to the public beach.

Just south of Malibu lies the popular public beach of **Santa Monica.** The famous pier there is a lively, if trashy, boardwalk, sort of a Coney Island West. Parks along **Ocean Avenue** provide a classic vista at dusk when the red sun sets over the shimmering Pacific. And a drive north on **Topanga Canyon Boulevard** traverses a marvelous stretch of L.A.'s largely unheralded Pacific wilderness.

The **South Bay,** encompassing **Manhattan, Hermosa** and **Redondo Beaches,** comes closest to the California immortalized by the Beach Boys. The endless summer of surfboards and T-birds—a lifestyle created by the baby boom generation in the wake of 1950s prosperity—lives on at their old haunt, Manhattan Beach. On Friday nights the main drag revs to life, still the premier cruise spot that inspired George Lucas' *American Graffiti.*

San Pedro marks the beginning of a long stretch of industrial waterfront, a clamorous panorama of tankers and shipyards. Offshore oil rigs, some cleverly disguised as island high-rises, guard **Long Beach.** The dock here berths the restored luxury liner **Queen Mary** and Howard Hughes' bizarre military boondoggle, the **Spruce Goose.**

Streets of the Stars

Of equal importance to the beach in the Los Angeles mythos is **Beverly Hills.** If a deep tan and bleached hair represent an unfettered life of outdoor leisure, the sumptuous estates of Beverly Hills symbolize an ultimate triumph over the work ethic. That triumph generally is known as "stardom." Beverly Hills allows stars to manifest their stardom, and inspires hopefuls with an example. Window-shopping along famed **Rodeo Drive,** customers interested in a $50 T-shirt may need an appointment.

Until the 1940s the **San Fernando Valley** was regarded as a refuge for those who either couldn't afford, or didn't wish, to become absorbed by urban Los Angeles. With the postwar proliferation of tract homes, however, the Valley came to typify L.A.'s characteristic suburban sprawl.

The vast expanse of subdivisions provides a suitably bland setting for Stephen Spielberg's chiller *Poltergeist.* (Justice prevails when one particularly insipid house is sucked up into thin air by evil spirits.) And the area was finally incorporated into the L.A. mystique in the late 1970s when Moon Zappa's hit song, "Valley Girl," defined the budding youth culture that flourished amid the shopping malls of such prosperous communities as **Sherman Oaks, Encino** and **Woodland Hills.** Nonetheless, vestiges of the Valley's frontier character remain. A drive through the mountainous desert of the **Tujunga Canyon** region is ample testimony that Los Angeles has a great deal more to offer than beach sand and health spas.

One of America's more famous backyards.

THE PACIFIC COAST HIGHWAY

Santa Barbara marks the arbitrary border of Southern California, beyond which the influence of Los Angeles wanes. At Gaviota, US Highway 101 veers abruptly to confront the inland mountains, suggesting the rural character of communities from here to San Francisco.

Just beyond, the **Pacific Coast Highway** (State Highway 1) cuts across the gentle Santa Ynez range toward the colorful fields of Lompoc. The coast reappears at Pismo with an impressive panorama of blue water curving around a duned beach, bordered by cultivated fields that reach toward the distant mountains. From here State 1 continues along the water's edge to San Simeon, site of William Randolph Hearst's palatial abode.

Myth of Tradition

The most striking aspect of **Santa Barbara** is its distinctive Mediterranean architecture. Other amenities make this Southern California's favorite resort town: miles of beaches, ideal hang gliding cliffs, a cosmopolitan collection of boutiques. But the ubiquitous white-washed adobe, tile roofing and iron grill-work permeate Santa Barbara with a charming, and quite unique, sense of historical immediacy.

The joke, as usual, is on the tourist. Santa Barbara's Andalusian past is not a lingering heritage but an utter fabrication. As one local journalist has written, "the city and its architects were able to create a myth of a tradition, which turned out to be far more believable than the realities of factual history."

Factual history has it that an energetic woman named Pearl Chase, arriving in 1909, was distressed by the shabby appearance of her new home. When an earthquake leveled the town in 1925 Chase sprang into action, founding the Architectural Board of Review to draft a new building code. Today Santa Barbara's commercial buildings *must* have tile roofs and stucco exteriors white-washed in one of three approved shades.

Sleepy **Lompoc,** reached via the Pacific Coast Highway, is ennobled by the presence of the **La Purisma Conception,** the state's 11th mission. But Lompoc shows its true face across town—and an extraordinary one it is. The cultivated fields on the outskirts of town are a veritable bouquet of magentas, pinks, golds and purples. Lompoc's flower fields, glorious bands of color reaching toward the mountains in either direction, supply the nation with floral seeds.

Legends of clams the size of dinner plates lend **Pismo Beach** an air of mystery. "That was a long time ago," uttered with a faraway look in the eyes, is the common local response to such tales. Long ago indeed; upon inquiry into Pismo's clammy past, one wonders just what all the fuss is about.

The clams, smaller than dinner plates but plentiful nonetheless, disappeared in the early 1980s. Unrestrained harvesting and predatory sea otters, newly protected by law, obliterated the bivalve population.

One would expect economic disaster to follow the disappearance of Pismo's claim to fame. Instead, the sole effect seems to have been an increase in shellfish prices at local restaurants. What remains in the wake of the Pismo clam

Spanish roofs in Santa Barbara.

is a humble seaside village, abounding in quiet beaches and friendly shops selling T-shirts, knicknacks and suntan lotion.

Welcome to the Pleasuredome

Looking up at **Hearst Castle** from the parking area, it's clear that Hearst chose a site of exquisite beauty for his pleasuredome. The Castle, nestled amid a flurry of imported greenery, occupies the pinnacle of an imposing mass of grassy hills overlooking the sea. From this vantage point one feels much like a Medieval vassal in the shadow of the local lord's fortress—quite possibly the impression Hearst intended.

Constructed on the old family campground, the Castle was designed by architect Julia Morgan to satisfy Hearst's request for "something a little bit more comfortable." Beyond its ample comforts, however, San Simeon is an elaborate showcase for Hearst's extensive collection of historical art. The buildings themselves incorporate authentic Roman frescos, Spanish ceilings and turrets from Portugal, with stunning attention to detail, into one tenuous whole.

Inside the Castle there's no relief from the onslaught of visual delights. Covering every inch of wall and floor space, wedged into every crevice, is a little piece of history and a tribute to human artisanship. Throughout the ages, the wealthiest kings and clergymen of Europe and Asia acquired these tapestries, marble statues and silver place settings. One of America's wealthiest men gathered them all into this dizzying hodgepodge of opulence.

The man himself is an enigma. Orson Welles attempted to illuminate Hearst's character in his masterpiece, *Citizen Kane*. The dramatization appears to be accurate, save one crucial point: Rosebud, Welles' symbol of a lost childhood that Hearst never really missed. As tour guides at San Simeon explain how "Mr. Hearst preferred the High Gothic style" and "Mr. Hearst enjoyed German comic strips," the picture emerges of a man possessed of enormous powers of discrimination and very little taste. If nothing else the tour amply confirms Lincoln Steffens' observation that, above all, "this man had a will."

Lifestyle of the rich at San Simeon.

THE RUGGED
CALIFORNIA COAST

North of San Simeon the Pacific Coast Highway skirts along mountainsides that fall sharply into the sea. Below is a wonderland of eroded cliffs and arching rock formations, a playground for pudgy sea lions, flocks of shore birds and frolicsome sea otters. The pristine peninsula of Point Lobos affords an opportunity to explore this in-between realm of crashing surf and twisted cypress trees.

Easing gently from the wilderness toward San Francisco's densely populated hills, the Highway passes the Monterey Peninsula. A short drive west will be rewarded with fine dining, shopping and exploring in Carmel, where a number of San Francisco artists and writers created their utopia after the earthquake. The city of Monterey is a little slice of local history and a big chunk of latter-day exclusivity. Farther north, Castroville invites the adventurous to probe the arcana of the edible thistle.

The stretch of coastline between San Simeon and the **Monterey Peninsula** is known as **Big Sur,** a legendary wilderness of holistic healing retreats and remote homesteads inhabited by third generation pioneers. The area was barely accessible to traffic until 1937, and even now the sheer cliffs hugged by the highway occasionally slide into the sea, leaving residents in complete isolation until the road is rebuilt.

The terrain is decidedly rugged, convincing more than one visitor that Sur's is the most beautiful shoreline in the state. Dark, thicketed mountainsides rise steeply from the sea, serrated by primeval stream gorges. Clinging to the hillside, State 1 wraps around these canyons, faced alternately with cascading falls and ragged shoreline, sometimes with glimpses of the undulating coastal profile extending for miles ahead. Infrequent guard rails, looking suspiciously flimsy, are a small comfort in the face of the menacing rocks below.

Inland Forests

Eventually State 1 leaves the sea for a taste of the **Los Padres National Forest,** through the southern tip of the coastal redwood belt. It's easy to forget that the

On the jagged edge: the crashing Big Sur surf, left; and right, Point Lobos State Preserve.

ocean is less than one mile (1.6 km) away, though it can be reached via several trail systems through the forest and adjoining state parks. In many ways the area is best seen on foot, for it is just this combination of forest and seashore that makes Big Sur so intriguing.

If there's one indispensable stop between San Simeon and Carmel, surely it is **Point Lobos State Preserve.** Although Point Lobos may be seen in a few hours, the overwhelming serenity of its seaside wilderness invites an entire day's visit.

Several short footpaths traverse the rock-strewn headland revealing a plethora of extraordinary landscapes, including one of two existing groves of ghostly Monterey Cypress trees. To wander along one of these sandy paths is a feast for the senses. Luxurious wildflowers cover the rocks with splashes of yellow and purple, complementing a bouquet of floral fragrances that mingle in the salt air. Melancholy bird calls and the gentle flapping of gulls overhead play in subtle counterpoint to the waves crashing against the shore.

The magnificent **Bird Island** lies just off the shore, its camel-humped spine

covered with black cormorants. These huge dark seabirds leave their perch on the rock occasionally to skim the waves, looking for small fish amid the swirling brown masses of sea vegetation. Mats of this rubbery stuff, which you've seen washed up on the beach all up the coast, collect around mysterious stone arches worn into ancient rock formations by the restless sea. Close by, the waves break against **Sea Lion Rocks,** giving an impression of slow motion, as do the black cormorants hanging on the ocean breeze.

The artists, writers and bohemians who fled to **Carmel** in the wake of the San Francisco earthquake had in mind only to preserve the natural surroundings of their new home. In their zeal these early residents outlawed highrises, neon signs, traffic lights, parking meters—anything possessing the foul taint of city life, including artificial house plants. They never guessed that their ordinances, combined with the proximity of chi-chi Monterey, would spawn this delightful outdoor shopping mall.

Although to residents, Carmel must be the most wonderful—not to mention exclusive—community on earth, to visitors it is a center of unmitigated afflu-ence where charm is equalled only by dollar value. Clothing and jewelry are plentiful, but the town is famed for locally produced *objets d'art.* Still lifes, ceramic bowls and stuffed animals vie for the sightseer's short change.

In the daylight the town's elegant dwellings, lining tidy streets that even split here and there to accommodate an old tree, are a jumble of quaint styles. Particularly striking is a stone tower built by poet Robinson Jeffers from rocks found along the shore.

Monterey's History Walk

Padre Serra's initial attempt to establish a' mission in this area, the **San Carlos Cathedral,** may be seen along **Monterey's Path of History.** (The good Padre eventually relocated to escape the unholy effect of soldiers from the nearby presidio on his Indian converts.) This walking tour of historic buildings highlights the classic Monterey style: a distinctive blend of whitewashed adobe, Mexican folk art and pragmatic New England carpentry.

At the path's waterfront end, **Cannery Row** basks in the glow of John

State Highway 1 hugs the coastline.

Steinbeck's brilliant novel of the same name. What Steinbeck celebrated, however, were "weedy lots and junk heaps, sardine canneries of corrugated iron, honky tonks, restaurants and whore houses," not a tacky tourist trap. Steinbeck's world withered with the mysterious disappearance of the sardines in the mid-1940s, about the time the movie version of Steinbeck's *Sweet Thursday* was filmed here.

A visit to Cannery Row is redeemed by the **Monterey Aquarium,** which exploits to wonderful effect the marine life found in a Grand Canyon-sized trench just offshore. Wall-length tanks house solitary sharks, regal salmon and schools of tiny fish amid beds of kelp that writhe with the simulated tides.

Fully one third of Monterey's famed **17 Mile Drive** borders luxurious private homes—aside from the entrance fee, little different from a drive through any affluent neighborhood. And given the exquisite Big Sur coast, the shoreline along this private road is quite expendable. The gnarled grove surrounding **Cypress Point**—besides Point Lobos the only place in the world Monterey Cypress grows—does possess a rare beauty, however. But if you're under time limitations (or offended by the cover charge) it's safe to say you won't be missing anything.

Amid the agrarian fields bordering the Monterey Bay, signs advertising locally grown artichokes may inspire an excursion northeast on State 156 to **Castroville,** the "Artichoke Capital of the World." Here the famous California Artichoke Advisory Board determines the proper alchemy for producing artichokes of optimum size, shape, consistency and color.

Marked by a huge cement rendering of the local pride and joy, the **Giant Artichoke Restaurant** serves delicious deep-fried leaves. By-the-bag bargains at the adjoining produce stand are irresistible (even if you hate the darn things) and make great gifts for vegetarian friends in San Francisco.

Incidentally, Marilyn Monroe, teetering at the edge of stardom in 1947, was crowned Castroville's original Artichoke Queen. She was only the first in a distinguished line of young women to embody the town's bounteous crop of the noble thistle. Surely Castroville has something on the ball.

Farmland meets ocean, Big Sur.

SAN FRANCISCO: DREAMS OF GOLD

The heady flush of gold fever still runs through San Francisco's veins. The city has had a wild glint in its eye ever since the forty-niners stampeded into town, increasing the population from 450 to 25,000 in a single year. The seeds that have since flowered into this garden of ethnic groups, architectural styles and liberal attitudes were sown in the years between 1849 and the turn of the century.

The promise of gold lured both the wealthy and the desperate of several nations, and to this day immigrants continue to stream in. Italians have made **North Beach** the Little Italy of San Francisco. Panning for gold in areas left behind by the whites, and later building the trans-American railroad, Chinese immigrants established the largest **Chinatown** outside of Hong Kong. Afro-Americans occupy the decayed **Western Addition** alongside a growing Japanese population. And while **Mission Dolores** is the sole remnant of the original Spanish colonists, the recent influx of Mexicans maintains the Latin roots of the **Mission District.**

The gold rush left San Francisco a latter-day Sodom and Gomorrah. Itinerant sailors and failed prospectors turned the bayside into a nest of opium dens, brothels and gambling houses. The notorious Barbary Coast, spanning the port towns of the Pacific, was centered in **Jackson Square,** now an office complex. Here unwitting sailors, drugged with treated whiskey at the local pub, were "shanghaied" to man ships bound for the Far East.

To the west on **Nob Hill** and **Pacific Heights** the city's railroad barons and successful prospectors lived in turn-of-the-century splendor, perched safely above the vice and iniquity. These remain the wealthiest areas of San Francisco, retaining a few of the early Victorian mansions. One of them, **Mark Hopkins House,** is now a luxury hotel.

Urban Inferno

The mad crescendo of wealth and vice reached a shattering climax in 1906: the great San Francisco Earthquake left the city in utter ruin. The quake itself was relatively harmless; it merely toppled the mansions of Nob Hill and ruptured every water main in the city. With water diverted from fire department's hoses, however, the ensuing blaze destroyed 28,000 buildings and left more than 600 dead.

Up from the Ruins

From the devastation a new city arose like a phoenix from the pyre, plumed in a rich diversity of cultures. The conflagration seared away San Francisco's penchant for violent disorder and forged instead an underlying attitude that yesterday's gold might disappear with tomorrow's tremor.

A physical manifestation of this attitude was erected in the mock-optimism of the 1915 Panama Pacific International Exposition. The **Palace of Fine Arts,** an exquisite facade of Classical Revivalist domes and columns, was built not of ageless stone but of plaster and *papier mâché.* Its irony, like that of San Francisco itself, is that the flimsy structure prevailed for 50 years and now stands, refurbished, for the pleasure of all.

Cable car, San Francisco treat and daily transport.

284

The Dispossessed

Continuing a tradition of hospitality for those seeking gold at the end of the rainbow, 20th-century San Francisco has welcomed the nation's dispossessed and alienated. The bohemians arrived in the 1930s. Later the Beats, led by Jack Kerouac and Lawrence Ferlinghetti, settled **Telegraph Hill.** Ferlinghetti's **City Lights Books,** one of the nation's most endearing bookshops, stands nearby on Columbus Street. The hippies colonized **Haight-Ashbury's** slum, which has since undergone an uncharacteristic gentrification. And most recently the gay population has emerged, revitalizing **Castro Street** and assimilating fully into San Francisco's economic and political life.

A penchant for high living makes San Francisco a premier restaurant town—it has the highest number of eateries, per capita, in the world. The ethnic melting pot has bubbled over in a plethora of cuisines. From an exotic luncheon of dim sum in Chinatown to pastries (accompanied by Caruso on the jukebox) at **Cafe Puccini** in North Beach, San Francisco's profusion of good food and enticing ambience is inexhaustible.

Forty Hills

Even the city's geography—an unruly collection of 40 hills—reflects a giddy attitude. Not only do the hills carve the city into a number of unique neighborhoods but their slopes afford extraordinary views at every turn. The skyscrapers of the **Financial District,** among them the landmark **Transamerica Pyramid,** cut a particularly impressive profile from the eastern corner of **Mission Dolores Park.** The city spreads inland beneath **Coit Tower** on Telegraph Hill, while the crest of **Twin Peaks** faces the Bay from a distance.

Teams of horses pulled carts up these steep slopes until compassion for the beasts inspired Andrew Hallidie to invent the cable car in 1869. Periodically out of service for repairs, the system was last renovated in 1984.

The melancholy dirge of fog horns also fills the air after a summertime warm spell. Then the **San Francisco Bay** generates a thick gray fog that creeps through the **Golden Gate Bridge** to en-

Downtown Frisco through the Golden Gate.

velop the city. On clear days, however, the Bay's sparkling blue is visible in all directions, imparting a feeling of space amid the urban clutter.

The riches of the Bay Area include **Berkeley,** whose University of California campus remains a perennial hotbed of activism, both political and intellectual, and the newly revitalized port of **Oakland.** (**"The First And Last Chance Saloon** is the only cool thing in Oakland," insists one Berkeleyite, referring to author Jack London's favorite haunt.)

Indefinable Riches

As a place for dining, shopping, admiring architecture, museuming or simply living, San Francisco has as much to offer as any urban center. It has a special indefinable quality as well. It's something in the way the low buildings wrap around the undulating hills. Something in the town's acceptance of misfits and oddballs, who in turn make unique and meaningful social contributions. And it may well be the same thing that led tens of thousands of prospectors, empty-handed after toiling in the mines, to remain and make San Francisco a home. Their spirit infects everyone who enters with a *joie de vivre* that makes this, as the Visitor's Bureau constantly proclaims (with such assurance that you just wish it weren't true), "everybody's favorite city."

Marin County, directly across the Golden Gate Bridge, is the reputed origin of the hot tub and a style of affluent hedonism unparalleled since the Roman Empire. Crossing the bridge, however, not human opulence, but Marin County's wealth of natural beauty is most striking. The bay view is a magnificent composition of sparkling water studded with islands below the rising expanse of grassy headlands that crowd a blue sky.

Nowhere are Marin's natural riches more luxurious than at **Muir Woods. Mount Tamalpais,** with its stunning 360-degree vista of the Bay Area, reveals the surrounding territory to be equally elegant. Like a fond farewell from the Marin headlands, **Muir Beach Overlook** (marked "vista point" from State 1) is one final, spectacular close-up of the Marin coastline before the beautiful drive to Point Reyes.

Victorian style on Alamo Square.

YOSEMITE NATIONAL PARK

The mighty Sierra Nevada dominates the eastern California landscape from the Tehachapi mountains northward to the snowy jewels of the Cascades. At the middle of this enormous corrugation in the earth's crust, 160 miles (257 km) from San Francisco, lies **Yosemite National Park.** The Park's area encompasses natural wonders ranging from numerous exfoliating granite domes, shedding layers of rock like massive igneous onions, to the 2,400-foot (730-meter) plunge of Yosemite Falls, to the giant sequoias of Mariposa Grove—"too many," in the words of naturalist **John Muir**, "for ink and narrow paper."

Muir has been Yosemite's most eloquent spokesman. Born in 1839, he devoted his youth to exploring the Sierra Nevada, and his later years to conveying the depth of his enthusiasm for it in a number of books. From observations of the surrounding geography, Muir evolved his then-radical theory regarding Yosemite's glacial origins. His ideas since have gained acceptance, and evidence of Yosemite's former rivers of ice can be seen in the broad U-shaped valleys, sloping moraines of debris left in the rocky wakes of creeping glaciers, and the shining patina of reflective "glacial polish" of many granite formations.

Finding Yosemite's ecology threatened by overgrazing, logging and mining as early as 1890, Muir began a campaign of letters and magazine articles that led to the establishment of the National Park Service and federal protection of the territory.

Most visitors come to see the **Yosemite Valley,** a wide, flat parkland sheltering the headwaters of the Merced and Tuolumne Rivers and surrounded by a soaring rim of granite. The valley's formations are among the best known and most spectacular: the parallel peaks of **Three Brothers**; **Half Dome**, its inward face sheared evenly by glacial forces; **El Capitan**, the largest granite monolith in the world. The valley's ample amenities include campgrounds, hotels, fine restaurants, stores, stables and free buses from the visitor's center to various trailheads. Seven-hundred miles (1,120 km) of hiking and horse trails probe the diverse environments that exist between the lush river gorges and the subglacial tundra.

The best camping weather occurs between June and October. Regulations regarding group size, length of stay, building fires and tent location ensure preservation of the pristine backcountry. Mandatory camping permits may be obtained free of charge at any ranger station. Reservations are available until they constitute 50 percent of the park's capacity, after which entry into the park is allowed on a first-come-first-served basis. Winter snow blocks several roads, but winter camping is allowed.

[Yosemite can be reached from San Francisco via the Bay Bridge (I-80 east). Exit onto I-580 east shortly thereafter, and continue eastward on I-205 just outside of Tracy. At Manteca take State 120 east all the way to Yosemite Village, the commercial heart of the Yosemite Valley.]

CALIFORNIA'S NATURAL SPLENDOR

An extraordinarily beautiful coastline accompanies State 1 until it veers inland 200 miles (320 km) north of San Francisco. Weather-beaten shacks, once logging ports, are scattered between the more substantial communities of Mendocino and Fort Bragg.

Point Reyes National Seashore, 15 miles (25 km) past the white crescent of **Stinson Beach**, is an oasis of unique geological and ecological features. Reyes' elongated triangle of wilderness is cleaved from the coast by **Tomales Bay**, which just happens to follow the celebrated **San Andreas Fault**. It appears that the park now lies some 310 miles (500 km) from its original home beside the Tehachapi Mountains.

Understandably, the Fault forms the basis for any discussion of the park's bountiful natural splendor. Point Reyes stands atop the eastern edge of the great Pacific plate, which, along Tomales Bay, grinds northward against the continental American plate at a rate of three inches (10 cm) each year—building up tremendous stresses beneath the Earth's surface. Reyes was the epicenter of the devastating earthquake of 1906 which shattered San Francisco and shunted the park itself 16 feet (five meters) to the northwest.

A 40-minute drive due west on Drake Highway to the **Point Reyes Lighthouse** is the most convenient way to see the park. The highway crosses oyster beds and dairy farms before crawling along a duned spit that juts into the Pacific.

Whale Watching

The lighthouse itself occupies a precarious spot among crags of conglomerate rock, perched at the bottom of 300 cement steps that descend toward the violent waves. Whales are a common winter sight here, passing on their yearly migration to Baja. You can hear harbor seals barking from the left hand beach throughout the year, and murres, looking like miniature penguins, reside on the rocky ledges below.

Few other roads interrupt the wilderness, particularly south of the lighthouse, but the entire peninsula is crisscrossed by hiking trails that lead to countless secluded lagoons, marshes, bluffs and beaches.

Back to the Coast

Bodega Bay's secluded inlet marks a return to the shoreline, offering a quiet drive around the cove perimeter to take in its abandoned docks and storm-worn fishing boats. During the early 1800s, the indigenous Miwok Indians coexisted here with a colony of Russian fur traders, but little has changed since the Mexican government disposed of both. Bodega harbor served as a backdrop for Alfred Hitchcock's classic film, *The Birds*, in 1962. More recently, the village made headlines as the northern terminus of Christo Javacheff's 1976 art piece—the "wrapping," in colorful nylon, of some 22 miles (35 km) of coastal territory.

The violent **Sonoma/Mendocino** coast is a fog-drenched, wave-chiselled wonderland of chimneyed seastacks (rocks worn from the eroded coastline) and sheer sandstone cliffs. Frequent roadside overlooks become irresistible

Drakes Beach, Point Reyes National Seashore.

distractions as the stacks take on forms ever more enchanted. Seabirds perch in oblivious elegance upon hundreds of islets strewn amid the frothing waves, contemplating beached tree trunks and cliffs carpeted with crimson wildflowers. Weathered general stores and gas pumps along the way are remnants of the "dog hole ports" where timber, logged along the coast, was gathered for shipment to mill towns.

Founded by a shipwrecked German sailor in 1851, the city of **Mendocino** exudes the flavor of a New England lumber town. Once a bustling seaport, its saloons provided an ideal spot for the hardworking logger to squander his pay.

Though the logging industry has long since petered out, the city experienced a renaissance in the 1950s when its depressed economy and picturesque setting attracted a cadre of prominent San Francisco artists. The historic district now flourishes as a quiet collection of fine restaurants and antique shops. The town has also been popular with the Hollywood crowd, serving as a set for *Summer of 42* and the film adaptation of John Steinbeck's *East of Eden*.

Jug Handle State Reserve provides an informative diversion between Mendocino and the fishing village of Fort Bragg. One of several state parks stretching along the coast from Sonoma to Sinkyone, Jug Handle stands out as the site of a five-step "ecological staircase." Scientists believe that the coast, responding to underground forces, has been rising steadily for half a million years at a rate of 100 feet (30 meters) every 10,000 years. Meanwhile the ocean has carved out successive terraces, each housing its own ecosystem. An unusual "pygmy forest" occupies the final step, where 100-year-old trees grow to a mature height of only a few feet in a natural bonsai garden.

A procession of dull commercial buildings lines the approach to **Fort Bragg**, but a right turn just beyond the **Noyo River** crossing delivers traffic at the river's colorful estuary. Bragg's old harbor, featured in the 1966 comedy *The Russians Are Coming*, is a salty carnival of seafood restaurants, bait and tackle outlets and dry docks. The Noyo's mouth moors a lively display of commercial vessels packed like sardines in a can, particularly in foul weather.

Clouds sit over inlet, Point Reyes.

LAND OF THE GIANT REDWOODS

Desolate, wind-swept dunes crowd the shore before State 1 jogs inland to join US 101. The eastward detour spans forested coastal hills alongside the rough-and-tumble **Eel River** before descending to **Leggett**, home of the fabulous **Drive Thru Tree**. This attraction is only the first of far too many, ranging from the sublime (**Humboldt Redwoods State Park** itself) to the ridiculous ("the amazing **One Log House!**"), that haunt the sequoia groves south of Redwood National Park.

The woodland between Leggett and the Oregon border is redwood country, and the trees have touched every facet of life here. Redwood's superiority as a building material inspired the "carpenter's gothic" style of Ferndale's cottages. Eureka was built upon the fleeting prosperity of the lumber industry. US 101 continues through the lush forests of Redwood National Park and into Oregon beyond Crescent City.

The pride of this territory is the **Ave-nue of the Giants**, a 33-mile (53-km) alternative to the highway through dense corridors of monumental redwoods. These trees are part of a narrow "redwood belt" stretching 500 miles (800 km) along the coast—the only place in the world where these trees grow. Three hundred feet (90 meters) high and 20 feet (six meters) in diameter, they are the world's tallest trees. Thriving in the thick coastal fog, some live for more than 2,000 years.

The redwoods inspire not only passing tourists, but the entire livelihood of the Humboldt community. Sculptors carve the wide timbers into life-sized wooden grizzly bears for sale along the roadside. Others, for a hefty admission fee, show off the stout trunks growing in their backyards. Logging trucks carrying both raw timber and finished boards are a constant reminder that the trees are an economic necessity as well as a natural wonder.

Conservation vs. Exploitation

Pacific Lumber Company's **"Demonstration Forest,"** at the northern end of the Avenue, is a palpable symbol of the

Avenue of the Giants, Richardson Grove in the Redwood Forest.

tension between conservation and exploitation. The self-guided nature trail is a thinly veiled bit of public relations intended to ease visitors gently into the conception of this magnificent forest as a well-managed renewable resource.

Redwood has long been prized for its density and deep color, and despite slumps in the building industry and competition from more common trees such as cedar, it remains in demand. The logging industry, born in tandem with the gold rush, made hardly a dent in the redwood belt until the advent of power saws in the 1940s. The new technology made it possible to clear acres in a single day. Forty years are required to raise a stand of redwoods for such uses as pulp and press board.

It takes 500 years to develop the fine grain and blood red tint that have made the wood itself so popular; virgin forest remains at a premium. Conservationists estimate that the trees are logged at two and a half times the rate of regeneration, even while a tourist pamphlet calmly asserts that "more redwoods grow each year than are harvested." Considering a lag time of 500 years, both statements may well be true.

Water tower in Orick.

Five miles (eight km) southwest on Mattole Road stands a picturesque village of refurbished Victorian dwellings known as **Ferndale**. Settling the newly cleared redwood forest in the 1850s, Ferndale's original Danish dairy farmers gave way to successive waves of Portuguese and Italian immigrants. The houses, storefronts and chapels they built, abounding in characteristic fretted gables and turreted bay windows, still line the streets. Their lively two-tone color schemes are complemented by manicured rose gardens and sculpted hedgerows.

Ferndale's back streets, where old buildings have been allowed to retain their weathered dignity, add a welcome dose of authenticity. A remarkable terraced cemetery commemorates bereavements as long ago as 1870 in a far corner of town. These quaint, historical surroundings are complemented by a number of antique shops and restaurants, making Ferndale the perfect stop off the beaten track for a night's bed and breakfast.

As a haven for Victorian architecture cosmopolitan **Eureka** is far better known, though far less deserving. Among a score of 19th-century structures dotting the city, its chief claim is

the absurdly ornate **Carson Mansion**, a monument to one of the "lumber barons" responsible for developing the coast. The highway skirts Eureka's prosperous industrial and commercial districts, paralleling the insulated waterfront that makes this the principal port between San Francisco and the Columbia River. A survey of the Humboldt and Arcata Bays is available crossing the Samoa Bridge, or in greater depth touring their waters on the ferryboat *Madakat*.

North of the fast-food-encrusted tail end of Eureka's commerical strip, US 101 edges **Patrick's Point State Park**, a network of trails crossing the rocky bluffs to the beachcomber's paradise of **Agate Beach**. Semi-precious stones, including quartz, jasper and jade, glint among the waves alongside bleached white tangles of driftwood.

From here to Redwood National Park the roadway spans several curious natural causeways partitioning the waves from a succession of freshwater lagoons. Shifting tides built up these barriers across the mouths of small inlets which, fed by mountain streams, gradually have become shallow surfside lakes. Thanks to winter storms that

breach the seawall, these lagoons are naturally stocked for brief periods with halibut, steelhead, salmon and other ocean catches.

Freshwater Lagoon, at the border of Redwood National Park, is crowded with recreational vehicles and lawn chairs. The lagoon environment is better appreciated from a secluded primitive campground at the north end of **Stone Lagoon**. Here Stone Lagoon's seaward edge may be traversed on foot, rough surf on one side, wooded lakeside wilderness on the other. This frustrated estuary, a near collision of fresh- and saltwater, of woodland and beach sand, is a stunning example of nature's ingenuity in resolving her conflicts.

Roadside Elk

Redwood National Park, enveloping the highway like a damp, verdant cocoon from Orick to Crescent City, is easy to drive straight through. To do so, however, would be to neglect the wondrous realms passing on either side hidden behind a curtain of moss-covered trunks. Perhaps the first hint might be a herd of noble Roosevelt elk, grazing unhurriedly along the roadside at **Elk Prairie**. But by then, several opportunities to succumb to this forest's exquisite magic would have passed.

Among the least dispensable excursions is a drive down the narrow, potholed Coastal Trail, along **Golden Bluffs Beach** to **Fern Canyon**. After a winding descent through a dense woodland of almost tropical fecundity, the trail emerges at the foot of Golden Bluffs' sheer sandstone cliffs. The bluffs border dunes strewn with gnarled driftwood, bleached white by the ocean surf.

A path from the Fern Canyon parking area slogs inland from the mouth of Home Creek. A few bends farther on, the stream bed explodes in a mass of vibrant foliage. The pebbled ground is, quite suddenly, the floor of a ravine bordered on either side by sheer, fern carpet cliffs.

Fir trees, some 40 feet (12 meters) overhead, peek over the edge of impenetrable leafy walls that glisten with moisture. In places the fern curtain has become unfastened, falling in sheets to reveal the wall's underlying texture of compressed pebbles—and emphasizing the fragility of the scene.

Pretty as a picture, Gingerbread Mansion in Ferndale.

NAPA VALLEY: WINE COUNTRY

Nineteen-seventy-six was a banner year for the wine-makers of **Napa Valley.** In a blind taste test conducted by Parisian wine connoisseurs, a bottle of red wine from the Napa's Stag's Leap Vineyard managed to beat out a bottle of Maison Lafitte-Rothschild, much to the chagrin and surprise of the French. An upstart wine from California had upstaged a grand old bottle from the Old Country. The consequences, both fiscal and emotional, were remarkable; California wine was on a roll. The new-found confidence of American wine-makers is perhaps best glimpsed in the Napa Valley, a region which produces the majority of California's fine wines.

Just an hour's drive north of San Francisco, Napa Valley is blessed with a perfect climate for wine-making. The summer days are long and hot with virtually no precipitation, and the nights are cool and dewy. The great disparity in temperature allows the

grapes of Napa Valley to develop with just the right balance of sweetness and acidity. The valley's soil is rich in minerals which are essential for the maintenance of sturdy vines.

But though the physical charms of the valley are extraordinary, it must be admitted that perhaps the luckiest element of the Napa success story has been the availability of several millennias' worth of wine-making knowledge from Europe to America. The wine-makers of Napa are an extremely well-educated bunch. This is not to imply that Napa is wholly indebted to the traditional knowledge of Europe, for, with typical American technological know-how, the oenologists of the Valley have helped develop new techniques for the cultivation and fermentation of wine, such as the use of stainless steel storage tanks and computer-regulation.

The majority of the nationally famous Napa Vineyards are located on the stretch of State 29 which runs through the center of the valley with the town of **Napa** at its southern end and **St. Helena** at the northern end. Some of the better-known of these vineyards are **Christian Brothers, Inglenook** and **Robert Mondavi.** Virtually all of the vineyards offer free tours of their operations followed by wine-tasting sessions in which a variety of wines are served up to a usually eager crowd. The quality of the tours, not to mention the wines, varies considerably from vineyard to vineyard, so do try to visit a few wineries.

Smaller artisanal vineyards are scattered throughout the Valley. The homey atmosphere of these small operations might come as a welcome relief after the experience of the crowds which flock daily to the bigger wineries. The wine at some of these small vineyards is often of higher quality too.

If the omnipresent talk of wine and food begins to get cloying, stop in at the **Silverado Museum,** located at 1490 Library Lane in St. Helena. The museum is filled with memorabilia relating to the life of the writer Robert Louis Stevenson. And if you happen to be in Napa at the end of July be sure to stop in at the Napa County Fair, a rip-roaring hog-wild country event.

INLAND OREGON

US Highway 199 northeast provides the most direct path to Oregon's magnificent Crater Lake. Time spent negotiating its scenic hairpins is amply rewarded with visits to Oregon's marble caves and the gold rush town of Jacksonville. From Crater Lake, State 138 cuts westward through the Umpqua National Forest, where Interstate 5 leads toward the collegiate atmosphere of Eugene and Corvallis.

At **Cave Junction** State 46 lurches into the Siskiyou foothills, ascending laboriously to the **Oregon Caves National Monument**. The 75-minute underground tour, a walk through the inside of a mountain, reveals a subterranean smorgasbord of calcite draperies, stalactites and stalagmites.

Oregon Caves is perhaps less developed than many other commercial cave attractions, with much more climbing of ladders and many fewer red, blue and green lights. Yet it is not without its outstanding idiosyncratic formations, most notably **Paradise Lost**, a sanctuary hung with massive flowstone boulders, dangling like succulent fruits of the earth's interior.

Beyond the fast-food joints of Cave Junction, US 199 eventually reaches a valley from which gentle mountain ranges rise impressively in all directions. This ring of mountains somehow gives an impression of an enormous sky overhead, much more vast than before. Shortly, State 238 intervenes, leading directly into the foothills on its way to Jacksonville. The mountains stand particularly boldly against the sky when you're this close, though these wooded slopes exude a welcoming quality—in stark contrast to the more aloof snowy peaks rising in the distance.

If the intensity of Santa Barbara's obsession with period architecture seemed relaxed to reasonable proportions in Ferndale, historic **Jacksonville** is positively laid back. Though the chamber of commerce's brochure insists that residents have preserved their heritage out of love and respect, it appears more likely that this sleepy town awoke, like Rip Van Winkle, to find that its centenarian aspect had a dollar value.

Since gold was discovered here in 1851 the town has had its ups and downs, the former consisting of a 10-year boom, the latter of floods, fires and epidemics. Through it all Jacksonville managed to avoid becoming another ghost town and retained several original buildings.

The architecture here is frontier Western: nothing fancy. The effect, however, is quite charming. Brick shoeboxes and wood slat sheds sporting tall facades to cover their slanted roofs are mostly in need of a fresh coat of paint. Lacking the scrubbed down, gussied up look of other "historic" towns, Jacksonville is on to something more friendly and down-to-earth.

Just outside of Jacksonville, State 238 passes through the eyesore of Medford. Following the signs for 99 north, State 62 splits off toward Crater Lake. **Mount McLoughlin's** snow-streaked peak rises directly on the right, towering above the foreground ranges with solemn dignity, despite competition from gas stations and truck dealerships.

State 62 ascends the Cascade Range's western slope along the lively **Rogue River** to **Lost River Reservoir**. Beyond, a flat corridor of highway lined with stately evergreens offers side roads into the **Rogue River National Forest**, and provides a backdrop for the first glimpse of Crater Lake's dramatic peak.

A Sacred Place

The history of **Crater Lake** is shrouded in ancient geological upheavals and Klamath Indian legends. Its sapphire blue punch bowl, adorned by spectacular lava and pumice formations, is unique even among the volcanic riches of the High Cascades. Native Indians—for whom this was a sacred place—recorded the mountain's final eruption an estimated 6,840 years ago in tales of a jealous battle between rival gods. At that time the mountain spewed more than 100 times the magma ejected by nearby Mount St. Helens in 1980, spreading sheets of ash and pumice boulders over 25 miles (40 km) and the blasting out the lake's basin.

Creeping glaciers had long since carved the valleys that have become the twin crescents of **Kerr** and **Sun Notches**. Later, lava seepage molded such features as **Devil's Backbone**, a belt of

Wizard Island on Crater Lake, the second-deepest lake in North America.

ragged spires extending to the crater's rim along the western wall, and the stony masts of the **Phantom Ship**. Continued activity raised a central cone of cinders, now **Wizard Island**. Finally erosion washed away the ash flows, leaving behind hardened cylindrical vents where hot gasses had escaped: the diabolical chimneyed fumaroles of **Annie Creek**.

Lake of Sapphire

The basin, or caldera, collected rain and melted snow—no other source feeds the lake—eventually reaching a permanent depth of nearly 2,000 feet (600 meters). The water is remarkably free of dissolved minerals and suspended particles, absorbing light over the entire spectrum and reflecting from its depths only the shortest wavelengths, which we see as blue.

On summer mornings the crater is bathed in thick fog which clears in the noonday sun, so visitors would best be either late or patient. By mid-July the **Rim Drive** circling 35 miles (56 km) around the caldera is free of snow. Three other roads radiate from the cra-

ter, making numerous circuit hikes possible via a network of footpaths that honeycomb the park. The magnificent lake itself is traversed by tour boats which stop at Wizard Island and the Ghost Ship.

Following State 138 in the direction of **Diamond Lake**, young evergreens give way to an older forest of exceptional beauty. Along the **Umpqua River** gorge this forest nearly obscures a series of spectacular rock formations. Chimneyed and terraced rock faces, covered with a patchwork of brilliantly colored mosses, line the foothills that rise capriciously to either side until the road veers away from the river at Glide.

On the highway into **Roseberg**, sheep dot the soaring hills, which resemble the bluegrass slopes of Tennessee. Frequent rainfall, reputedly predicted according to the number of goats on nearby **Mount Nebo**, embues the pastures with an almost iridescent sheen. I-5 continues north, rising and falling with the land like a four-lane roller-coaster and affording tremendous views of its increasingly wooded contours.

Cradled amid dark, wooded hills and crisscrossed by the **Willamette River**,

Phantom Ship on lake with no outlet.

Eugene suffers from a split personality. A sizable lumber industry, encouraged by copious resources and an accommodating river, has given the city a heartland working-class pride and a taste of industrial blight. At the same time, the presence of the **University of Oregon** has whetted the population's appetite for urban refinements, not to mention the influx of dollars that goes with a college town economy.

The collegiate aspect dominates Eugene's character, leaving the lumber industry to become something of a civic neurosis. The University of Oregon occupies only a small percentage of the city's total area but everyone agrees that without it Eugene probably would not exist.

The campus itself is an attractive aggregate of old-fashioned brick-and-green quadrants and newer concrete buildings. Casual dress is preferred over stylized preppie uniforms by the students who are hard-working and career-minded — not the party-animal zanies depicted in *Animal House*, the fraternity sendup shot on this campus in 1978.

Eugene's repressed industrial urge has emerged as the sister town of **Springfield**. Scarred by railroad tracks and smokestacks, Springfield is indeed a sister — the ugly half-sister that Eugene does its best to ignore. Eugenites complain of industrial odors emanating from the east, though much of the town's work force lives there in order to escape high rents. A drive across the river yields an interesting view of the lumber industry in action.

Eugene has been growing rapidly in recent years. Services and a burgeoning high-tech industry are beginning to vie with the university for economic dominance. The city boasts several large shopping centers and a spanking new mall. There's no historical pretention here — beyond blocks of charming, if unmanicured, older homes, the architecture is strictly modern makeshift.

But like the uneasy laughter of a mild mannered madman, an occasional nervous tic belies Eugene's calm exterior. A chamber of commerce blurb crows about "freeways . . . turned into landscaped parks." A noble sentiment to be sure — but there's something vaguely pathological about the result: a sprinkling of quaint picnic tables amid a manicured public lawn, bordered on all four sides by roaring expressways.

State 99 passes through Eugene's industrial outskirts before splitting into eastern and western forks. The western route (99 W) traverses the picturesque **Willamette Valley**. Distant low-lying mountains border the Willamette region's fertile fields all the way to **Corvallis**, the actual and nominal (in Latin) "heart of the valley." Corvallis is the unpretentious home of **Oregon State University** and a well-established high-tech industry. Hewlett Packard is the largest employer after the school, trailed by several smaller companies.

Following signs to the coast on US 20, a detour onto State 34 climbs through a rash of foothills to **Mary's Peak Road**. The road snakes past several striking overlooks, all of which pale in comparison with the view from the top — bald Mary dominates the gentle hills of the Oregon Coastal Range, towering 4,000 feet (1,200 meters) above the valley. The weather station atop Mary's grassy crown affords a panorama that stretches, on clear days, as far as the ocean. From this point the sky is inestimably vast and the horizon so distant as to disappear entirely into the patchwork of hills, forests and farms below.

Train load of logs.

PORTLAND:
THE RIVER CITY

Portland, Oregon: The City of Roses, The River City. These names evoke visions of placid natural beauty carved with the bustle of a riverfront. The vision of beauty has reigned since the famous Lewis & Clark Expedition blazed a frontier trail to the American Northwest. In the 1840s came Amos Lovejoy, who conceived the second vision of Portland amid the lush forests and snowcapped peaks where the **Willamette River** joins, the **Columbia River** at short remove from the Pacific Ocean.

Portland was a natural—its strategic location and mild climate guaranteed its fortune as a Pacific port, even when it was known crudely as "Stumptown." Lovejoy and Francis Pettigrove, Portland's co-founders, have lived in local legend for the means by which they renamed Stumptown: a flip of a coin. Pettigrove, the victor, commuted to Stumptown the name of his native city: Portland, Maine.

Most important to Portland's livability and inspiring vistas is the city's resistance to the concrete explosion. Blissfully marked by about 160 parks and hostile to view-blocking high-rise development, Portland has maintained respect for the wild forests and white-capped mountains in which it is cradled.

From landscaped blocks downtown—notably the Plaza Blocks and the Park Blocks—to the unspoiled forest of Washington Park and Forest Park, Portland has attracted plant-lovers and hikers. **Washington Park,** the most active of these urban oases is the focus of outdoor activities and entertainment in the summer, while in the spring it draws diverse crowds to its **Rose Test Gardens.** These are the most highly regarded of Portland's many brilliant rose gardens. The Rose Festival in June is centered here, but extends throughout the beautifully adorned settings within the city limits.

Maclealy Park, nestled under N.W. Cornell Road, is a pedestrian-only park laced with hiking trails, perfect for a picnic and/or communion with nature and its wildlife. The grand and spectacular **Forest Park** is at the northwestern end of the scenic Wildwood Trail and replete with other hiking and riding paths.

Washington, Maclealy and Forest Parks are all inferior to the western bank of the Willamette River, in the hillier half of Portland, where stunning views are plentiful and scenic drives are not to be missed.

Although Portland was originally configured about the westbound Columbia River, the northbound Willamette has become its most important avenue. Eleven bridges arch over its waters, and all but two accommodate pedestrians. Morrison Bridge lands at its west end in a rapidly redeveloping waterfront marked with shops, restaurants, markets and restored 19th-century structures.

The "old city" lies, like the best parks, to the west of the Willamette. It is common to find salmon fishers casting lines off the green between Front Avenue and the river while sailors and water-skiers weave about the liquid thoroughfare.

[Portland is located near the border with Washington on I-5, about 75 miles (120 km) from the Pacific coast on US 26.]

OREGON'S NORTHERN COAST

In contrast to the agricultural and timber economies of the Willamette Valley, Oregon's northern coast subsists on fishing and tourism. Newport leads a parade of resort villages that continues to the Columbia River. There the port of Astoria serves as Oregon's northwestern outpost and gateway to the Washington wilderness.

Fifty miles (80 km) west of Mary's Peak on US 20 a sudden, sparkling view of the Pacific marks the entrance to **Newport**. Serving as a seaside resort since the late 1800s, Newport comes by its tourist trade honestly. **Main Street**, however, is the familiar blaring parade of roadside detractions. Side streets are of great help in appreciating the considerable charm of the place.

Yaquina Bay's north shore houses the obligatory waterfront shopping area crammed with seafood restaurants, fish markets and boat charters. On the sound a rustic old lighthouse occupies the high ground and is reputedly haunted by the echoes of a mysterious murder. Stan Mooney, a summer caretaker, points out "some reddish brown spots at the bottom of the spiral staircase; some say they're the blood. They've been wiped away, but they keep coming back. Of course other people say they're just rusty water dripping down from the pipes. I don't know."

Devil's Punchbowl

Eight miles (13 km) north on US 101 the relentless waves have created **Devil's Punchbowl**, a limestone sinkhole formed by the collapse of a network of seacaves. From here the ocean frequently is obscured by a succession of seaside villages that regard the tourist trade with a certain grim determination.

An ominous mount of stone on the western horizon invites a detour along the **Three Capes Scenic Loop**, to the foot of **Cape Kiwanda's** enormous conical seastack. From the shoreline rises an imposing sandstone cliff right out of Frank Herbert's planet *Dune*, its windy contours and shades of red and beige accentuated by the mouth of a seacave.

At the cliff's foot the rocky sea bed has been carved into a garden of distinctive mushroom formations; starfish cling to mollusks along their stems. More fascinating still are the numerous pristine tide pools, windows into a fantastic marine world teeming with colorful corals and crabs, fragile anemones and inquisitive fish. This is the kind of spectacle seen in the picture books that adorn suburban coffee tables, inspiring disbelief that such a place might truly exist.

The Loop returns to US 101 alongside the rugged mountains of **Oregon Coastal Range**. These peaks were first described in the voluminous notes of Meriwether Lewis and William Clark, whose pioneering expedition across the northwest took a break for one bitter winter at **Fort Clatsop** in 1805. An evocative reconstruction of their rustic little holiday inn stands at the **Fort Clatsop National Memorial**, six miles (10 km) southwest of Astoria.

Canning to Tourism

The entire history of the Northwest Territory is carved into a column that overlooks the **Columbia River** at **Astoria**, the first American settlement west of the Mississippi. The column, erected in 1926, faces the town's industrial waterfront, where the mighty Columbia River meets the Pacific, and offers a bird's eye view of the estuary, Clatsop Spit and the surrounding mountains. On clear days the flattened peak of Mount St. Helens is visible to the northeast.

Steep hills lined with humble Victorian homes attest to the prosperity that once blessed Astoria's bustling port. But things have changed; these days the town's dominant industry is, according to a local woman, "unemployment."

Now Astoria is trying to attract tourists. And surely the city's prominent role in Stephen Spielberg's kiddie adventure *Goonies* has furthered that cause. The local historical society has renovated a few Victorian mansions, and the **Maritime Heritage Museum** is reputed to house the best maritime exhibit north of San Francisco. Nonetheless, Astoria remains an elegant, if weathered, old port town, a link between the prosperity of the past and the uncertainty of changing times.

THE PEAKS OF THE WASHINGTON

Between the Columbia River and Seattle rise two of the **Cascade Range's** crowning glories. **Mounts St. Helens** and **Rainier** tower above a wide inland swath of protected wilderness that covers a quarter of Washington State, and gives the region an untamed quality absent in the south. The two snow-capped domes stand in stark contrast, however; Rainier's magnificent peak is a rambunctious celebration of ragged high country splendor, while St. Helens broods in the ashen aftermath of its 1980 eruption.

State 401 connects with 4 east north of the Columbia to parallel the river bank, along peaceful marshes and through desolate "tree farms" that cry out for the sheltering redwood groves. Near Cathlamet, Mount St. Helens reveals itself, a snow cloaked lord standing over the wooded hills that guard the river. State 503 east (reached via I-5 south) skirts the southern boundary of **Mount St. Helens National Volcanic Monument**.

The Great Eruption

The cataclysm that shook St. Helens on May 18, 1980 provided scientists and laymen alike with a glimpse of the violence that forged the spectacular Cascade Range. The destruction spread over 150 square miles (390 square km), clogging the Columbia with debris and flattening forests more than 17 miles (27 km) away. The blast incinerated 1.5 cubic miles (4 cubic km) of the mountain itself—its proud peak was reduced by 1,370 feet (415 meters) and marred by a gaping crater 1,700 feet (500 meters) long. A minor eruption in geological terms, St. Helens' convulsion released a quantity of energy 500 times that of the blast at Hiroshima.

Local entrepreneurs turned the eruption into a second gold rush, sweeping the ash that fell like snow into vials to be sold to the tourists who flocked from all over the nation. Since then, however, tourist traffic has dwindled. Instead of the well-paved arteries usually provided by the National Park Service, a few poorly marked, potholed single-lane gravel roads probe hesitantly into the

volcanic wasteland. With patience, a map (obtainable free of charge at either of two Information Stations) and a sturdy set of shock absorbers, visitors can explore this virtual moonscape of ash and pumice in splendid solitude.

At the mountain town of **Cougar** State 503 becomes County Road 90 Cougar makes a convenient stop for the flashlights and spare batteries required if one wishes to explore **Ape Cave**, a fascinating two-mile (three-km) lava tube accessible via County 83. Ape Cave was formed when cooling molten rock hardened into a surface crust while the lava beneath continued to flow, leaving its drainage path behind.

A Sense of Apocalypse

It's a relief to see sunlight again, and Mount St. Helens' shining cone. Approaching the peak, however, relief turns gradually into a disturbing sense of awe. Eight miles (13 km) on, County 83 deadends at **Lahar Viewpoint**, washed out by the torrent of melted snow that raged down St. Helens' southern slope, opposite the crater. Here the mountain faces the elegant

Mt. Rainier from below, left, and above.

crests of **Mounts Hood** and **Adams**, a scarred, brooding giant. The deluge carved an enormous gash into the mountainside, scattering boulders and ashen mud across its expanse and sweeping the forest aside in a tangle of uprooted trees.

Despite a noticeable bulge that developed on St. Helens' northern face just before the eruption, the magnitude of the blast was completely unexpected. The resulting incineration can be surveyed from County 99, 25 miles (40 km) north of Pine Creek Information Station on County 25.

A gnawing sense of apocalypse looms along the 17-mile (27-km) trek to **Windy Ridge**, five miles (eight km) from St. Helens' crater—as close as visitors are allowed. The area claimed by the volcano is fringed with groves of defoliated evergreens, standing against the bald mountainscape like hoary tufts of an old man's hair. Patches of bare earth are littered with the remains of uprooted trees, scattered in a horrifying game of pick-up sticks.

Still closer the stark contours of the foothills are covered with scores of tree trunks laid across the earth with appa-

rent care, all in a single direction as though combed flat. Amid the devastation a miner's car still lies where it had been parked—battered and scorched, grotesquely twisted.

At Windy Ridge only the towering mountain itself interrupts the pallid landscape. Its ominous crater beckons with quiet menace, the domain of some savage god. At its foot the once-bustling resort of **Spirit Lake** lies slain, a logjam of severed trees. And overhead, a plume of smoke—a final belch of repose as Mount St. Helens drifts back into its troubled slumber.

Outdoorsmen's Paradise

A drive, at least, through **Mount Rainier National Park** is a rewarding step on the way from St. Helens to Seattle. County 25 continues northward to Randle, where US 12 leads eastward past a succession of magnificent rock faces and saw-toothed peaks to the park's southeastern entrance.

Mount Rainier's boundaries define an outdoorsman's paradise, a patchwork of ragged peaks, glacial canyons, snow-fed lakes, stunning cascades and towering virgin timber. Its rounded dome is shrouded year-round in a luminous blanket of glaciers, the largest in the United States. Below the snow line, alpine meadows sprinkled with wildflowers and honeycombed with snowmelt rills provide a home for mountain goats, bears and deer.

Ringed by unobtrusive access roads and crisscrossed with hiking trails, Rainier affords the best backpacking, fishing and climbing north of Yosemite. Four developments (Ohanapecosh, Sunrise, Paradise and Longmire) are easily reached by car and offer relief from the park's predominately back-country aspect.

State 123 edges Rainier's eastern boundary, ascending through pristine forest toward the rocky, snow-crested spires of **Cayuse Pass**, where it meets State 410. Beyond the junction the mountain's gleaming dome towers directly behind, smooth and rounded like a great white bald head. That enormous peak remains in the rearview mirror through **Enumclaw**, where State 164 continues west, past **Auburn's** intersection with I-5, and throughout the metropolitan area that stretches north into Seattle.

left, ash-covered landscape near Mt. St. Helens. Right, Mt. Rainier watches over farmlands near Enumclaw. Following page: Show poster at the Buffalo Bill Historical Center, Cody, Wyoming.

TRAVEL TIPS

GETTING THERE

BY AIR

The vast majority of overseas visitors to the United States arrive by air. Direct overseas flights regularly arrive in New York, Boston and Washington on the east coast, Miami in the South, and Los Angeles and San Francisco on the west coast. New York and Los Angeles can be reached daily from Europe, Asia and South America. If your destination cannot be reached directly, connections can be made to almost any city in the U.S. on an American airline (see "National Airlines" for listings).

Transportation from airports to their metropolitan centers is convenient. You can travel by bus, taxi, subway/train and, in a few cases, helicopter. While trains and buses are probably the least expensive way to reach your destination, taxis are more convenient. Be aware that there are some unscrupulous cab drivers who will attempt to overcharge foreigners. Ask fellow travelers what the fare should be before engaging a driver.

Although flying overseas is never cheap, there are several ways to make your trip as economical as possible. Flying with small airlines is becoming an increasingly popular way to save money – if you don't mind giving up some of the amenities you are more likely to find on the major carriers. Charter flights and Advanced Purchased Excursion Fares (APEX) are also options worth looking into. The drawback to charter flights is that you must book your departure and return dates well in advance, and changes in schedule may be heavily penalized. APEX is less restrictive than charters, but you have to fit your trip into minimum and maximum length requirements, and you have to book about a month in advance.

NATIONAL AIRLINES

American Airlines	212-431-1132
Continental Airlines	212-974-0028
Delta Airlines	212-239-0700
Eastern Airlines	212-980-5000
Northwest Orient Airlines	212-736-1220
TWA	212-290-2121
United	212-867-3600

BY SEA

Even though few people choose to travel by sea these days, there are still a few companies that offer transatlantic and transpacific services. Regular passenger service between New York and Southampton, England is available from Cunard Line, which sails the luxurious *Queen Elizabeth II*. P & O Lines sails any one of several ships across the Pacific, but schedules are irregular. The best thing to do is to contact the company directly.

SHIPPING COMPANIES

Cunard Line	212-880-7500
P & O Lines	213-553-7000

BY RAIL/ROAD

The U.S. can be entered by bus, car, train and foot. Canadians entering the U.S. need only provide proof of citizenship at the border. Mexicans must show a valid visa.

Both Trailways and Greyhound have buses entering the U.S., Mexico and Canada. Amtrak (train) makes connections with trains in Canada. The most inexpensive way of entering the U.S., however, is still by car. It is also the most convenient, allowing you to determine your own destination.

TRAVEL ESSENTIALS

VISAS & PASSPORTS

Most foreign travelers to the U.S. must have a passport, visa and, depending on where they are coming from, a health record. In addition, they must make prior arrangements to leave the country. Those exempt from these rules are:

– Canadian citizens entering from the western hemisphere.
– Mexican citizens entering from Mexico or Canada with border crossing cards.
– British subjects from Bermuda or Canada entering from the western hemisphere.
– Certain government officials.

Any person who enters the U.S. can visit Canada or Mexico for a period of less than 30 days and still be re-admitted into the U.S. without a new visa. Visas can be obtained from any U.S. embassy. If a visitor loses his or her visa while in this country, a new one may be obtained from the embassy of the visitor's respective country. Extensions are granted by the Immigration and Naturalization Service.

MONEY MATTERS

Foreign currency can rarely be used in the U.S., nor can it be exchanged for U.S. monies in most parts of the country. Upon arrival you should have at least some money in U.S. currency in small bills on hand. In general, you can change money at your port of entry, major hotels, or large banks in a major city. The best rate of exchange can be obtained at a bank.

The basic unit of money in the U.S. is the dollar ($1.00). The dollar is made up of 100 cents. There are four coins you are likely to encounter, each of which is worth less than a dollar. The penny is of the least value; it is worth one cent ($0.01). The nickel is worth five cents ($0.05). The dime is worth ten cents ($0.10). And the quarter is worth 25 cents ($0.25).

There are seven denominations of paper money as well. They are all the same size, shape and color, so be sure to check the dollar amount printed on the face of the bill. The denominations are $1, $2, $5, $10, $20, $50 and $100. For the most part, prices are written in decimal form. So, for example, if an item is worth 19 dollars and 99 cents, the price will be written as $19.99. If you ask a shopkeeper how much the item costs, he or she might delete the names of the denominations and simply say, "nineteen ninety-nine", or, to use a common slang word, "nineteen bucks and ninety-nine cents".

CUSTOMS

Whether or not they have anything to declare, all people entering the country must go through U.S. Customs. It can be a time-consuming process, but to speed things up be prepared to open your luggage for inspection and keep these restrictions in mind:

1) There is no limit to the amount of money you can bring in with you. If the amount exceeds $10,000, however, you must fill out a report.

2) Anything that you have for your own personal use may be brought in duty- and tax-free.

3) Adults are allowed to bring in one liter (1.06 quarts) of alcohol for personal use.

4) You can bring in gifts valued at less than $400 duty- and tax-free. Anything over that is subject to duty charges and taxes.

5) Dogs, cats and other animals may be brought into the country with certain restrictions. For details contact the U.S. consulate nearest you or write to the Department of Agriculture.

IMMIGRATION & CUSTOMS OFFICES

U.S. Customs
1301 Constitution Ave. NW
Washington, D.C.
Tel: 202-566-8195

U.S. Immigration and Naturalization Service
425 I. St.
Washington, D.C. 20536
Tel: 202-633-1900

GETTING ACQUAINTED

In the U.S. there are four different time zones, each separated by one hour: the Eastern Time Zone, the Central Time Zone, the Mountain Time Zone and the Pacific Time Zone.

On the last Sunday in April the clock is moved ahead one hour for Daylight Savings Time. On the last Sunday in October the clock is moved back one hour to return to Standard Time.

CULTURE & CUSTOMS

It's important to show your appreciation to those who have rendered services on your behalf. The customary way of showing one's appreciation is to tip those in the service trade who do good work for you. The final and the only tasteful rule in tipping is that the tip should be fair and commensurate with the service provided. Remember, most people providing these services depend on your tips to a make a living.

The rate for tips is generally 15 to 20 percent of the bill. This applies to bartenders, waiters, barbers, etc. The general rule for tipping baggage carriers is about 50 cents a bag.

Doormen do not need to be tipped unless they provide a special service for you. Hotel maids need not be tipped unless you stay for several days or require special services. The rate is about a dollar or two per day.

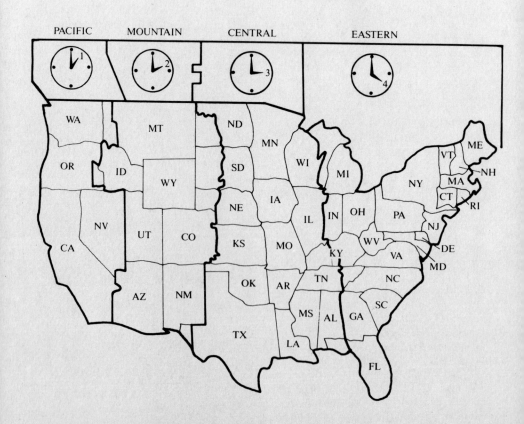

WEIGHTS & MEASURES

Despite a brief effort to convert to the metric system, the U.S. is still using its system of inches, feet, miles, ounces, pounds, etc. The following are some conversions that might come in handy:

1 inch = 25 millimeters
(12 inches = 1 foot)
1 foot = 0.3 meters ·
(3 feet = 1 yard)
1 yard + 0.9 meters
(5,280 feet/1,760 yards = 1 mile)
1 mile = 1.6 kilometers
1 ounce = 28 grams
(16 ounces = 1 pint)
1 pint = 0.45 liter
(2 pint = 1 quart)
1 quart = 0.9 liter
(4 quarts = 1 gallon)
1 pound (lb.) = 0.45 kilograms

CLOTHING SIZES

MEN		WOMEN	
Suits		**Suits/Dresses**	
U.S.	Metric	U.S.	Metric
34	44	8	36
36	46	10	38
38	48	12	40
40	50	14	42
42	52	16	44
44	54		

Shirts		**Blouses/Sweaters**	
U.S.	Metric	U.S.	Metric
14	36	32	40
14½	37	34	42
15	38	36	44
15½	39	38	46
16	40	40	48
16½	41	42	50
17	42		

Shoes		**Shoes**	
U.S.	Metric	U.S.	Metric
7	39	5	35
7½	40	5½	35
8	41	6	36
8½	42	6½	37
9	43	7	38
9½	43	7½	38
10	44	8	39
10½	44	8½	39

BUSINESS HOURS

Normal business hours begin between 9 and 10 a.m. and come to a close between 5 and 6 p.m. Although workers take lunch and coffee breaks, there is usually no interruption of service. Many shops stay open after 6 p.m., sometimes as late as 9 or 10 p.m.

Banks open by 10 a.m. and close at 2 or 3 p.m. Many banks stay open later one or two days a week, sometimes to 6 or 7 p.m. Most banks are open Saturday mornings. At present, the most convenient form of banking is by machine. Though most foreign travelers wouldn't have a reason to open an account in the U.S., those who do should note the advantage. There are also machine tellers for credit card holders. American Express has been particularly aggressive on this front.

HOLIDAYS

During the holidays listed below, post offices, banks, government offices and many shops and restaurants are closed:

New Year's Day
January 1

Martin Luther King, Jr.'s Birthday
January 15

President's Day
Third Monday in February

Memorial Day
Last Monday in May

Independence Day
July 4

Labor Day
First Monday in September
Columbus Day
Second Monday in October

Veteran's Day
November 11

Thanksgiving Day
Fourth Thursday in November

Christmas Day
December 25

COMMUNICATIONS

NEWSPAPERS

Every major city has at least one daily newspaper. Some newspapers like *The New York Times* and the *Washington Post* are local publications but are distributed nationally. *USA Today* is the only national daily newspaper. In addition, every large city has a city paper or magazine that is particularly useful to travelers because they list current cultural events, restaurants, nightclubs, movies, plays, etc.

TELEVISION

There are three major national television stations in the U.S., over 1,000 local stations and hundreds of cable networks. Television in the U.S. is mostly commercially sponsored, so every few minutes programs are interrupted for advertising spots. Although not as popular as the commercial networks, public television offers alternate viewing without commercial interruption. News broadcasts generally air around noon, 6 p.m. and again at 10 or 11 p.m.

RADIO

There are more than 7,000 radio stations in the U.S. Again, most are commercial. Most feature a music, sports or talk-show format with news and weather break every hour or so. There are stations that specialize in news broadcasts, where news is updated throughout the day and supplemented by feature stories on topical subjects.

POSTAL SERVICES

The postal system in the U.S. is an efficient government-run operation. Post offices are generally open from 8 in the morning to 5 in the afternoon on weekdays and until noon on Saturdays. They are closed on legal holidays. The cost of sending a letter or package is determined by the way in which it is sent (e.g., air, surface, overnight delivery). The following postal rates are subject to change.

Inside the U.S., Mexico and Canada
Letters: 25 cents first ounce; 20 cents each additional ounce
Packages: $2.49, lst class for packages up to 11 ounces; $1.50, 3rd class for packages up to 16 ounces.
Post cards: 15 cents

Foreign countries
Airmail letters: 45 cents per ½ ounce
Airmail postcards: 36 cents
Aerograms: 39 cents

Overnight delivery
Parcels: $8.75 for items up to 8 ounce; $12 up to 2 lbs.; $15.25 up to 5 lbs.

Stamps may be purchased at any post office and, at a slightly higher rate, at many hotels, airports, bus terminals, drugstores, etc. If you are uncertain of your destination in the U.S., mail can be sent to you care of General Delivery. The post office will hold your mail for as long as a month. You'll have to show identification in order to pick it up. Contact a local post office for details.

TELEPHONE & TELEX

In the U.S., a telephone number consists of ten digits: a three digit area code, a three digit exchange and a four digit number (e.g., 212-123-4567). When dialing a long distance call, all ten numbers must be dialed and prefixed with the number 1. For local calls simply dial the three digit exchange and the four digit number. If you have any questions dial the operator, 0. If you are having trouble finding a number call 555-1212 for information. These numbers are the same everywhere in the U.S. For long distance information dial 1-area code-555-1212. For overseas calls, you have to dial the international access code-country code-city code-local number.

Pay phones can be found almost anywhere. They are located at every hotel, airport, bus station and service area and at most restaurants and filling stations. Local calls start at 20 cents. Calls to information and the operator are free. To save yourself money while on the road, you might want to call collect. Dial 0-area code-exchange-local number. The operator will come on the the line. Tell the operator that you would like to make a collect call and state your name. The party you are calling will then have the option of accepting or refusing the call. Collect calls are more expensive than direct-dial calls, but they are often useful.

If you are unable to phone overseas, cannot wait for mail to reach the intended party or want a printed verification of the communication, you can telegram or telex your message. Both Western Union and International Telephone and Telegraph (ITT) provide such services. You can go to a local office or simply phone in your message.

ITT	800-325-6000
Western Union	800-257-2241

EMERGENCIES

SECURITY & CRIME

The U.S. is as safe a place as any to vacation, but there are a few common sense rules you should keep in mind.

• In general, large urban areas are more dangerous than small, rural towns.

• Do not walk alone in cities after dark, especially in areas that are uncrowded.

• When driving at night be sure to keep your doors locked, and do not be naive about helping strangers in questionable circumstances.

• Never leave valuable visible in a parked car. Lock them in the trunk if you can't take them with you.

• If you're staying at a hotel, put large amounts of cash or jewelry in the hotel safe rather than leaving them in your room.

• Rather than carrying cash, carry traveler's checks or credit cards. Keep a record of the check numbers so that you can be reimbursed if the checks get lost or stolen.

MEDICAL SERVICES

In general, medical services in the U.S. are very good. They are also very expensive. A patient can spend several hundred dollars a night for a hospital room with additional fees for x-rays, laboratory tests, medications, etc.

Don't expect doctors to make house calls. It's all but unheard of these days. If you are feeling ill or have an accident, call the operator and find out where the nearest hospital is located. Then, you can either get yourself over to the hospital's emergency room (open 24 hours) or if it's more serious, have an ambulance pick you up.

It's important for you to have some sort of insurance when traveling. Unless you go to a free clinic or a county hospital, you will have to show that you can pay for your treatment. Make certain that you know what your policy covers and have proof of the policy with you at all times. Contact a travel agent for all of the latest information on insurance policies available to visitors from abroad.

GETTING AROUND

DOMESTIC TRAVEL

Air travel is convenient between urban areas, reasonably priced and a big time-saver. Because of the distances involved in traveling across the U.S., a combination of air and land travel is advisable, especially if you want to visit more than one region. There are an abundance of airlines that fly between

311

most American cities. Major carriers offer a fairly high standard of comfort, but smaller airlines are becoming more and more popular because of their competitive prices (see below for listings).

In addition to the larger airlines there are hundreds of smaller airlines that fly to more remote destinations. The aircraft used by these airlines are generally smaller, holding from 3 to 20 passengers. There are also several thousand private planes available for charter which can take you most anywhere.

For those in a hurry, Chicago, San Francisco, Los Angeles, Newark and New York have helicopter taxis for hire to and from their airports.

REGIONAL AIRLINES

Ozark Airlines	212-586-3612
Piedmont Airlines	800-251-5720
Republic Airlines	212-581-8851
U.S. Air	800-428-4253
Western Airlines	800-221-1212

PUBLIC TRANSPORT

BUSES

Buses are the cheapest way to travel in the U.S., and they provide the most extensive system of travel routes. The motor coach network consists of suburban lines, city lines and two major national lines.

The two national bus lines are Greyhound and Trailways. Both offer the same standard of service and are competitively priced. Between the two lines you can travel almost anywhere in North America. Both companies offer 7-day, 14-day and 30-day passes for unlimited travel in the U.S. and Canada. Passes can be extended for an additional cost of about $10 per day. With few exceptions, Greyhound honors the Trailways Eaglepass and Trailways honors the Greyhound Ameripass. Discounts are available for children (12 and under travel half price, under 5 free when accompanied by an adult), senior citizens, groups and disabled persons. Both also offer sightseeing and tour packages.

Greyhound	212-971-6322
Trailways	212-971-6322

TRAINS

Traveling by train offers the comfort of being able to stretch out, walk around and see the countryside while remaining relatively inexpensive. Amtrak (Tel: 800-872-7245) handles most of the nation's passenger service. It makes connections between some 500 cities.

No matter where you're traveling, you'll find a train more comfortable than a bus. Amtrak provides comfortable and efficient service that's comparable to the most modern trains in the world. Still, due to the deteriorating situation of the nation's railways, trains are occasionally prone to delays. Depending on the destination, the time saved by choosing a train over a bus may be minimal.

Amtrak offers a number of discounts: Children under two travel free; children 11 and under travel at half fare when accompanied by an adult; senior citizens and disabled persons get up to 25 percent off on roundtrips, 15 percent off on one-ways.

PRIVATE TRANSPORT

BY CAR

Traveling by car is the most convenient way to see the States. Highways are well-maintained, tariffs are minimal and gasoline is relatively cheap. There are several national car rental companies for long-range one-way trips (see "Car Rental"). These large rental agencies provide the widest selection of cars and the most extensive services. They are also the most expensive. Regional rental agencies tend to cost less, but their selection and services are generally limited. Still, they may be perfectly suitable for local roundtrip driving.

In most cases, you must be at least 21 years old to rent a car, and you must have at least one major credit card. Always take out insurance, both collision and liability. Insurance may or may not be included in the base price of the rental. It usually costs somewhere between $25 and $150, depending on the type of coverage. It's also a good idea to inquire about an unlimited mileage package, especially on a long trip. If not, you may be charged 10 to 25 cents per mile in addition to your rental fee.

As you plan your trip, keep the following information in mind: There are four inter-states that run across the width of the U.S. From north to south they are **I-90** (from Boston, Massachusetts, to Seattle, Washington), **I-80** (from New York, New York, to San Francisco, California, **I-40** (from Greensboro, North Carolina, to Barstow, California) and **I-10** (from Jacksonville, Florida, to Santa Monica, California). Although these roads are the fastest way to cross the country, they are also among the least scenic. The speed limit on highways nationally is 55 miles (88 km) per hour, although some states have raised it to 65 miles (105 km) per hour within their borders. In residential and business districts the limit varies between 25 miles (40 km) and 35 miles (56 km) per hour.

Finally, if you're planning to drive any distance, it's a good idea to join the American Automobile Association (AAA). In addition to emergency road service, the AAA offers maps and guidebooks, insurance, bail bond protection up to $5,000 and a $200 arrest certificate.

CAR RENTAL

Avis	800-331-1212
Budget	800-527-0700
Dollar	800-521-6868
Hertz	800-654-3131
National	800-227-7368
Thrifty	800-331-4200

AUTOMOBILE CLUBS

American Automobile Association
811 Gatehouse Rd.
Falls Church, VA 22047
Tel: 703-222-6334

Exxon Travel Club
P.O. Box 3633
Houston, TX 77253
Tel: 703-222-6334

Mobil Auto Club
P.O. Box AA-32
Evanston, IL 60204
Tel: 800-621-5581

BY MOTORCYCLE

Traveling by motorcycle is cheaper than traveling by car. It's also more dangerous, uncomfortable, leaves little room for luggage and is limited by road and weather conditions. If you intend to ride a motorcycle, wear a helmet. Laws requiring the use of helmets vary from state to state, but common sense dictates that both drivers and passengers wear one at all times. Call any local motorcycle club for more information on helmet laws and group outings.

BY BICYCLE

If you have the time and stamina, there's probably no better way to get around than bicycling. If you are going cycling for any length of time it's advisable to get some routing information. For shorter treks, local riding clubs are a good place to start your inquiry. For longer trips you can check with national organizations for touring assistance like American Youth Hostel, Inc., Bike centennial and League of American Wheelmen.

If you plan on traveling to your starting point, you can get your bike there via train, bus or plane. The only condition is that you box your bike and package it. It is advisable to call ahead to check if boxes are available at your terminal. Otherwise, visit a local bicycle shop.

Bike Centennial
P. O. Box 8308
Missoula, MT 59807
Tel: 406-721-1776

League of American Wheelmen
P. O. Box 988
Dept A
Baltimore, MD 21203
Tel: 301-944-3399

BY RECREATIONAL VEHICLE

Traveling in a recreational vehicle (RV) can be one of the more expensive ways to vacation. There are several classes of RVs. The largest is the full-blown motor home or house trailer. These mammoth vehicles provide nearly all of the amenities you find at home including bathroom, kitchen, running water and closet space. The next step down is the converted van or minibus. In this setup, three to five people can sleep in tight but comfortable quarters. The smallest RV is a pop-up or trailer tent. In this case, a car hauls a small unit that opens into a tent.

It's not clear what the advantage of the pop-up is over a good, modern tent, especially considering that it's an added strain on your car and quite difficult to maneuver. The smaller converted vans can be fun, and, unlike the pop-up, are not difficult to handle. Still, given the investment, it's not as cheap as spending the night in a budget motel. The same holds true for the larger mobile homes. A mobile home is a big investment. Even if you buy or rent a used one, the costs are quite considerable.

For further information concerning RVs check with local dealerships, or contact: Camping World or the Recreational Vehicle Association listed below.

Camping World
Beach Bend Rd.
P.O. Box CW
Bowling Green, KY 42101
Tel: 800-626-6189

Recreational Vehicle Industry Association
1896 Preston White Dr.
Reston, VA
Tel: 703-968-7722

HITCHHIKING

Hitchhiking is probably the most dangerous way to travel and certainly the most unpredictable. Hitchhiking is illegal on all highways and interstates and on many secondary roads as well. However, if you do decide to hitch, it's best to do it from an exit ramp (if legal) or at a highway rest stop rather than on the road itself. For long distances, it's advisable to make a sign clearly stating your destination. To find the safest situations, check ride services and college campus bulletin boards for ride shares.

WHERE TO STAY

HOTELS & MOTELS

What you end up spending for a night's lodging depends on where you are and what you need. You can spend anywhere from $10 at a youth hostel to several hundred dollars at a five-star hotel. Fortunately, there's a middle ground of reasonably priced hotels and motels that offer good service and pleasant, clean rooms. What money buys can vary radically from one place to another. You can expect to spend more in a large city than in a small one for a comparable room. Still, you have a good chance of spending the night in decent surroundings without leaving broke.

If you're going to stay in a large city or in a resort area during its peak season, be sure to make reservations well in advance. Its customary to hold a room until 6 p.m. If you're late, play it safe and phone ahead. A good way to make sure you won't loose your room is to make your reservations by credit card. This way, your hotel is assured of payment.

Although not the cheapest places to stay, hotels and motels are the most popular and convenient. There are a good number of quality national and regional chains (see "National Hotels & Motels") as well as hundreds of independent ones. You can expect to pay about $75 for two in a hotel, $50 for two in a motel and $30 for two in a budget motel, keeping in mind that prices vary considerably depending on location.

In general, regional and national chains provide a consistent standard of quality. Most offer toll-free phone numbers that allow you to make reservations from any location free. On the whole, chains offer clean, comfortable rooms, and the budget establishments are usually a great bargain. Many motels have laundry facilities, restaurants or coffeeshops on or near the premises. And most if not all the ones you would consider staying at have telephones and television sets. Nearly all motels have parking facilities as do most hotels. In general parking is free, but there are exceptions, especially in big cities. Cots and cribs are usually available at a minimal additional cost.

Most hotels offer room service. Pools, saunas, tennis courts, and bars are not uncommon in the larger and more expensive ones. Meeting rooms and suites may also be available, and some furnish telex services, fax machines and secretaries for a substantial additional cost.

NATIONAL HOTELS & MOTELS

Best Western	800-528-1234
Hilton	800-445-8667
Holiday Inn	800-465-4329
Marriot	800-228-9290
Quality Inn	800-228-5151
Ramada	800-228-9822
Sheraton	800-325-3535
Hyatt	800-228-9000

BUDGET MOTELS

Budget Host Inns	800-626-7064
Friendship Inns International	802-532-1800
L-K Restaurants and Motels	614-387-6300
Motel 6	213-961-1681
Red Roof Inns	614-876-9961
Regal 8 Inns	618-242-7240
Scottish Inns of America	615-693-6611
Suisse Chalet International	800-258-1980
Super 8	800-843-1991
Days Inns of America	404-320-2000

BED & BREAKFAST

Country inns have become very popular in the last 10 years throughout the country, particularly in northern California and New England. They are usually situated in rural settings and offer an enjoyable alternative to travelers who have grown tired of more standard lodging.

Often converted from old mansions or farmhouses with 5 to 15 rooms, these inns offer a highly individual experience. No two inns are alike, and in most inns no two rooms are alike. Many of them are private homes that the residents have decided to open up to visitors.

Many bed-and-breakfasts have shared bathrooms and very few have televisions or telephones in the room. Rentals run anywhere from $35 to $100 and usually include breakfast. If you're interested in this type of lodging, it's advisable to check local bookstores for a publication that lists the inns in a given area.

CAMPGROUNDS

Campgrounds throughout the country provide a wide variety of outdoor accommodations. They range from primitive areas marked off for tents and sleeping bags to elaborate facilities with utility hook-ups for RVs. Some even have restaurants, playgrounds, pools and planned activities.

Most state parks, forests, national parks, monuments and seashores provide minimal camping facilities: a place to park your vehicle, a spot to throw down your tent and/or sleeping bag, public restrooms and outdoor cooking facilities. Fees for these public campgrounds range from $1 to $ 4 per site.

Private campgrounds can also be found in most areas of the nation, mostly in close proximity to popular parks and commercial attractions. These cost an average of $5 per person and usually offer sites for RVs, coin-operated laundry machines, toilets and play areas for children. The largest private campground association is Kampgrounds of America (KOA) with over 600 nationwide camps. A list of their facilities costs $1 and can be obtained by writing to the company directly. Most campgrounds are extremely busy during the summer months and spaces are usually allotted on a first-come-first-served basis. In some cases, it's possible to make reservations.

CAMPING ASSOCIATIONS

Appalachian Mountain Club
5 Joy St.
Boston, MA 02108
Tel: 617-523-0636

Kampgrounds of America (KOA)
P.O. Box 30162
Billings, MT 59114
Tel: 406-248-7444

Sierra Club
530 Bush St.
San Francisco, CA 94108
Tel: 415-776-2211

U.S. Forest Service
Department of Agriculture
Washington, D.C. 20250
Tel: 202-447-3760

U.S. Park Service
Dept. of the Interior
Washington, D.C. 20240
Tel: 202-343-4747

YOUTH HOSTELS

There are only several hundred youth hostels in the U.S. Unlike Europe, they are concentrated in several regions of the country and non-existent in others. It's best to contact American Youth Hostels to find out if there are any in the region where you're traveling.

Youth hostels are among the cheapest places to stay, usually under $10 for the night. They're great places to meet students and other budget-minded travelers. One drawback for some is that they are fairly restrictive in their regulations. The vast majority close during the day, and the maximum stay is three days. There is also a curfew usually between the hours of 10 p.m. and 12 a.m. Sexes are segregated at all hostels except the few with family accommodations. Smoking and drinking alcohol are prohibited.

American Youth Hostels, Inc.
1332 I St. NW
Washington, D.C. 20005
Tel: 202-783-616

YMCA & YWCA

The Young Men's and Young Women's Christian Association provides inexpensive overnight accommodations ($12-$30 for single, $22-$35 for a double). Ys are generally clean and safe places to stay. In addition, you have access to the many recreational facilities they have to offer. Most Ys have a pool, gym, track and weightlifting equipment. They are popular places for students and those seeking inexpensive lodging.

Most Ys that provide overnight accommodations are located in downtown areas of cities. Though the facilities themselves are usually secure, the neighborhoods in which they are located may not be. Also, if privacy is important, the Y might not be the best place to stay, since you might have to share bathrooms and/or sleeping quarters. Reservations can be made in advance by contacting the YWCA or YMCA directly.

Young Men's Christian Association (YMCA)
224 E. 47 St.
New York, NY 10017
Tel: 212-755-2410

Young Women's Christian Association (YWCA)
1135 W. 50 ST.
New York, NY 10020
Tel: 212-621-5115

FOOD DIGEST

There are several inexpensive options for travelers looking for a place to eat. While the large fast-food chains offer consistency and economy, they rarely offer the best nutritional value. You can usually depend on independent diners and family restaurants for hearty, inexpensive, home-cooked meals.

The finer, more expensive establishments generally maintain a dress code. The most exclusive require jackets and ties for men and dress pants or dresses for women. If you're not sure about the dress code, simply call the restaurant. In big cities be sure to make reservations at the better restaurants.

THINGS TO DO

NATIONAL PARKS

The 26.5 million acres (10.6 hectares) of unspoiled lands that comprise the national park system are administered by the Department of the Interior and the National Park Service. There is an admission fee at most national parks – $1-$3 per vehicle, $0.50 for bicyclists and hikers. But visitors can save money by purchasing a Golden Eagle Passport at any national park.

This card costs $25 and provides free entry or substantially discounted admission to all national parks and monuments in the U.S. for one year. Senior citizen discounts are available for those 62 years or older who are entitled to Golden Age Passports free of charge. Blind and disabled persons may also obtain free Golden Access Passports, which provide free or reduced admissions.

NATIONAL FORESTS

The 189 million acres (75.6 hectares) of national forest in the U.S. are administered by the Department of Agriculture and the U.S. Forest Service. They are multipurpose areas, with timbering, mining, livestock grazing and ski areas frequently found within their borders. There is no fee to enter the forests.

NIGHTLIFE

A wide range of nighttime entertainment is also available in most cities and large towns, including nightclubs, bars, discos, ballrooms, live theater and movies. Gambling is legal in select countries of Nevada and in Atlantic City, New Jersey. Prostitution is illegal in all states with the exception of Nevada. Possession of non-prescription drugs is also illegal, and penalties can be quite severe. Probably the best way to find out what's happening at any given time is to ask the local residents; otherwise, check the daily newspaper.

FURTHER READING

GUIDE BOOKS

Bailey, John. *San Francisco Insider's Guide*. Berkeley: Non-stop Books, 1980.
Brown, Vinson, and David Hoover. *California Wildlife Map Book*. Naturegraph Publishers, 1967.
Buryn (ed.). *Vagabonding in the USA: A Guide for Independent and Foreign Travelers*. Buryn Publishers, 1983.
Butchart, Harvey. *Grand Canyon Treks*. Glendale, CA: La Siesta Press, 1976.
Camphouse, Marjorie. *Guide to the Missions of California*. Pasadena: Ward Ritchie, 1974.
Cleberd, Frances. *Hidden Country Villages of California*. San Francisco: Chronicle Books, 1977.
Delehanty, Randolph. *Walks and Tours in*

the Golden Gate City. New York: Dial Press, 1980.

Editors of Bon Appetit magazine. *America's Best Restaurants: A Reader's Choice Selection of Where to Eat in San Francisco.* Los Angeles: Wilshire Marketing Corp., 1982.

Fancher, Betsy. *Savannah: A Renaissance of the Heart.* New York: Doubleday & Co., 1976.

Federal Writers Project. *California: A Guide to the Golden State.* New York: Hastings House, 1939.

———. *The WPA Guide to New York City.* Pantheon, 1984.

Fischhoff, Martin, et al. *Detroit Guide: 5th Edition.* Detroit: Detroit Guide, 1983.

Fleming, Jack. *Desert Hiking Guide.*

Fradkin, Philip L. *California: The Golden Coast.* New York: Viking Press, 1974.

Greene, A.C. *Dallas USA.* Dallas: Texas Monthly Press, 1984.

Hobson, Archie (ed.). *Remember America: A Sampler of the WPA American Guide Series.* New York: Columbia University Press, 1985.

Hornbeck, David. *California Patterns: A Geographical and Historical Atlas.* Mayfield, 1983.

Leadabrand, Russ. *Guidebook to Rural California.* Pasadena: Ward Ritchie, 1972.

McWilliams, Carey. *Southern California: An Inland on the Land.* Santa Barbara: Peregrine Smith, 1973.

Milne, Terry. *The Ultimate Bay Book.* San Francisco: California Living, 1979.

Mohlenbrock, Robert H. *The Field Guide to US National Forests: Enchanted Lands for Hikers and Campers.* New York: Congdon & Weed, 1984.

Okun, Janice, and Eleanor Ostman. *Don't Miss: A Restaurant Guide to 50 American Cities.* New York: Harper & Row, 1986.

Peirce, Neil R., and Jerry Hagstrom. *Book of America.* New York: Warner Books, 1984.

Ristow, William. *The San Francisco Bar Book.* San Francisco: Downwind Publications, 1981.

Rundback, Betty, and Nancy Kramer. *Bed & Breakfast USA.* New York: E. P. Dutton, 1986.

Seymour, Catryna Ten Eyck. *Enjoying the Southwest.* New York: Lippincott, 1973.

Sterling, E. M. *Western Trips and Trails.* Boulder, CO: Pruett Publishing Co., 1981.

Sunset Books. *Ghost Towns of the West.* Menlo Park, CA: Lane Magazine and Book Co., 1971.

Thomas, Earl. *Back Roads of California.* New York: Clarkson N. Potter, 1983.

Weisberger, Bernard A. (ed.). *WPA Guide to America.* New York: Pantheon, 1985.

Wurman, Richard Saul. *LA/Access.* San Rafael: Presidio Press, 1982.

———. *NYC Access.* Los Angeles: Access Press, 1983.

———. *San Francisco Access.* San Rafael: Presidio Press, 1982.

HISTORY

Beck and William. *California: A Histroy of the Golden State.*

Brown, Dee. *Bury My Heart at Wounded Knee.* New York: Holt, Rinehart & Winston, 1971.

Carr, Henry. *Los Angeles, City of Dreams.* New York: D. Appleton-Century, 1935.

Chapman, John L. *Incredible Los Angeles.* New York: Harper & Row, 1967.

Cleland, Robert Glass, and Glenn S. Dumke. *From Wilderness to Empire: A History of California.* New York: Alfred A. Knopf, 1959.

Cole, Tom. *A Short History of San Francisco.* San Francisco: Monte Rosa, 1981.

Connell, Evan S. *The Son of the Morning Star: Custer and the Little Bighorn.* Berkeley: North Point Press, 1985.

Cowan, Walter, John C. Chase, et al. *New Orleans Yesterday and Today.* Baton Rouge: Louisiana State University Press, 1983.

De Tocqueville, Alexis. *Democracy in America.* New York: Random House, 1981.

Erdoes, Richard. *Saloons of the Old West.* New York: Alfred A. Knopf, 1979.

Forbes, Jack D. *Native Americans of California and Nevada.*

Goode, Kenneth G. *California's Black Pioneers.* Santa Barbara: McNally and Loftin, 1976.

Hansen, Gladys. *San Francisco Almanac.* San Rafael: Presidio Press, 1980.

Lerner, Max. *America as a Civilization.* New York: Simon & Schuster, 1957.

Leslie, Warren. *Dallas Public and Private.*

Grossman Publishers, 1964.

Lewis, Meriwether, and William Clark. *The Journals of Lewis and Clark*. Houghton and Mifflin, 1963.

Murray, Ken. *The Golden Days of San Simeon*. New York: Doubleday, 1971.

Parkes, Henry Bamford. *The American Experience*. New York: Random House, 1959.

Pettitt, George. *Berkeley: The Town and Gown of It*. Berkeley: Howell-North Books, 1973.

Smithsonian Institution. *The American Land*. Washington, D.C.: Smithsonian Institution Press.

————. *The National Museum of American History*. Washington, D.C: Smithsonian Institution Press.

Smith, Henry Nash. *Virgin Land: The American West as Symbol and Myth*. Cambridge: Harvard University Press, 1950.

ARTS

Andree, Herb, and Noel Young. *Santa Barbara Architecture*. Santa Barbara: Capra Press, 1975.

Dobie, J. Frank. *Guide to Life and Literature of the Southwest*. Austin: University of Texas Press, 1943.

Evans, Walker. *Walker Evans First and Last*. New York: Harper & Row, 1985.

————. *Photography for the Farm Security Administration 1935-1938*. New York: Da Capo, 1975.

Frank, Robert. *The Americans*. Aperture, 1978.

Gebhard and Winter. *A Guide to Architecture in Los Angeles and Southern California*.

Lawrence, D.H. *Studies in Classic American Literature*. New York: Penguin Books, 1977.

Leydet, Francois. *Time and The River Flowing: Grand Canyon*. New York: Ballantine Books, 1968.

Marcus, Greil. *Mystery Train: Images of America in Rock 'n' Roll Music*. New York: E.P. Dutton, 1976.

Morris, Wright. *The Territory Ahead*. Macmillan Co., 1957.

Murray, Albert. *Stomping the Blues*. New York: Random House, 1976.

Scully, Vincent. *Pueblo: Mountain, Village,*

Dance. New York: The Viking Press, 1972.

Tashjian, Dickran. *William Carlos Williams and the American Scene 1920-1940*. New York: Whitney Museum of American Art, 1978.

Willis, Ellen. *Beginning to See the Light*. New York: Alfred A. Knopf, 1981.

LITERATURE

Agnee, James, and Walker Evans. *Let Us Now Praise Famous Men*. New York: Ballantine Books, 1978.

Anderson, Sherwood. *Winesburg, Ohio*. New York: Penguin Books, 1976.

Brammer, Billy L. *The Gay Place*. New York: Random House, 1984.

Brown, Rosellen. *Tender Mercies*. New York: Alfred A. Knopf, 1978.

Cather, Willa. *My Antonia*. Houghton Mifflin.

Connell, Evans S. *Mrs Bridge*. New York: The Viking Press, 1959.

Conroy, Frank. *Stop-Time*. New York: Penguin Books, 1977.

Cooper, James Fenimore. *The Leatherstocking Saga*. New York: Avon, 1980.

Crane, Hart. *The Bridge*. Liveright, 1970.

————. *The Complete Poems of Hart Crane*. Liveright, 1966.

Dos Passos, John. *USA*. New York: New American Library, 1969.

Dreiser, Theodore. *Sister Carrie*. New American Library, 1962.

Farrell, James T. *Studs Lonigan*. New York: Avon, 1976.

Faulkner, William. *The Sound and the Fury*. New York: Random House, 1967.

————. *The Town*. New York: Random House, 1961.

Hawthorne, Nathaniel. *Twice Told Tales*. Airmont.

Hemingway, Ernest. *In Our Time*. New York: Scribner, 1930.

Irving, Washington. *The Sketch Book*. New American Library.

James, Henry. *The American Scene*. Indiana University Press, 1968.

Jenkins, Peter. *A Walk Across America*. Fawcett, 1983.

Jewett, Sarah Orne. *The Country of the Pointed Firs*. Avon, 1977.

Kerouac, Jack. *On the Road*. New York: Penguin Books, 1976.

Lee, Harper. *To Kill a Mockingbird*. New

York: Warner Book, 1982.

Melville, Herman. *Moby Dick*. 1851.

Mencken, H.L. *The American Scene: A Reader*. New York: Random House, 1982.

Miller, Arthur. *Death of a Salesman*. New York: Penguin Books, 1976.

Morris, Jan. *Destinations*. New York: Oxford University Press, 1980.

Morris, Willie. *North Toward Home*. Boston: Houghton Mifflin, 1967.

Morris, Wright. *The Field of Vision*. University of Nebraska Press, 1974.

Muir, John. *Wilderness Essays*. Gibbs M. Smith, 1980.

Percy, Walker. *The Moviegoer*. Avon, 1979.

Pirsig, Robert. *Zen and the Art of Motorcycle Maintenance*. New York: William Morrow, 1974.

Rudman, Mark (ed.). *Secret Destinations: Writers on Travel*. National Poetry Foundations, 1985.

Sinclair, Upton. *The Jungle*. New American Library, 1973.

Stegner, Wallace. *The Sound of Mountain Water: The Changing American West*. New York: E.P. Dutton, 1980.

Steinbeck, John. *Travel with Charley: In Search of America*. New York: The Viking Press, 1962.

Thompson, Hunters S. *Fear and Loathing in Las Vegas*. New York: Warner Book, 1983.

Twain, Mark. *The Adventures of Huckleberry Finn*. Dell, 1960.

——. *Life on the Mississippi*. New York: Penguin Book, 1985.

Whitman, Walt. *Leaves of Grass*. Bantam Books, 1983.

Williams, Tennessee. *A Streetcar Named Desire*. New York: New Directions Book, 1980.

Wilson, Edmund. *The Portable Edmund Wilson*. New York: The Viking Press, 1983.

Wolfe, Thomas. *Look Homeward*. Angel. Scribner.

USEFUL ADDRESSES

TOURIST INFORMATION

NORTHEAST

Connecticut
Dept. of Economic Development,
210 Washington St.,
Hartford, CT 06106
Tel: 800-243-1685.

Maine
Maine Publicity Bureau,
97 Winthrop Ave.,
Hollowell, ME 04347
Tel: 207-289-2423.

Massachusetts
Massachusetts Division of Tourism,
Dept. of Commerce and Development,
100 Cambridge St.,
Boston, MA 02202
Tel: 800-343-9072 (out of state), 617-7272-3201 (in state).

New Hampshire
Office of Vacation Travel,
105 Loudon Rd., P.O. Box 856,
Concord, NH 03301
Tel: 603-271-2666.

New York
Division of Tourism,
99 Washington Ave.,
Albany, NY 12245
Tel: 518-474-4116.

Vermont
Travel Division,
134 State St.,
Montpelier, VT 05602
Tel: 802-828-3236.

MID-ATLANTIC

Delaware
State Visitors Service,
630 State College Rd.,
Dover, DE 19901
Tel: 800-441-8846, 800-282-8667 (out of state).

Maryland
Office of Tourism Development,
1748 Forest Dr.,
Annapolis, MD 21401
Tel: 800-638-5252, 800-492-7126 (out of state).

New Jersey
State Division of Tourism,
CN 826, Trenton, NJ 08625
Tel: 609-292-2470.

Pennsylvania
Bureau of Travel Development,
416 Forum Bldg.,
Harrisburg, PA 17120
Tel: 800-323-1717.

Washington, D.C.
Traveler's Aid Society,
1015 12th St., NW 20009
Tel: 202-347-0101.

West Virginia
Travel Development Division,
State Capitol,
Charleston, WV 25305
Tel: 304-348-2200.

SOUTH ATLANTIC

Florida
Florida Division of Tourism,
402 Collins Bldg.,
Tallahassee, FL 32304
Tel: 904-487-1462.

Georgia
Dept. of Industry and Trade,
P.O. Box 1776,
Atlanta, GA 30301
Tel: 800-241-8444.

North Carolina
Travel and Tourism Division,
430 N. Salisbury St.,
Raleigh, NC 27611
Tel: 800-438-4404.

South Carolina
Dept. of Parks, Recreation and Tourism,
Suite 113, Edgar A. Brown Bldg.,
1205 Pendleton St.,
Columbia, SC 29201
Tel: 803-758-8735.

SOUTH

Alabama
Bureau of Publicity and Information,
532, S. Perry,
Montgomery, AL 36104
Tel: 800-633-5761, 800-392-8096 (out of state).

Kentucky
Capital Plaza Tower,
Frankfort, KY 40601
Tel: 502-564-5335.

Louisiana
Tourist Commission,
P.O. Box 44291,
Capitol Station,
Baton Rouge, LA 70804
Tel: 504-342-8119.

Mississippi
Division of Tourism,
P.O. Box 849,
Jackson, MS 39205
Tel: 800-647-2290.

Tennessee
Tennessee Dept. of Tourist Development,
P.O. Box 23170,
Nashville, TN
Tel: 615-741-2158.

GREAT LAKES

Illinois
Office of Tourism,
222 S. College St.,
Springfield, IL 62706
Tel: 217-782-7139.

Indiana
Tourism Development Division,
440 N. Meridian,
Indianapolis, IN 46204
Tel: 304-232-8860.

Michigan
Travel Bureau,
P.O. Box 30226,
Law Bldg.,
Lansing, MI 48909
Tel: 517-373-1195.

Minnesota
Minnesota Tourist Information Center,
Dept. L, 480 Cedar St.,
St. Paul, MN 55101
Tel: 612-348-4330.

Ohio
Office of Tourism, Ohio Dept. of Economic
and Community Development,
Box 1001,
Columbus, OH 43216
Tel: 614-466-8844, 800-BUC-KEYE (out
of state).

Wisconsin
Division of Tourism,
P.O. Box 7606,
Madison, WI 53707
Tel: 608-266-2161.

GREAT PLAINS

Iowa
Iowa Development Commission
250 Jewett Bldg.,
Des Moines, IA 50309
Tel: 515-281-3251.

Kansas
Dept. of Economic Development,
503 Kansas Ave., 6th Floor,
Topeka, KS 66603
Tel: 913-296-3181.

Missouri
Missouri Division of Tourism,
P.O. Box 1005,
Jefferson City, MO 65102
Tel: 314-751-4133.

Nebraska
Nebraska Dept. of Economic Development,
P.O. Box 94666,
Lincoln, NE 68509
Tel: 402-471-3111.

Oklahoma
Oklahoma Tourism and Recreation Dept.,
500 Will Rogers Bldg.,
Oklahoma City, OK 73105
Tel: 405-521-2409.

South Dakota
Division of Tourism,
221 S. Central,
Pierre, SD 57501
Tel: 800-843-1930, 800-952-2217 (out of
state).

Texas
Texas Division of Tourism,
Dept. AAA, Box 12008,
Austin, TX 78711
Tel: 512-465-7401.

ROCKY MOUNTAINS

Colorado
Division of Commerce and Development,
State Office of Tourism,
1313 Sherman St.,
Denver, CO 80203
Tel: 303-866-2205.

Idaho
Touridaho,
Capitol Bldg., Room 108,
Boise, ID 83720
Tel: 208-334-2411.

Montana
Montana Highway Commission Advertising Dept.,
Highway Bldg.,
Helena, MT 59601
Tel: 800-548-3390.

Wyoming
Wyoming Travel Council,
I-25 at College Drive,
Cheyenne, WY 82002
Tel: 307-777-7777.

SOUTHWEST

Arizona
Arizona Office of Tourism,
3507 N. Central Ave., Suite 506,
Phoenix, AZ 85012
Tel: 602-255-3618.

Nevada
Nevada Dept. of Economic Development,
Capitol Complex,
Carson City, NV 89701
Tel: 702-885-4322.

New Mexico
Tourism and Travel Division,
Bataan Memorial Bldg.,
Santa Fe, NM 87503
Tel: 800-545-2040, 505-827-5571 (out of state).

Utah
Utah Travel Council,
Council Hall/Capitol Hill,
Salt Lake City, UT 84114
Tel: 801-533-4000.

PACIFIC COAST

California
California Office of Tourism,
1030 13th St., Suite 200,
Sacramento, CA 95814
Tel: 916-322-1396.

Oregon
Travel Information Section,
Oregon Dept. of Transportation,
Salem, OR 97310
Tel: 800-547-7842.

Washington
Travel Development Division,
General Administration Bldg.,
Olympia, WA 98504
Tel: 206-753-5600.

EMBASSIES

Should you run into some sort of problem, contact your embassy in Washington, D.C. or your consulate in other major cities. They should be able to help you or at least recommend the appropriate course of action. See below for embassies located in Washington.

Australia
1601 Massachusetts Ave. NW
Washington, D.C. 20036
Tel: 202 797-3000

The Bahamas
600 New Hampshire Ave. NW
Washington, D.C. 20037
Tel: 202 338-3940

Barbados
2144 Wyoming Ave. NW
Washington, D.C. 20008
Tel: 202 939-9200

Belgium
3330 Garfield St. NW
Washington, D.C. 20008
Tel: 202 333-6900

Canada
1746 Massachusetts Ave. NW
Washington, D.C. 20036
Tel: 202 785-1400

Denmark
3200 Whitehaven St. NW
Washington, D.C. 20008
Tel: 202 234-4300

France
2535 Belmont Rd.
Washington, D.C. 20008
Tel: 202 AD4-0990

Germany
4645 Reservoir Rd.
Washington, D.C. 20007
Tel: 202 331-3000

Great Britain
3100 Massachusetts Ave. NW
Washington, D.C. 20008
Tel: 2020 462-1340

Greece
2221 Massachusetts Ave.
Washington, D.C 20008
Tel: 202 NO7-3168

India   .
2107 Massachusetts Ave. NW
Washington, D.C. 20008
Tel: 202 265-5050

Ireland
2234 Massachusetts Ave. NW
Washington, D.C. 20008
Tel: 202 483-7639

Israel
1621 22nd St. NW
Washington, D.C. 20008
Tel: 202 483-4100

Italy
1601 Fuller St. NW
Washington, D.C. 20009
Tel: 202AD4-1935

Jamaica
1666 Connecticut Ave. NW
Washington, D.C. 20009
Tel: 202 387-1010

Japan
2520 Massachusetts Ave. NW
Washington, D.C. 20008
Tel: 202 234-2266

Luxembourg
2210 Massachusetts Ave. NW
Washington, D.C. 20008
Tel: 202 265-4171

The Netherlands
4200 Linnean Ave. NW
Washington, D.C. 20008
Tel: 202 244-5300

New Zealand
19 Observatory Circle, NW
Washington, D.C. 20008
Tel: 202 265-1721

Norway
3401 Massachusetts Ave. NW
Washington, D.C. 20007
Tel: 202 333-6000

Portugal
2125 Kalorama Rd.
Washington, D.C. 20008
Tel: 202 C05-1643

South Africa
3051 Massachusetts Ave. NW
Washington, D.C. 20008
Tel: 202 232-4400

Spain
27 Fifteenth St. NW
Washington, D.C. 20009
Tel: 202 C05-0190

Sweden
600 Hampshire Ave. NW
Washington, D.C. 20037
Tel: 202 965-4100

Switzerland
2900 Cathedral Ave. NW
Washington, D.C. 20008
Tel: 202 HO2-1811

ART/PHOTO CREDITS

INDEX

Atchafalaya Swamp, 212R
Atlanta, 187
Atlanta By Pass, Georgia, 184
Atlantic Ocean, 39, 176
Atmore, 193
atomic bomb, 237
Auburn, 302
Aunt Fanny's Cabin, 187
Austin, Stephen, 229
Austin, Texas, 214, 222, 224
automobile, 57, 275
Automobile Consumer Profile, 18
Autry, Gene, 27
Avenido Benito Juárez, 234
Aztec, 255

B

Babe Ruth Birthplace/Maryland Baseball Hall of Fame, 145
Bacon, Henry, 151
Badlands, South Dakota, 79, 80, *80,* 81, 82, 83
Badlands National Park, 80
Bad River Indian Reservation, Wisconsin, 69
Bagdad, 255
Baja, 288
Baja Peninsula, 272
Balboa Park, 272
Baldwin, 193
ballistic missile, 237
Baltimore, Maryland, 145
Baltimore Museum of Art, 147
Barbary Coast, 284
barley, 104
barn, 65
Barn and Farm Museum, 162
Barnett, Newman, (Sculptor of the *Broken Obelisk*), 219
Bat Cave, 229
Battery, 168
Battle of Bloody Marsh, St James Island (1742), 178
Battle of Little Bighorn, 92
Battle of Mobile, 198
Báton Rouge, (capital of Louisiana), 207, 209
Baum, L. Frank, 48
Bayfield, Wisconsin, 69
Bayfield Peninsula, Wisconsin, 69
Bayou La Batre 200
bayous, 203, 209
Beach Boulevard, Biloxi, *200*
Beach Boys, 276
Bear, Chief Henry Standing, 86
Beatty, Warren, 40
Beaufort, 169
Beaumont William, M.D., 66
Beauvoir, 201
Bela Union Theatre, 87
Bellamy, Francis, (writer of the "Pledge of Allegiance"), 48
Belle Fourche River, 90
Belle Isle, 57
Bellingrath Gardens, ("The Garden For All Seasons"), 199
Bellisimo, Theresa, 51
Bellow, Saul, (writer), 60
Belly, Chief Rotten, 92
Benjamin Franklin Parkway, 141

Benjamin N. Duke Memorial Flentrop Organ, 162
Benton Harbor, 63
Benz, Carl, (automobile maker), 57
Benzonia, Michigan, 64
Berkeley, (University of California), 286
Bessemer, Michigan, 68
Bethania, 161
Betsy Ross House, 140
Beulah, Michigan, 64
Beverly Hills, 277
Bicentennial Center for the Performing Arts, Salt Lake City, 85
Big Apple, 59
Big Belt Mountains, 102
Big Bend Park, 232
Big Creek Baldy Lookout, 110
Big Creek Baldy Mountain, 110
Bighorn Basin, 44, 95
Big Mama's Cafe, 68
Bighorn Mountains, 90, 94
Bighorn National Forest, 94
Big Meadows Lodge and Campgrounds, 155
Big Mountain, Montana, 107
Big Sur, 281, 283
Bill Williams Mountain, 258
Billy the Kid, 237, 240
Biloxi, 200
Birds, The, 288
bison, 99
"Black Belt", 193
Black Canyon City, 255
Blackened Redfish, (Cajun Cuisine), 213
Blackfeet Indian Reservation, 104
Blackfeet Indians, 109
Black Hills, South Dakota, 79, 80, 83, 84, 86, 87, 89
Black Hills National Forest, 89
Black Maria, 137
Black Robes, 111
Black Swamp, 55
Blessing of the Shrimp Fleet, 198, 200
B.L.U.E.S., 61
Blue Earth River, 75
Blue Highways, 29
Blue Ridge Mountains, 155, 156
Blue Ridge Parkway, 158, 161
Blyn, 123
Boardwalk, 167
boating, 188
Bob Marshall Wilderness, 109
Bodega Bay, California, 288
body-surfing, 167
Boehm porcelain, 199
Bonanza Trail, 101
Bond, Bill, *(150 Years of Texas),* 224
Bonney, William a.k.a. Billy the Kid, 242
Boone, Daniel, 17
Booth, John Wilkes, 152
Borglum, Gutzon, 84, 86
Boscobel, 40
Bozeman, John, 101
Bozeman, Montana, 101
Bozeman Trail, 90, 91
Brainerd, Erastus, (journalist), 116
Brando, Marlon, *24,* 28
Brandywine Valley, 142
Bread of Life Mission, 117
Breckenridge, Colorado, 107
Breckenridge Joe, (artist), 112

C

H

I

J

K

L

M

Q – R

T

Y – Z

A
B
D
E
F
G
H
I
J
b
c
d
e
f
g
h
i
j
k
l